THE GOD WITHIN SPEAKS

AN INNER PILGRIMAGE TO THE SOUL OF WISDOM

HAZEL SINANAN

BALBOA.
PRESS
A DIVISION OF HAY HOUSE

Balboa Press books may be ordered through booksellers or by contacting:

Balboa Press
A Division of Hay House
1663 Liberty Drive
Bloomington, IN 47403
www.balboapress.com
1-(877) 407-4847

Printed in the United States of America.

ISBN: 978-1-4525-8078-4 (sc)
ISBN: 978-1-4525-8080-7 (hc)
ISBN: 978-1-4525-8079-1 (e)

Library of Congress Control Number: 2013915389

Balboa Press rev. date: 9/27/2013

To my Divine aspect and celestial friends who lovingly inspired the wisdom in this book, that I may re-give to humanity, through the sharing.

Special gratitude is extended to Candace Frieze who supported and encouraged my work and gave me the opportunity to reach out to thousands of people around the world. It is with **Unconditional Love, Absolute Light and Abundant Hope** that I offer these teachings, which I pray will inspire others to find the Divine within themselves, and draw from the well spring of knowledge and wisdom which always existed within them.

To my parents Charles and Roma Sinanan, I honour, for giving me habitation for my soul and for providing me with the tools to become self sufficient and sustaining in God's service.

TABLE OF CONTENTS

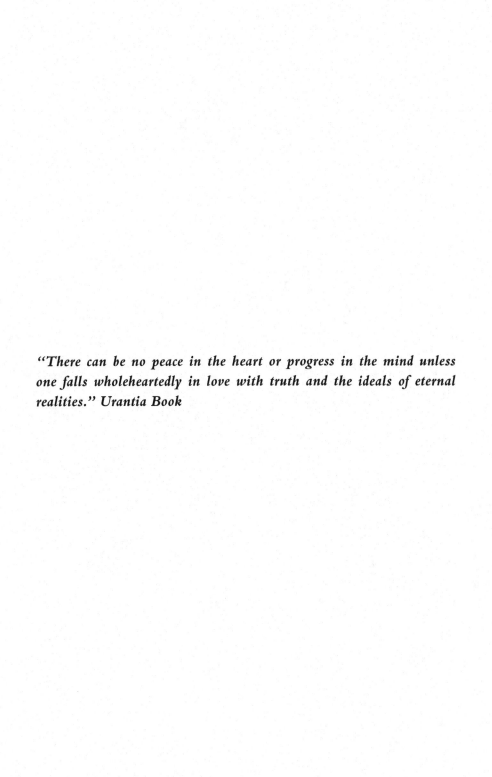

"There can be no peace in the heart or progress in the mind unless one falls wholeheartedly in love with truth and the ideals of eternal realities." Urantia Book

GLOSSARY

Creator of All That Is

The Universal Father is the Source of all creation, the First source and Center of all things and beings. Also referred to, as Universal intelligence, ONE LIGHT, ONE MIND and CENTRAL SUN. The Creator of All That IS, is the first part of the Trinity which comprises the Universal Father, the Eternal Son and the Infinite Spirit.

Reference to God as "HE" is simply due to mass perception. God has no gender. God is energy and consciousness. You can say Father/Mother, God/Goddess, for it is the energy that responds. In this book I refer to God as HE.

Many people do not like the term God. It can be used interchangeably with any of the other terms referred to above, or whatever name you seek to call the Infinite energy of the ONE.

Christ Michael

Christ Michael who is also known as Jesus Christ, is a Paradise Creator Son of the Universal Father and the Eternal Son.

HE is called Christ Michael Aton. Aton means "THE SUN GOD". Aton is actually a part of HIS very long universal name. Christ Michael is the Sovereign and Creator Son of the Universe of Nebadon, which is the local universe to which Planet Earth belongs. Christ Michael's presence is with us, through the spirit of truth HE bestowed upon the Earth during Pentecost.

Nebadonia

Nebadonia is the Mother Spirit of the local universe of Nebadon. She is also known as the Creative Spirit and is the essence of the Infinite Spirit (part of the Trinity). She assists the Creator Son, Michael, in the administration of the local universe of Nebadon. HER presence is with us through the Holy Spirit.

Father Melchizedek

The Creator Son Michael and the Creative Spirit Nebadonia created the original Melchizedek known as Father Melchizedek. Father Melchizedek subsequently collaborated with the Creator Son and the Creative Spirit to bring into existence the entire group of Melchizedeks.[1]

Machiventa Melchizedek

Machiventa Melchizedek is the Melchizedek who incarnated on Earth during the time of Abraham. He is the Melchizedek referred to in the Bible. He is currently the invisible Planetary Prince for Earth.

Ascended Masters

Ascended Masters are enlightened beings who have successfully raised their vibration to a certain frequency of light and no longer have to experience physical birth and death. They serve humanity from a higher plane of existence. The Masters who give the messages in this book are part of the Chohans (Teachers) of The Seven Rays of Life. Each of us is guided by the powerful forces at work within these Rays, and as

---

[1] For further information on the Spiritual hierarchy see the Urantia book— www.urantia.org

such, these Chohans can be looked upon as our spiritual mentors. The Chohans of the Seven Rays of Life are of the stature of Archangels.

Master St. Germain

He is the Chohan of the Seventh Ray. This Ray is the transmuting ray and is used for Purity, Truth, and Freedom—Freedom of one's God self. He teaches man to *"espouse his inalienable divine right to live in accordance with his highest conception of God."* The Ray known for what is called Ceremony means *"commemoration and adherence unto the Law of Truth, a celebration of new beginnings."*[2] He is known as the Master Alchemist and has bequeathed the Violet Ray[3] (Violet Flame) to be used to transmute all that is negative, being the baser elements of the human nature, so that, we may embody the ascended Christ beings that we are and live in Christ consciousness.

Lady Master Nada

She is the Chohan of the Sixth Ray and is the bringer of truth of communications on soul levels. The Sixth Ray also represents Ministration and Service. She tutors souls in mastering qualities of peace, service and brotherhood. She assists with the mastery of speech, interpretation, communication and delivery of the WORD. She helps all who are devoted to serving the needs of God's children in every branch of human services.

She has taught that *"the natural course of one's life is always the preferring of the love of God and the service of that God incarnate."*[4]

---

2   The Rainbow Masters—The Magnificent Seven

3   The Violet Flame is an aspect of Pure consciousness. It is the "Sacred fire" that can be used to transmute all that is negative. It can be used to free the lower aspects of consciousness until it is transformed into Christ consciousness.

4   The Rainbow Masters—The Magnificent Seven

Master Lanto

He is the Chohan of the Second Ray and is known as the Sage. His, is the ray of wisdom. He teaches students how to raise their vibration by embodying the flame of life within the innermost chamber of the heart. His teachings focus on the attainment of higher consciousness through the golden ray of Creator's light.

Archangels

Archangels are the offspring of the Creator Son and the Universe Mother Spirit. They are the highest type of high spirit beings produced in large numbers in a local universe (such as Nebadon). They are committed to assisting mortals in their ascending career. On earth at this time there is a great gathering of the Archangels. *"Your planet has become a divisional headquarters for the universe administration and direction of certain archangel activities having to do with the Paradise ascension scheme."*[5]

Archangel Michael—is known as the Prince of the Archangels and defender of the Christ consciousness in all God's children. He is the Archangel of protection, and once called upon to do so, he protects souls from the adversaries of God. He is also "The Archangel of the Resurrection" and is serving the planet Earth as part of the Correcting Time (Earth's transition); whereby he, with his contingent, will assist souls who are ready to be resurrected to eternal life. He is also known in the celestial realms as the Archangel **of** Michael, meaning Michael of Nebadon.

Man—Reference to Man means the race of Man, which includes both genders.

Soul—The Soul can be seen as the non-physical energetic interface between body and Spirit. The Soul is that which has "God potential".

---

[5]   Urantia Book Paper 37

The soul's destiny is to ascend to the fullness of God. Through mortal experiences, the soul has the opportunity to evolve in God awareness through the ministrations of the "Spirit of Life and Truth" within. When the soul is imbued with the reality of Spirit, God awareness, wisdom and creativity are birthed. When the soul fuses with Spirit, "soul potential" becomes "spirit actualities" which include immortality and fixation on divine qualities. This fusion constitutes the mystery of making God and man one. The soul is sometimes referred to as the Soul/Mind complex.

As Elizabeth Clare Prophet said in her book "St Germain on Alchemy, Formulas for Self Transformation" *"The rejoining of soul with Spirit (of God) is the alchemical marriage that determines the destiny of self and makes it one with immortal Truth."*

The soul has the potential for immortality depending on the choices made by the incarnate being. The soul can be lost but the spirit referred to below can never die.

Spirit—refers to (1) The spirit of the Father (the divine spark of God or Father fragment within the core of each ensouled being). It is the "I AM" presence within. It is this "Spirit" with which the soul must fuse at some point in its ascending journey (2) The Spirit of the Son is the Spirit of Truth, bestowed by Michael of Nebadon during the event referred to as the Pentecost. The *"Spirit of Truth comes really to lead all believers into all truth, into the expanding knowledge of the experience of the living and growing spiritual consciousness of the reality of eternal and ascending sonship with God. The term "baptism of the spirit" signifies the conscious reception of this gift of the Spirit of Truth, and the personal acknowledgment of this new spiritual power as an augmentation of all spiritual influences previously experienced by the God-knowing soul."*[6] (3) The Holy Spirit, which is the spirit of the Infinite Spirit, (3rd person of the Trinity) expressed through the Universal Mother Spirit (Nebadonia).

---

[6]   Urantia Book Paper 194

Higher self—There are various aspects to the Higher self above the incarnate being. There is the Soul, Over-soul, Christ self and then God self. Ultimately the Higher self is the exalted aspect of "self"; the I AM presence and Christ self. The Higher self can be seen as the *"perfected future manifestation of Spirit reaching back through time to help out extensions of itself still in the linear past."* [7] The Higher self can provide intuitive guidance and wisdom to assist the soul on its ascending journey.

"I AM" presence—refers to the "Higher Presence of Divine Authority" individualised in each ensouled being.

Karma—is the Law of Cause and Effect. Karma involves the balancing of energies. It could be viewed as a spiritual debt that must be paid. Man must stay on the karmic wheel through the soul's reincarnation until all Karmic cycles are balanced. Man determines his karmic fate through his thoughts, feelings, expressions and deeds. Man can accelerate the clearing of karma through the use of the Violet flame of transmutation.

---

[7]   Montalk.net

PREFACE

I have learnt from the Father that one of the most thrilling and inspiring human experiences is searching for truth. I did not know this ten years ago when I started engraving my candles with the words "God's Truth". I was seeking the highest truth without necessarily having a comprehensive understanding of what that involved.

It was through myriad experiences over the course of many years that I realised the one truth I was seeking, and which was in fact revealed to me, was the truth of Love. I found the truth of Love in God, by HIS very existence within me. I discovered love within myself which enabled me to explore its truth and reality. I realised that I did not have to seek love outside of myself to have it or experience it. In being Love, I would inevitably create and attract Love of the highest vibration.

"The God Within Speaks" is inspired by the teaching mission given to me by the Father in 2010. My mission is to inspire others to walk the path of freedom through the seeking of truth; to boldly explore the inner terrain of their "god" mind to uncover divine intelligence.

It is not my purpose through this book to impose or foist my truth upon others. I simply teach that, that which we all long for—"Freedom in love and in life," can be ours if we know that God is the pathway to that freedom. In fact I have come to know God as Truth and Freedom, for the truth always liberates. The Father taught me *truth will always be recognised by your spiritual consciousness.* The god within each will reveal higher knowledge, wisdom and truth, should we ably cultivate a relationship with that "inner god".

No one can teach you how to know God. God's messengers have all provided at some point or the other, route maps to higher consciousness which eventuates in a state of "Christness". God is Light and Light is All there really is. Master St Germain has taught elsewhere that *"To know God man must know what Light is, energy, gravitation and God's processes in the building of bodies which manifest HIS presence and HIS purposes."*[8] This will assist in an intellectual comprehension of God. To know the spiritual God, we must experience HIM by severing our consciousness from the awareness of our body, and become ONE with HIM. This state can be experienced through meditation.

To know God you must have an interest and desire to know self. When people tell me that they don't really believe in God, I ask whether they believe in themselves or know themselves. I simply say to them, *"seek to know yourself; seek the truth of yourself first, and in so doing you will find God."* However, you must also be born of the spirit; this means having the knowledge that man is at his highest, spirit. Those who are born only of the flesh and know only things of the flesh cannot appreciate or know deeper spiritual realities. When you can accept that you are spirit in reality, you will begin to seek the ways of spirit, which will inevitably lead to an exhilarating discovery of the infinite spirit of God within you. Vitally, it is through life's experiences that the opportunity to find self and God in self, presents itself.

It is through my mortal experience that I discovered God within myself, HIS love, wisdom, beauty, peace faith, patience and charity. When you find God within yourself, you will begin to experience HIM in a real and abiding way, and you will come to know HIS qualities and attributes as yours. There will be no affectation, compulsion or need, to imitate a God you are taught of, through religion or tradition. Discovering God through your mortal experience will enable you to awaken to your inherent nobility and eventually merge in unity with your highest self. When you begin to know God you will begin to know love. You will desire to live HIS Law of Love, for in that love there is only freedom. Master St Germain taught elsewhere that *"there is every kind of freedom in love; for there is no hatred, anger, jealousy, covetousness*

---

[8]   Phoenix journals

or hypocrisy where there is all enveloping love."[9] When you know God you will know this kind of freedom in love.

I have been taught by the Father that HE speaks to HIS children through the language of light, which is wordless; light, being the language of inspiration. When our desire to know God through ourselves and know ourselves through God, is genuine, and our intent in seeking is pure, revelations of spirit become a natural part of our journey. The Father will reveal HIMSELF in multiple ways. HE has always said that the call compels an answer. HE will answer, but we must fine tune our abilities to hear HIM.

The teachings in this book are spiritual insights I received from my Higher self, the Creator of All that is, Christ Michael, the Mother Spirit, the Ascended Masters and the Archangels. These are the teachings and wisdom I use to guide my daily life. As the moments pass, my inner awareness and connection with the Father grows. Desire to feel the presence of God every moment of my life feeds my discipline; and my passion for truth becomes my passion for the god within me. The truths revealed to me through my mission are truths which align me with HIM. HE has taught me that Truth is neither magical nor mystical, it just is. Disbelief by others cannot change what is truth.

Each through his/her mortal experience will, if there is a desire, find self and God; and in so doing receive insights into spiritual realities in measure of his/her readiness. God is the ultimate truth and it can take us eternity to know HIM fully. Should we desire to awaken to the spirit of truth within us, our journey on this earth plane will be a fulfilling one.

When we can become one with the will of God, we can experience the Kingdom of God within us on earth. We will find that in truth there is no death and we will know life only in God. We will come to

---

9   Phoenix journals

know ourselves as HIM. We will be free of the bondage formed by the consciousness of death.

There is only freedom in knowing God–WHO is all Light, Life, Truth, Wisdom, Knowledge and Power. This is our heritage, our right, and the truth of who we are.

Truth frees us from misconceptions, disinformation, lies, false paradigms and limited perceptions; thus enabling us to identify the Truth of who we truly are; that is, pure consciousness—GOD.

In keeping with my mission, the messages in this book are meant to inspire readers to take the journey of truth, and be open to spiritual revelations. As you seek truth from the highest source within you, you will be astounded yet warmed by the discovery of who you are, why you are here, and greater realties which transcend our inhabited dimension.

Through the tests in our lives, lessons are learnt which births awareness of truth already existing within ourselves.

"It is the comprehension of truth that constitutes the highest form of human liberty."[10]

Our celestial counterparts are working on "overdrive" to awaken humanity. As the earth is being prepared for her ascension, so too, is mankind. There is a level of spiritual awakening which man must experience in readiness for the ascension process. Through the teachings in this book, readers are encouraged to open their minds to a higher or cosmic perspective on certain matters, issues and topics, and to begin to seek after the highest truth of ALL THAT IS.

Many pieces in this book address aspects of Love. The Creator desires HIS children to know, that Love is the highest form of frequency or

---

[10]   The Urantia Book

energy. It is the basis of Creation, the basis of spirit and therefore the basis of man. The type of love addressed in this book is the love that centres all things in balance and harmony. To truly know love is to know God and the ecstasy of eternal ONENESS. I have been taught that the nature of God/Creator is to give out HIS love for re-giving. Love is the energy flowing from God to each of us; if we desire to attain the presence of God we must cause that love to be re-given and returned to God. The Law of Love translates into the Law of Balance.

Balance is that which keeps all things in equilibrium and harmony. If we desire to have harmony in our lives, we need to honour the Law of Love by ensuring that what we seek and are given by God, we re-give equally. In other words, the giving and re-giving must be equal and in balance with each other. If we seek peace and happiness from God, we must re-give peace and happiness in our interchange or transactions with others. In this way the Law of Love will work and balance be maintained.

"The God Within Speaks" does not tell a story, but contains revelations received through my god mind, which brings a higher perspective of life and matters we encounter in life. It is my sincerest desire that each who read this book will receive enlightenment, and in particular an understanding that each is Sovereign with God powers and attributes, which, if accessed, can be used to fashion a divine life on earth enabling them to "BE" the three fold flame of Wisdom, Power and Love.

Spiritual growth is continuous for there is always something new to learn. When we are ready to receive and be taught, knowledge will be presented to us and that which we may have come across in the past may find a new resonance with our souls. Remember the saying, *"Greatness is the ability to hear new information, not with mind to disprove or disbelieve, but to see how it might be true."*

I encourage each reader to give permission to the god within to speak through you; not only will the energy of your words change, but truth will become your passion.

May your journey on the path to freedom be paved with God's Truth.

Blessed be in Love and Purest Light.

TRIBUTE TO THE SOURCE

YOU play the tenuous strings on my evolutionary heart,
Where YOU create a masterful composition
Blending YOUR cosmic culture with the
tuneful longing of my desire
To coalesce in a vibratory range,
Pleading harmonious tunes drawn from the ethereal pocket.
With untold skill YOU conduct the symphony of love
That classical rendition of a heart pulsing to the
rhythmic beat of its celestial heritage.
Such perfection in presence
Those deft and lighted fingers convert riotous
notes into compassionate chords
And fires the frequency of the ascendant scales
Until a matchless crescendo erupts in the ecstasy of ONENESS
And I am left satiated in the energetic display of YOUR mastery.
My indigenous heart screams encore as it rises in surrender
Offering itself in boundless service,
That YOU may perfect its tune through YOUR artful strum
And channel the harmonious passion of its nature
To transcribe the lyrics of YOUR heavenly composition,
That other hearts may be inspired to allow the Master entry
That they too, may find their eternal tune in YOU.

I AM THAT I AM

In divine love birthed from YOUR perfection within.

INTRODUCTION

"The God within Speaks" is a book about the author's spiritual journey, transformation and unfolding, and her discovery of her inner divine essence, being the repository of all knowledge wisdom and truth. The first four chapters of the book charts the initial steps in the author's spiritual awakening which combines her divine experiences, encounters and lessons learnt. This prelude is intended to assist readers in connecting with the author's experience and energy, as well as, comprehending the purpose of the book, which is to encourage the readers to seek absolute truth from within by forging a relationship with their divine essence. The book is meant to inspire others to take inward steps through intent, desire and action to allow their Higher selves to work and live through them, thus facilitating higher consciousness which will open them up to the flow of the Mighty Source.

The book shows that when one is able to connect and receive guidance from one's Higher self, one's purpose in life becomes clearer. As the author unites her mind with that of her Higher self, allows her Higher self to think with her, and surrenders to the insights of her higher mind, wisdom flows. The result is inspired thinking which manifests in wisdom teachings aimed at opening up the minds of the readers to contemplate new perspectives, and act as a catalyst for truth seeking. In the Chapter, Exhortations of the Master, there is reference to a simple technique, on how to connect with one's Higher self using energy signatures in the left hand.

The Chapter 'Lessons from Nature' is meant to show how the Divine communicates with us through every life force in Creation, and how we have the ability to connect with every life force to learn a divine lesson.

The messages in this book seek to encourage each reader to remove the word 'limitations' from one's vocabulary, and espouse cosmic thinking of eternal realities, which is, that man is God in manifest and is limitless, eternal and free.

Overall, the Higher self teachings aim to impart wisdom which can be translated into one's daily living or practice. They are meant to inspire others to desire to discover their true essence and seek wisdom and knowledge, which is TRUTH, to enable them to live empowering and fulfilling lives. In other words all can do what the author has done; tap into a higher consciousness and reap truth for themselves which will open up their awareness, and motivate higher connections with spirit. This will enable spiritual independence to be achieved, eventually. To this end, the author has in the appendix, created a powerful Energy Clearing meditation to enable readers to un-create false paradigms or limiting beliefs which preclude them from connecting with their god selves. The author is also aware of how challenging it is for many to relax for the purpose of connecting with divine energies, and has thus created a Hypnosis meditation to facilitate relaxation and divine connection. Persistent use of these meditations will bear fruit as the participant follows the process.

The Chapter "Conversations with the Master" offers an intriguing insight into how each has the ability to connect with the Master within and seek answers to day to day issues and problems. The author's conversations with the Master within her yielded much wisdom and practical advice. There is no greater solace and wisdom that could be had than from one's true self, being the Master within.

The other chapters are channelled wisdom teachings from the Creator, the Christ, the Mother Spirit, various Ascended Masters and Archangels. Each message given is specially meant to bring clarity to the readers' thinking on certain subjects, and to open up minds to truths which may not be readily accepted. These messages support the resurrection of God or Christ consciousness within each soul during this time, when humanity and the planet are on the brink of ascending vibrationally into another dimension. The vibration which resounds from the teachings is distinct and peculiar to the energy which brings the message. The messages from these beings are by no means attached to any religion or religious figure. The author simply works with certain members of the Spiritual Hierarchy who have identified themselves to her by name/ title, and who have chosen to use her as a channel to reveal some cosmic truths. The underlying message in some of the teachings is that, the comprehension of truth will influence one to make changes in one's thinking, outlook and behaviour, and thus find one's freedom to live and be a truly empowered, divine being.

Some of the messages highlight that human perceptions are usually based on outer sensory perceptions, existing conclusions and opinions formed on limited information, being that which is observed or taught. True knowledge can only be known from the higher mind and needs no proof. The messages illustrate that perceptions can rarely be trusted to show truth unless they are formed through the inner or higher senses. It is time to recognise the limitations of human perceptions influenced by ego thinking, and choose to align ourselves with higher knowing. As we avidly seek the truth in all things, our claircognizance will awaken and we begin to know what the Creator/God/Source knows, and come to recognise the illusion of separation. The more we seek truth with pure intent the more we will receive in honesty.

The teachings are directed to reminding readers of the truth of who they are, and the implications as well as blessings of coming into remembrance. Some of the messages encourage readers to directly face the truth of matters or experiences, instead of brushing them aside and focussing on only the things which make them feel good. It is only when we can face the truth that we can find the courage to make changes, if necessary. Truth is not always easy to hear or bear. These messages should be read with an open mind and with the eyes and understanding of spirit, thereby negating what might be a negative reaction if read through the ego mind.

This book is dedicated to awakening within each reader the desire for truth, and the desire to seek the highest truth no matter how uncomfortable the process might be. In so doing, each reader may feel compelled to relinquish outdated beliefs and thinking, for revelations of spirit founded on the ONE truth. Ultimately, the teachings encourage the reader to desire to espouse his/her inalienable divine right to live in accordance with his/her highest conception of God, with whom they are ONE. The intention is to motivate the readers to seek the god within themselves, so that they too can begin to access higher knowledge and truth.

The messages in the book are conveyed through a combination of conversational style, anecdotes of personal experiences, visual language, analogies, prose and essay. The messages are presented as received. They encourage deep thought through the posing of questions, and introduce some new perspectives for contemplation with one's god self.

The book contains a wealth of wisdom, and the author has been told that if a reader is seeking inspiration or guidance on any day, he/she can simply sit in silence and express a desire for guidance, open the book, and the message he/she needs to hear or the inspiration, guidance or wisdom needed, will be in the Chapter at which the book is opened.

1

THE JOURNEY

I have travelled aeons through the labyrinth of life
and tasted the vagaries of its pliant moods.
I have ambled over many roads in a cloud of pallor
and missed the gentle fingers of light kneel to signal highlands free.
I have courted the wealth of life's pleasures and
charmed the winds of worldly cares,
Yet every track I have sojourned a blessed experience did it brew
Sometimes tasteless, savoury some,
But lessons did it cultivate
until that fateful call did rend the covers webbed around my soul
that I would hear the plaintive tunes caress the sleeping light awake
into the knowing of the truth.
Poised on the plateau of content, the radius of my wings extends.
Equipped with knowing I embark, to the sacred temple, that I Am.

I was born in Trinidad, an island in the Caribbean, and had a normal childhood growing up with three brothers, one sister and parents who served in the field of education.

Unlike many star seeds (those not of the Earth), I was not born conscious of my gifts. I do recall having a great love and empathy for children and would be moved to assume a motherly status towards them. One of my most vivid memories is the day my last brother, Barry, was born. I took over the role of mother at the age of six and treated him as my own. A few years later, when he became ill and had to be hospitalised, I recall kneeling at the bedside and praying to God for his recovery.

As a child I was fairly grounded, very sensitive, prone to being emotional and not very comfortable with the male presence. I lived in my own inner world at times with the propensity to day dream.

When my siblings were out playing, my preference was to read. As a teenager, my love for philosophy made me realise how different I was from others my age. A great source of inspiration to me was Khalil Gibran. My favourite book then was "The Prophet". I harboured thoughts of one day being able to write like Gibran did. Being a non-conformist with a keen sense of justice, I deplored injustice and had an aversion to violence and conflict. In my formative and adolescent years I exhibited the traits of a typical Virgo, being born on 15th September. It was clear (mostly because they told me so) that others found me difficult at times. In those days I did not particularly feel understood. Perhaps, this was born from my inability to understand myself or my role in this world. I always felt older than my age and was predisposed to being of a serious nature.

My religion was Presbyterian, and I have fond memories of attending Church and Sunday School as a child, and singing hymns. It became very obvious to me when I started High school that my knowledge of the Bible was very limited. There was little inclination on my part to study the Bible or to memorise passages or excerpts. Needless to say, my performance in the religious education class was average.

On a brighter note, my creative abilities began to evolve and I found myself writing poetry and prose and participating in the performing arts. My inclination for theatrics made it easy for me to express the "soul" in the writings of others, and of my own. I did have a great teacher in my mother, Roma, who had trained me and my siblings at an early age, in the art of public speaking and the recitation of poetry. However, my sense of fearlessness and courage to express my strong convictions and feelings was inherited from my father, Charles. My musical abilities were encouraged through the playing of the piano, and singing in the church and school choir.

The works of Chaucer, Shakespeare, Blake and Yeats greatly appealed to me. Their expressions moved my soul and inspired an interpretation through a deep perspective. It appears that, at an early age I was intuitive without knowing what that meant.

Religion taught me to know God outside of myself. HE was to be praised, honoured and obeyed. HE was to be worshipped in separation to self and seen as an entity way beyond the human form in a dimension or place called Heaven; never to be comprehended until one passed over through death and reunited with HIM.

The word spiritual held no importance to me at that time. Religion was taught and one was expected to conform to what was offered. In fact the word spirit was associated with either the Holy Spirit or those who were deceased. Having grown up in a cosmopolitan environment my siblings and I learnt to appreciate the religious persuasions of others, and participated in and enjoyed the festivals of other religious denominations.

My life changed when I entered into training for a career in the legal profession. My analytical side became enhanced but my creative abilities withered into dormancy. I had a fairly uneventful five years of studying to become a lawyer with the normal experiences one might necessarily undergo at University.

I entered the Legal profession in October 1994 and began my career as a lawyer. Being quite academic and analytical by nature made it easy for me to adapt to the profession in those early years.

My real spiritual journey commenced when I moved to England in 1998 to pursue a Master of Laws degree. Living by myself with very little support, in a foreign country much bigger than I had ever experienced before, took some getting use to. The pace of life and the culture was totally different to that which I was accustomed. However, adapting to my new life became easier over time, and after I completed my Master's degree I gained employment as a Solicitor.

As a Solicitor, I lived a fairly conservative life. I settled neatly in my new environment, having made a few lasting friendships. There were many unrealized expectations, some to my benefit, which eluded me until much later on. There were moments of the normal heart-wrenching emotion of pain and hurt. The frustration of injustice, the disappointment of selfishness and unappreciated kindness and love were all experienced. However, it was obvious to me that I was becoming a victim of these realities. It was difficult to appreciate or know at this time of my being, that my God, was paving a way for a rebirth within me, which would bring me to the point that I am at this moment. The limitations, the frustrations and disappointments brought me strength and purpose, and paved the path to a new awakening of the god in me, which I now realize has always been, as it is in all of us. It was at this time that the healing properties of forgiveness became a real experience and liberated me from the hold of anger, emotional pain, and imbalance.

It became clear to me then that I had to love myself first, by choosing to be free of the negative elements birthed through the experiences. Choosing peace of mind instead of pain and anger allowed me to forgive; not only in words and thought but with meaning and intent.

This enabled me to send love to the other parties who shared in the experience.

It was long after, that it dawned upon me that I was creating my experiences as a learning device. Being naive in many ways and not wise to the ways of the world influenced my trusting and loving nature. To me it was the only way to be.

The next experience spanned four years of my life. It is the lessons learned and growth achieved during this time which contributed to my character today. There may have also been karmic issues to be worked out through this experience. Through this emotionally arduous time my creativity was resurrected. I was baptised into the knowledge of the spirit world, taught myself how to heal others, and the Father (God) became my constant guide and companion. My mantras became *"Always will I set the Lord before me, HE is at my right hand and I shall not be moved"* and *"HIS grace is sufficient for me for HE shall perfect HIS strength in my weakness"*. These words were from the Bible and were a source of much solace to me during those trying times. It was during this time that my relationship with the Divine became stronger. Yet, in keeping with my religious upbringing I still treated the Father as an entity outside of myself.

I was also led to powerful spiritual people who opened doors to new information, which enhanced my understanding of spirit and spiritual matters. One such lady was Ana Robinson, an internationally renowned Spiritual Guide and prayer warrior who led me in the ways of spirit. She always maintained that I had a lot of work to do for God.

The tendency to see myself as a victim made me ask the question, "Why me?" I eventually saw myself as a participant in the experience that caused me to be stretched. This enabled me to discover my tenacity, strong will and God attributes. This experience proved to be the conduit to profound self discovery, character enhancement and spiritual enlightenment. Unknowingly, the divine lessons and wisdom revealed to me enhanced my understanding of the experience. During this experience the poem Stretched was written.

Stretched

Stretched to the limit, my heart cried
No more, no more, please stem the tide
Of pain and fears and challenges,
    I cannot bear.

HE must have heard my tearful plea
Because HE came and dried my cheeks.
HE soothed me with HIS loving touch
HE whispered words of timeless love.

My pain recedes, my hope restored;
Surely HE would end it now.
In my mind's eye I see a door.
Could it be the opening
I have been waiting for?

And then it came with resounding force.
The pain, poignant and raw.
My spirit waned and cried aloud
No more, no more
Deliver me, please save me now.

HE came to me and held my hand
HE said, MY child this is MY plan
Do not despair for you are saved
I deem you worthy of MY grace,
MY will shall never lead you through
The path where I cannot keep you.

I looked at HIM through loving eyes
And felt my Father's breath of life.
I then submitted to HIS will
And felt my spirit wax with pride,
As HE anointed me with peace
I felt my Father's grace released.

7

He looked at me and said, "MY child
Longsuffering you must achieve,
For the fruit of the spirit to be received,
No burden shall I give to you
Without the courage and the strength
And MY unfailing grasp to hold."

I understood my Father's plan
For my spiritual transformation.
Stretch me my Father, as far as you can
And I will bow to YOUR command.

It is said that you must be careful what you ask for. Even today I continue to be stretched in many ways, but it is clear that the goal for me was and is self mastery—mastery over my emotions, mastery over the illusion of myself in this world and God mastery. The Ascended Master Serapis Bey has taught that *"Time and space are the crucible whereby you must prove your God mastery and the alchemy thereof."* [11] Although, unaware of it at the time, I was attracting experiences in keeping with the goal of my soul. The lesson being taught was that, it is here and now, that I must bring it all into balance. It is through my life's experiences that the opportunity presented itself for me to overcome, find, create and sustain balance. In 2002, the world of spirit opened up to me and I became aware of the existence of spirit guides. They began to speak to me through my candles. I would engrave the candles with names, being the subject of my prayer, and the candles would burn into love hearts, initials or other prophetic words or figures. One night the flame on one of my candles was ablaze higher than normal, and I saw that the wick had formed into the shape of a love heart. It became clear to me then how powerful energy is and how through my thoughts and intent energy would respond to me.

---

[11]   The Rainbow Masters—The Magnificent Seven

My guides then began to give me vivid dreams which were encouraging to me, and also prophetic of the things which would happen for me and others. It was during this time that I started to engrave the candles with the words "God's Truth".

I remember one night awaking at some unknown hour and seeing a man standing at a corner of my bedroom. There was no fear. I said to him, "*I know who you are; you are here to look after me*". He was my guide in spirit. Not long after that, I remember musing to myself before going out on a date, as to whether my date would think I was beautiful. That evening whilst waiting for my bus to take me home, an unassuming man came up to me, handed me a rose and asked me if I believed in Angels. I answered "*yes*". He gave to me the rose and said, "*I am an Angel from God and I want you to know that you are beautiful.*" He then walked away and vanished into the night.

Eventually, my challenging experience came to an end and the healing began. My life progressed until the next two experiences which were less daunting, yet still emotionally painful. There were times when I felt that the lessons from my previous experiences did not serve me, as I was being swept away by my own inability to understand the reasons for these experiences. Perhaps, the true lesson was eluding me. Nevertheless, my faith in God remained strong and in fact I grew closer to HIM, trusting with an inner knowing that my patience and longsuffering would be rewarded. As a result of this faith, no matter how emotionally drained I felt at times, the choices made in response to the experiences were balanced and in keeping with the will of God.

It was one of my great convictions that before I departed from this life I would see the face of God and hear HIS voice. Many times during the night whilst asleep or in dream state I would hear myself praying.

In hindsight, it became clear that my experiences were a stepping stone for me in my search for love. It eventually culminated in the greatest love affair I would ever experience in my life.

Like most people, I wanted to be in a loving relationship which progressed to marriage and family life. My desire eluded me, notwithstanding my capacity to give and share pure love. One weekend I cried out to the Father asking *"why oh why have YOU forsaken me?"* Why was it that I was giving and giving and giving love to all who came into my life and HE could not lead me to someone who would reciprocate? What more could I do or give?

It was at this moment that my great awakening occurred. A light bulb was switched on within me and over the next few weeks HE filled me with HIS presence. HE filled me to the brim with such pure unconditional love that I have never since sought love outside of myself. This was the beginning of my baptism into truth. HE gave to me the knowledge that HE is within me, not outside of me, and that HE is all LOVE and that I am all love. He took away my need, filled what I thought was a void by simply awakening me to the remembrance of HIS presence within. My experience transcended an intellectual comprehension of HIS presence. I felt and experienced HIS energy in a real and abiding way. HE has become my very heart beat. HE is the seat of my soul, yet HE sits on the throne of my heart.

The journey up to that point had been gruelling at times, but I was being prepared through multitudinous experiences to evolve into my power.

With my acceptance of the Father's revelation, HE charted my path to the acquisition of Higher Knowledge and Truth. My real education was about to begin.

2

THE UNFOLDING

There was a profound feeling during the days and weeks following my awakening that life would never be the same for me again. My path led me to people and groups who would become instrumental in my growth and spiritual education. The shutters over my eyes were fully lifted and a desire to be educated by spirit and in spirit was overpowering.

This season in my life was the season of revelations. I began to feel presence around me. Whether travelling, teaching or just sitting at home, there was a presence around my head, my arms and my legs. I would feel feathery touches on my face, and my third eye and crown chakra would be buzzing. This was a new and exhilarating experience. It felt as if the presence was that of my spiritual and or Angelic guides. I did not know however, how to respond to the experience; it was simply comforting.

In hindsight I realise how important divine timing is. Readiness is always so crucial to the materialisation of change. For years, through my various experiences I was being prepared for this. My Angels and guides communicated to me through different ways in the past; such as dreams, candles, poetry and prose. Being more spiritually open now meant that their mode of communication could become personal.

During this spiritually fertile time, my hunger for truth (that which I was praying for, for many years) was being assuaged through published teachings which were brought by the Ascended Masters, the Archangels and Members of the Spiritual Hierarchy. I was certainly being taken through the stages of education necessary to bring me back into the remembrance of who I am. There was a resonance with the teachings which prompted a feeling of me travelling through my consciousness to an instant, where I too taught what was being taught to me now. There was an instinctual knowing that the teachings were truth. Most of the teachings were written in a language that was spiritually conventional, which appealed to me. I was also being taught about the Father's plans for the ascension of the planet and the wave of energy from the universe directed towards awakening and raising the consciousness of humanity.

On the eve of my birthday in September 2009, the Archangel Michael visited me. He came in a wisp of pure violet/pink energy and embraced me. I was elated. This day marked the beginning of endless visitations from the Angelic realm. The Angels would come from behind and embrace me in their presence and I would feel pure heat bathe my entire body.

They became my constant companions. I knew they were with me and felt their presence. At this point my telepathic abilities were not yet developed, so I decided to try automatic writing. The energy in my physical space was created through lighted candles and by inviting Angelic presence from the light of the Creator into the room. The visualisation of divine light filling the entire room mentally prepared me to receive communication from my Angels. My faith accepted that there were no boundaries. After all, they too wanted to communicate with me and I had been feeling their presence for many months. With the intent to connect with them I held on to a pen very loosely and said *"If there is Angelic presence in the room move the pen to the right."* After a few calls they moved the pen to the right. You will know when they enter as the pen begins to move without any effort on your part.

The Angels introduced themselves by name and gave me further information about their role in my life. I persevered in my efforts to connect with them in this way, and during many sessions they revealed my higher purpose. Most surprisingly they also revealed my soul's lineage, as a Melchizedek incarnate. It was many months later through a meditation that Archangel Uriel also confirmed that my soul was from the Melchizedek order and I bore the wisdom of the ages. A visitation from our star brothers through dream state one night further confirmed my lineage.

Before 2009 came to an end, through automatic writing, the Archangel of Michael connected with me and said that I was being prepared for a task for God. He confirmed that I was under HIS divine protection. Not long after through automatic writing "God" came through. The exact words written were *"Mighty God is present"*. HE spoke to me directly through this mode which was very heartening. I had asked HIM to hug me, and that night during an out of body experience whilst asleep, I saw myself standing on my bed. Suddenly, I was taken down to the side of the bed and realised that there were hands around me hugging me. I reached out behind me with my arms and felt a cloak. As suddenly as it happened, I was back in my body and wide awake. It was during this time that I was cultivating a very close relationship with the Father from within.

On the same night that the Father had appeared through automatic writing, my Higher self also made an appearance. She introduced herself and told me more about my role on earth. One night not too long after this experience, I had another out of body experience during sleep time. I was standing in my kitchen and an Angel lifted me up to the ceiling and brought me back down; then lifted me up again and took me across to the living area; and as I looked to the wall on the right there were wings on my back. These experiences provided impetus to connect more and more. I was taught that there are no limitations and I resolved to connect with my higher brothers and sisters of the celestial realm.

During the last few months of 2009 I felt energetically connected to the Ascended Masters; in particular the Chohans of the Seven Rays, the Archangels and the Father. Within myself there was a knowing that there was a higher purpose to be fulfilled in my life. A big picture began to emerge where I saw myself as part of the whole, as eternal and bearing the identity of spirit. In this context of higher understanding the things and desires I had in the past were no longer important. Service to God and humanity was my purpose for incarnating on this planet. I was not giving up anything, but truly embracing who I am and living my truth. I see myself and all my brothers and sisters of the soul, incarnate on planet earth, as extensions of the Father/Creator. There was an understanding that the Father could live through me if I allowed HIM to. HE has taught me that we are all messengers of the time; we are all prophets of the time and we must carry the word of God through our behaviour. HE has also taught that *"we are all sacred and in that sacredness*

we have an obligation and responsibility to all things to which we are connected".[12]
I answered HIS call and I asked HIM to use me for HIS glory and the greatest good of All.

In November 2009, whilst on holiday, the spirit of the Father within moved me and I wrote the following which can be used as a mantra or affirmation in one's daily life. It resonates a power within and the Mighty I AM truly responds.

Mighty I Am Presence

Mighty I Am Presence
Let YOUR trim wick of light reveal
That I may pour the oil of love
To stir the flame within my core.
Alive and vibrant I command
YOUR power within to expand
That warmth divine, that knowing all
That silver cord my link to God
From which all wisdom truth and light
Eternal in my soul resides.

Mighty I Am Presence
May YOUR realm be incarnate
That as I stand within YOUR might
Communion with my inner light
Shall move my consciousness beyond
The human octave of this form
That I may be that I Am
A manifestation of my God.

The Father has taught me that HIS will, is that it is our will to become God in manifestation. This is the goal of the journey to ONENESS.

---

[12]   Phoenix journals

The year 2010 was a year of bliss. I was blessed with the gift of telepathy and began in earnest communing with the celestial realm. When they desired to bring a message through me they would buzz me in the head. My Higher self initiated me in the wisdom of spirit and I began channelling divine wisdom.

I also began actively channelling the Masters, Archangels and the Creator Son (Christ Michael or Jesus Christ).

3

MY MISSION

3

MARRIAGE

My mission or purpose was given to me telepathically. One night I asked for clarification and guidance as to what should be done with the channelled material. That night through an out of body experience I crossed the veil and met the Creator Son—Christ Michael. HE asked me to record my mission, which is being done through this book.

My mission involves encouraging, inspiring and assisting others to become spiritually independent through the education of the mind, so that, the spirit within could be emancipated, that the soul may make a concerted journey towards enlightenment.

How many of us seek truth from external sources, for example, by reading copious numbers of spiritual or philosophical books? Spiritual literature is abundant and there is much information we can obtain with which we may resonate. We must be careful however that we don't get stuck in the paradigms of others without seeking validation ourselves.

How uplifting and soul rewarding it would be for each of us to discover higher learning and truth from within ourselves. Is personal experience not the most credible validation you can attain for truth?

During this time in the Earth's transition and ascension, many are awakening to their true selves, their spiritual being. Many are exploring spirituality, but what is spirituality? Master St Germain has taught that *"Spirituality is a progressive awakening to the inner reality of our being—our spirit self. It is a seeking after God and is the opening of the deepest life of the soul to the indwelling God presence."*[13] Truth, Knowledge and Wisdom come from the spirit of God within our soul. This is where you must go to discover, recover and be reminded of your supremacy. This is where your real treasure lies.

I am here to remind you of your natural identity, the real you. You are a Sovereign being through the birth of your immortal soul, made

---

[13]   Phoenix Journals

possible by the ONE Creator. You are not your physical body and your physical body is not you. You are mind/soul/spirit. Sovereignty is your soul's inheritance through the presence of "The Divine". All power lies within you, through HIM that gave your soul life. You are imbued with God powers and attributes, which, if accessed, can be used by you to create the life you desire.

I have been taught by our celestial brothers of the light that *"the entire purpose of life is finding God within ourselves, our talents, calling and sacred labour. Our bodies are merely a vehicle of consciousness loaned to us that we may prove our God mastery"*. [14] The Masters taught that the *"Physical body is an extension of the eternal mind for use of that mind in a physical environment to serve."*[15]

You may ask, how can God be within me when I can't see HIM or identify with HIM there? If you can accept that you have a soul created by God and that your soul is incarnate within you; then even though you cannot see your soul, you will know that it is the unseen part of you which works with you and through you to manifest itself through your experiences. Master St Germain has taught that *"The awareness of God in yourself is something above and beyond the form yet it registers within and upon the form."*[16] We can sense that which is physical through our outer sensory perceptions, but we can only "KNOW" that which is spiritual. This knowledge comes from the workings of our inner mind or what we will call the higher mind.

Should you in moments of solitude go within yourself by silently intending to commune with God, you will begin to sense the Divine within you. Through intent and perseverance you will eventually begin to feel a profound love enveloping you from within, and you will know that the Father is truly within you. It is only our thoughts that keep us

---

[14]   The Rainbow Masters-Magnificent Seven
[15]   Phoenix Journals
[16]   Phoenix journals

in separation from HIM. We are constantly connected with HIM and can never be apart from HIM. If you can understand this and begin to experience HIM living through you, in time you will come to know yourself as HIM and effort to be HIM knowingly. The Creator is not separate from HIS creation but is within all HE creates.

During the course of our life's journey we may have many truths reflective of where we are in our spiritual unfolding. There will come a point in our spiritual evolution where we will seek the highest truth. I come to teach that there is only one Truth, which is God; or to put it differently, the "consciousness" of what we refer to as God. There are however myriad routes or ways to access that Truth. We can access God and therefore Truth from within God's mind, which is within our mind. It is there that HIS Light resides, which holds the treasure of divine intelligence. The love, power and wisdom of God can also be found in our hearts.

When we are able to find the God within, a light bulb switches on and our true education begins; for higher knowledge comes from looking within. Our inner sensory perception will begin to unfold, our god minds become awaken and we become aware of our divinity as we start to receive the wisdom of divine intelligence. We shall only then come into the "Knowing" that God alone is knowledge, and that very God is within us. We can download from our god mind reams of wisdom to direct the course of our lives. Always on our spiritual journey must we realise that illumination is gradual, and each experience which breeds and results in enlightenment must be savoured.

We carry the temple of God within us. If we can find and gain entry into that temple, we can live in the energy of the Mighty I AM Presence. Our lives, accomplishments and growth will be framed in spiritual reality; and we shall come into knowledge of the Truth, that we and the Creator Source are ONE and that we too have the power to create and manifest as HE does.

4

BAPTISM INTO TRUTH—LESSONS LEARNT

During the last few years of my spiritual awakening, I learnt many valuable lessons.

I began appreciating the Law of ONE, meaning, recognition that there is only one consciousness, being the God or creational consciousness of which we are all a part. There is no inferiority, superiority, discrimination or inequality in the Law of ONE, for at a soul level "All are ONE and ONE is All". It is for us in this physical seat of consciousness to come into that understanding through the knowing of God within. It is only then that we will start to think and behave in a way that truly reflects our Higher selves.

I was also taught that observing the Law of ONE does not mean tolerating unbalanced behaviour. It simply means that we must love each other as God loves each and recognise that we are a reflection of each other. We must however be discerning of behaviour against God's laws, but at the same time be able to see that even though we are one consciousness, each may be at a different spiritual level in his/her journey back to the Creator Source. This in itself gives us an opportunity to help those who may not be as spiritually aware; and to recognise that each child of God will at his/her individually determined rate eventually reunify with the love of Source. The Masters have taught that *"One of the most important of Creation's Natural laws is that all life is equal. That is a fact which must be acknowledged before man can expect to find balance and growth in any enlightened community. You have to respect life-all life, not just your own."*[17]

We tend to be unconsciously aware of this; yet unable to apply it in a sustainable way in our daily living. Master Serapis Bey shared this very inspiring affirmation which I began to use every day:

Universal Mother
Weave me in the language of love
That brings me closer to loving my brothers and sisters in ONENESS

---

[17] Phoenix journals

Grow me in my ability to think feel and to act with a love that binds
All things together in beauty and creation.[18]

Repetitive use of this affirmation combined with my daily connections with the divine presence within, enabled an expansion in my consciousness to embrace all as one with me. I was able to focus not so much on the physical body of another but on the light within each, which is divine and which connects me to them. This inner vision allowed me in my daily travels to honour my brothers and sisters of the soul whom I encountered, and to embrace them in divine love whilst acknowledging how loved they too are by God. In other words regardless of their status, identity or circumstances, the one thing I knew we all shared was the reality of God within each of us. I honoured and honour the "Divine" within them in the knowledge of our ONENESS.

I also began to see every life force in creation as ONE with me; that included animals and nature. Through my recognition and understanding of my responsibilities to the god within me, I also began to recognise and understand my responsibilities to other life forces within creation. I forged a deep and abiding relationship with the Earth and came to know her not only as body but also as spirit. She too is a sentient being and we as humans are custodians of her body, responsible for her sustenance, balance, longevity and ascension.

Everything comprises energy and all things respond to energy. When we project negative thoughts and follow with negative words and actions, we affect our energy field, lower our vibrations and affect the energy of the collective consciousness including that of the Earth.

In order to minimise this we must assume responsibility and accountability for the effects of our thoughts and words.

---

[18] Phoenix journals

I was taught by my Angels the importance of assuming mastery over my emotions. When our emotions overcome us, wisdom deserts us. So the lesson is to assume control over our emotions and act in wisdom. This requires a sturdy discipline to be conscious or vigilant of our thoughts, reactions and responses.

Our life's experiences have the power to evoke reactions in absentia of our ability to sometimes see and know the reason for the experience. It may not be until after the experience has run its course that we are able to adopt a more balanced perspective, which enables us to extract the lesson or learning. What is needed is foresight and foreknowledge, so that, we may be able to embrace every experience as an opportunity to learn more about ourselves; or to remind us of what we already know and need to put into practice. Experiences provide us with opportunities to grow in our mastery.

We must therefore learn to see every experience as a healthy opportunity to shine our God light and master through emanation, our God attributes, notwithstanding that some of these experiences may be discomfiting. When the natural flow of our aura becomes disturbed, we can recall all the lessons we learnt through our past experiences. We can then access the wisdom which we have come to know through the Christ teachings or teachings from other revered beings such as Buddha and Krishna, and thus be able to restore inner harmony and equanimity.

I was being trained to see and act in truth. When I asked Archangel Michael to show himself to me; he said *"why do you need to see me, I AM of the ONE mind."* He was teaching me to "know" through my inner mind rather than relying on my outer senses for truth. When I asked my Angels to present themselves, they did so by appearing in the form of light geometric shapes. Again they were reinforcing the truth that they are simply energy and that my fantasies of them must be exchanged for a true understanding of their nature. Their response is a direct correlation to my ardent desire for truth in all things.

29

I was taught that all that we seek is within us. Peace, harmony and balance dwell within us and it is for us to take responsibility for ourselves, as no one else on earth can give us these things. A state of inner balance and a sense of peace and serenity could only be maintained if love directed all actions, feelings, thoughts and responses. The true essence of love was shown to me as the love of the God incarnate. In the event of inner disturbance I would go to the god within and seek guidance and restoration. I would always come out feeling balanced and joyful.

The reality is that our daily lives will not always be smoothly paved, but as much as we can we should endeavour to create our reality through positive projections, and hold on to those projections as a manifested reality.

The Father has said to me *"I will be your sword and I will cut down or part all impediments that seek to obstruct your spiritual course; and I will be the mirror of golden light which surrounds you to catch the whips of negativity hurled at you. I will purify through MY love that negativity and return it as light to its source."* How wondrous to know that we do not walk on our own, but with the Source of All within us. It is humbling, yet empowering to allow this force within to direct and guide our lives.

Each and every day I ask the Source to extend HIMSELF through me and to live though me in this physical world, that I may play my part in facilitating and being a conduit of cosmic energies in our physical dimension.

5

GIVING AND
RE-GIVING

I have been taught by the Father that the Law of Balance is the foundation of the universe and it is the basis of giving and re-giving.

Balance is the point of perfection, peace and stillness. All creation starts from a point of balance. When all is in balance there is unity and ONENESS. The rhythm of the universal mind is always in balance.

In human relations, if there is to be balanced unity one must give in service to another followed by equal re-giving by the other. Master St Germain taught elsewhere, *"As all men are ONE each one gives to the whole and the whole re-gives equally."*

If man were to observe nature he would realise that nature never takes but gives only. There is harmony in nature until it becomes disturbed by unbalanced actions.

I was blessed to witness the Law of Balance in action as reflected in nature when I visited a beautiful island resort in the Maldives. This afforded me the opportunity to experience total communion with the God incarnate. Whilst I was on the island I was conscious of the Father every moment. This was inevitable, for the natural beauty of the island boasted the presence of God. Through my inner vision the magnificence of our Creator became clear, and HIS presence was evident in all creation as HIS delightful face would present itself in all natural life.

I understood what "Balanced rhythmic interchange" meant when I saw how all of nature interacted through the giving and re-giving of themselves. The ambling wind massaged the tepid waters of the ocean and worked in harmony with the tides to generate symmetric waves, whose rhythm matched the universal heartbeat. Only the majestic trees could hear the music of the melodious wind for they danced and swayed to its vibrant tempo, generating a coolness that provided a welcome relief from the effervescent sun.

The beauty of the ocean lay in the myriad colours which clothed its length and breadth, a result of the holy union between the angling sun, the indigo blue sky and the prosperous ocean. The milky jade of the shoreline preceded the tenacious emerald and aqua turquoise eyes of an ocean, that sees it all. The sun has given life and beauty to God's creation and the ocean has re-given of its love by providing a home for the sea animals, and sustenance through the plankton and phytoplankton. The chlorophyll within plants in the ocean and on land magnetically draws the golden rays of sun light which they photosynthesise into chemical energy, and subsequently release oxygen from which other life forms benefit. Do you see the harmonious working of God's creation?

Even the ivory sands offer comfort and shelter to the baby crabs that astutely create and bury themselves in holes which provide a natural haven. My heart jumped for joy as I witnessed daily the herons plodding along the shoreline picking for food, but mostly enjoying for long periods of time the beauty of the ocean as they stared intently and in silence at the blooming waves. I marvelled at the body structure of these birds. I witness at dusk the stingrays harmoniously swimming close to shore with baby sharks and other unique fish and marvelled at the verdant imagination of our Father and HIS attention to detail.

I walked amongst the dense forest thanking the trees and other plants for the oxygen they provide and the home and food they willingly offered to the little creatures. Gratitude was given to the singing birds for bringing joy to the forest through their whistling renditions. It was as if the birds were serenading the trees in love and gratitude for providing them with shelter.

Appreciation was extended to the trees and plants for their fertility and the fruit and food they birth; and I reminded them to thank Gaia (the Earth) and the Father for the life given to them, for they too are fruits of the Earth's bountiful womb.

A few times I was accosted by lizards which ran across my path; admittedly I am not endeared to them. I complained about their presence as they tended to camouflage nicely with the sand, earth and trees, so they often took me by surprise. The voice of Christ Michael echoed that it is not for them (the lizards) to facilitate me by staying out of my way for I was in their natural habitat. It was for me to facilitate them. They were merely accommodating me. What a wonderful lesson that was in respecting every life force in creation. I still did not get use to them, but I stopped complaining!

Some of the branches of the trees were wilting and close to decay, which marred the face of the trees with a sickly energy. I knew that these trees must be pruned and the decaying branches removed that the beauty of the other branches might be seen. The leaves were sagging for thirst whilst the scorching sun continued its tirade, so, through the god within, I prayed that these leaves would be rescued by the rain. That night for the first time during my visit the heavens poured in answer to my prayer. I gave thanks that the leaves would find renewed life.

When the day retired to rest and the dying scarlet embers of evening became draped by the sombre veil of darkness, a litany of crisp stars pierced the unseeing eyes of the ebony sky and assured the earth that the heavens were looking after "All" during the night. A cosmic flavour filtered through and I was mesmerised by the parading stars which flirted with me at every turn as I lavished attention and accolades upon them.

I was humbled by the dedication and love that the workers on the island applied to their daily chores. Their faces lit up when I smiled with them or enquired of their day. They live insulated lives on the island resort, with no family and scarcely any time off. I thanked God for their humble experience and prayed that the presence of divinity which abounds their island would be discovered by each within himself. I encountered one young man who on the day of our encounter had turned thirty. He had no one to celebrate with. His family lived in India and had not remembered his birthday, and his only brother who also worked on the island did not remember too. Yet this young man was not fazed. He accepted it with a smile and we talked of God. He confided in me that he had a small temple in his room, and he prayed every day. He had a very enquiring mind and it became evident to me from his disclosures that he was clairvoyant. He could see spirits. Yet, he lived in an environment where his abilities cannot flourish through guidance, for he cannot understand its significance.

This holiday brought real enlightenment as I truly experienced ONENESS with God and with All. I remembered Master St Germain's words from a journal which I had read: *"The entirety of creation is a manifestation of love. Every effect of motion in Nature is a manifestation of the Nature of God, for Nature gives of its all in every action and re-gives equally in every reaction. Nature never takes—for God never takes. Nature always gives equally for God always gives equally. God's equally balanced giving for re-giving is never violated in Nature for Nature is an extension of God's nature."*[19]

I also called to mind Christ Michael's teaching that we must take the time to look at the flowers, their colours and contours through a magnifying glass. HE says *"Look at the heart (seed) of the blossom and realise the perfection and see the feeling which is reflected in your soul of how each colour and hue reflects on your being. I promise you if you begin to see the world through the magnifying glass and realise its perfection of that which Nature presents, you will never be out of communion with God."*[20]

I was blessed to experience the perfection of God's nature, and understood that continuous meditation simply means continuous God awareness. I am now resolved to journey every moment knowingly and with that feeling of ONENESS that God is in me and I am in HIM; and if HE has created the abundance on earth and I am in HIM, I too have created this abundance and must therefore be a worthy custodian of Our Creation.

---

[19] Phoenix journals
[20] Phoenix journals

My Father and Creator, how awe inspiring and magnificent YOU are! Words cannot express the pure ecstasy I feel when my soul touches YOURS. May the union of our souls be locked in the purity of our love, for as YOU have given life to my soul, I re-give to YOU my life in service.

"I am favoured of YOU, my Creator. I am of the inner Mind. I Know YOUR joy and I am exalted in YOU. I have all knowledge and all power. That which I desire to know or to have or to give is mine to know, to have or to give. My dwelling place is in YOUR high heavens. Be in me that I may be YOU-knowingly. I am in your Light, O my Father. Enfold me ever in YOUR light that I may not again feel the heaviness of the dark upon my heart. Dissolve my separateness and make me ONE with YOU that I, too, can ever be in the giving."[21]

---

[21]   Phoenix journals

6

REALITY VS ILLUSION

My Higher self and I were having a conversation about Reality and Illusion, as it is said so often that our world is an illusion. The following is her explanation.

Behold, the world is yours. The landscape of your thoughts will define its meaning for you. Only you can embrace what is real and determine that which is illusionary. Your eyes through which you see the outer world tells you that what you see must be real, for you can touch and feel it to prove its existence. You, therefore, believe that what you see is real.

What if I told you that your world is simply a mirror of the thoughts of the Creator of All That Is, and that your world as it is now is a mirror of your thoughts?

Whatever you create starts with an idea followed by thoughts. You then channel energy through your efforts to give it form through the creation of matter; that which you can see, and feel through touch. This matter becomes a mirror of your thoughts. You think it as an idea, then visualise it and then you create it. Is your creation real? That depends on what you see or know as real.

You live in a world that is a closet of illusions. There is no reality in matter. Matter serves a temporal need. It is part of the greater experience in the worlds of time and space. It is transient, albeit meaningful in its own way. Reality finds its home in the bliss of eternity, for that which is real is eternal in nature. That which is real cannot be destroyed or depleted. You must always return to that which is real.

Think of the Creator of All That Is as ALL that exists. How then can there be separation in reality? Think of the Creator as projecting HIS thinking through motion on a vast screen. HIS multiple thoughts are recorded on that screen and there appears to be life in HIS projections. Yet, what HE seemingly creates is in fact an illusion, that which simulates reality.

Think of when you go to the cinema. You sit in front of a very large screen. When the movie starts the screen becomes alive. An unseen projector electrically projects a spectrum of light and sound wave motion pictures unto the screen. With your outer senses you can see the actors and witness the events and scenes unfolding. You can actually become so engrossed in the movie that it appears to be real. If you were to walk up to the screen whilst the movie is playing you can neither touch the actors on the screen nor can you become a part of the movie. The reason for this is that what you are seeing and hearing is not real; it is an illusion. The movie is a mirror of what is projected through an instrument. If the projector is turned off so will the movie.

In the same way you should see God as the projector, who projects through HIS thinking, multiple ideas using light waves of motion, to create actors and scenes on the screen of life (time and space). HE has created a movie of sorts. If HE is to stop thinking you will not be here. It is your senses which make the experience real; just as in the cinema where you become so engrossed in the movie through your senses that you forget it is not real.

It is the senses of man which credits the illusion as real and creates the belief that man is separate from God. Should the players on the screen recognise that they are merely thought fragments and that the true universe in which they reside is that of the Knowing Universe as opposed to the sensing one, then that which is real shall become apparent.

The senses create the illusion of reality as all things seem tangible and natural. I ask you to ponder upon: What is natural about emotional or physical suffering or pain? What is natural about lack, poverty, disharmony and discord? Do you think that The Creator sent man to Earth to suffer or experience pain, all of which are created through and by the attachment to the outer senses and the physical structure of the ego? If God is all love, light, peace, balance and abundance, how can you be any less? How can you be less than whole and perfect? It is your senses that tell you otherwise. Your senses do not serve you in truth.

It is the players on the screen who makes the play real through forgetfulness of their Source. They feel that they have taken on a life of their own, but in fact there is only ONE life. Now, look at those who are awakened to the presence of the god within them. They know what is real and they know the true purpose of the play. They learn to access the universe of knowing and utilise the senses of the body for the purpose of experience.

Knowing that you are not separate from the Creator, knowing that your world is an illusion, knowing that all that is real is God, and knowing that God is in each, is the beginning of a journey based on truth.

As individuals in the play you instinctively know that you have the power to create. However, what you choose to create and how you choose to create, you deem "up to you". After all, many see themselves as separate from the Creator and therefore, they have the free will to exercise as they please.

Where your creations are fuelled or inspired by the depths of you, meaning your eternal soul; and love, being the emanation from your soul is woven into the picture you draw or paint, or the music you compose or the poetry you write; that part of you which is real is reflected within your composition or creation. In others words, your creation becomes an expression of your soul. Your production expresses the invisible you and it is that which gives beauty to your creation and becomes an inspiration to others. The real you will always shine through your creation, mesmerise the hearts of others, and draw that which is real within them to that which is real within you.

It is the unseen which connects you to your neighbour and not what you deem the "reality" of relationships. That which is real within you is connected to that which is real within your neighbour, even if you do not share a blood relationship; for all men and women are related through their eternal soul which comes from the ONE.

When you ordinarily look at another you see the mortal body which is the mirror of the Creator's thought. What you do not see is that the Creator is "within" HIS Creation; just as you are "within" yours. HIS intangible yet real presence is "within" the reality of you—your soul. The Creator is the unseen part of you, the dynamic beauty of you. It is HIS presence "within" you that enables you to create from the beauty of your soul through love; and just as you are in your creation, HE is there too, as you are one with HIM.

However, you must know that, just as that which the Creator creates "seems to be" real, so too that which you create "seems to be" real.

To be captivated by the illusionary world that surrounds you, limits your ability to enjoy true vision which will allow you to see beyond the veil of separation, and to transcend the "time capsule" which defines your earthly experience.

Man is spirit turned or brought inside out, for that which is real is always within. That which is within is the Source of creation and has All Knowing.

God and man is ONE and it is the illusion which seems to be more than ONE.

ONE

Into your sacred palm
my solemn hand imprints
that now YOU bear the memoirs of silent retreats.
I journey the breadth of time and space
where vistas unalloyed behold a reverence pure.
That place where the stirring melody of my soul's tuneful longing
draws the harmony of YOU

Where I am regaled by celestial auras
and nourished with delight as YOU wear my hand in YOURS
and speak in melodious questions to kindle the solitaire of wisdom.
When time is spent, the parting bugle heralds.
YOU show YOUR sacred palm which bears the imprint of MY hand
that I may know that time and space illusions,
cannot erase, the union of our melded souls
The ONENESS of OUR eternal being.

7

ONE HEARTBEAT

In one of my nightly meditations the voice within began to speak. I became carried away by the simplicity, yet poignancy of the message.

You are the beat of the universal heart. The heart centres you and is centred in you.

To access the universal rhythm within you, find your centre, your point of balance. Only then will you begin to feel the tempo of love that stills the universe, yet gives it life through seeming motion.

It is the pulse of the universal heart which you must re-discover. You must re-familiarise yourself with the subtleties of its vibrations, so that, you begin to feel a natural harmony responding within. The beat of the universal drum of life will welcome you home to the knowledge of the ONE heartbeat.

The universal heart cycles and re-cycles ruby rich love to every part of its being. It withholds nothing. It is matchless in service and selfless in giving. It tires not in its eternalness. It is constant in its calling of the children birthed by it; quietly summoning them to seek its timeless symmetry within themselves and know it as their own.

When you find, hear and begin to know the universal heartbeat within, you will know that the life in you is resurrected. Only then you will understand the vibration of immortality and experience that which you share with all men—THE ONE HEARTBEAT.

8

THE SILENT ECHO

One night as I sat with and in the Father's presence, HE said that HE desired to speak of the Silent Echo. I was intrigued by the topic, but experience taught me to listen and go with the flow of HIS thoughts.

Silence is not a feature which breeds comfort in a world that is braced within the parameters of activity. In this flurry, much is missed that can otherwise be a catalyst to man's supreme enlightenment. I will speak to you through the analogy of a heartbeat.

You cannot usually hear your heartbeat unless you sensitise your outer ears through the instrument of a stethoscope. You cannot feel your heartbeat, save perhaps through physical exertion. Your outer senses, must with the aid of something other than itself become attuned to your heartbeat. It does not mean that your heart is not beating. It beats whether or not you can hear or feel it. It keeps your physical body alive.

Likewise, I would like you to think of the celestial heartbeat. This heartbeat is evidenced through the knowing of your inner senses rather than your outer senses. Your inner senses can know it through the experiencing of its rhythm. As your inner senses become attuned, it will be able to hear and feel the celestial rhythmic heartbeat. It is most present and alive. Your inability to hear and feel it does not mean it is absent or non-existent; much like the beat of your physical heart.

To hear the celestial heartbeat you need to experience quiet endurance. This simply means that you must persevere with the intention and desire to hear and feel. This may be challenging for many who are pre disposed to being guided by the outer senses. It may take some time to acclimatise to the inner senses which you can begin to know through quiet communion. In this way they will respond, by providing you with insight, through inspiration and visions. As you engage in continuous communion with these senses, they become stimulated and begin to work for you. In time your inner awareness will grow as your inner senses become practiced. A whole new world (your inner world) will open up for you and you will begin to explore a new yet familiar dimension within yourself.

Your inner senses are governed by your higher mind or consciousness. It is these senses that will avail you of the cosmic or celestial heartbeat. This heartbeat tirelessly echoes into the consciousness of the children of the universe, prompting them to get in touch with the higher beat of life.

It is time to hear that silent echo and respond. If you cannot find this heartbeat, hear it, feel it and become one with it, you cannot find your immortal soul, and you cannot know life. As your physical heart keeps your mortal body alive, the celestial heart beat keeps your soul alive.

The Father said if I were to listen to my physical heartbeat I would hear the rhythm "I AM, I AM, I AM", for the physical heartbeat is a replica of the celestial beat.

9

JUST AS I AM

I was contemplating with my god mind a song that I had sung in church when I was a youth. The title of the song is *"Just as I am"*. I was not enthralled by the lyrics of the song, save the words "Just as I am".

As I pondered these words I heard "Fear creates disjointed thoughts which render many paralysed by perceived limitations. It is a hindrance to self progress. It decapitates the life inbred and hastens to concretise the feeling that you are as you are and must be accepted as you are. When others accept you as you are this validates acceptance of self. Too often this thinking prevents true evaluation of self.

You become reticent to change without appreciating that who you think you are, is not truly who you are. Reticence becomes the conductor of the morose as you remain in the mire of "That is who I am, how I am, and if you love me you must accept me as I am." This is the proverbial cop out phrase, in the absence of knowing what "Just as I AM" connotes.

Should you dissect the words you would know that "Just as" is simply "Just is". This translates "to be". Therefore Just as I Am can most aptly be translated to "BE that I AM" or "BE the I AM". Should you meditate on these words there will come a delightful twist in your thinking. Tune your thinking to a higher vibration and all that "I AM" will seep into your consciousness, that you may indeed reach for the "I AM" within you. The "I AM" is the "Higher Presence of Divine Authority".

The "I AM" teaches you to assume responsibility for self, your true self, and not the illusion of who you think you are, or the perceptions others may have of you, as foisted upon you.

The "I AM" is the individualised presence or God within each. The "I AM" of you is calling out to you to "BE WHO I AM", "BE THE I AM". This notion is often too heady or overwhelming for ones to embrace, in a culture that sees the "I AM" as God who dwells beyond man.

The aptitude of man must be tickled, so that, he reaches up to the highest point of himself where true life dwells. When you can be moved to say, "accept me just as I AM", you are saying to others that you recognise yourself as the I AM, that you are being the I AM, that you represent all that the I AM stands for, and they must accept the highest part of you which is the "Divine" essence. You are in effect espousing your inalienable divine right to be WHO YOU ARE. You do this without fear or favour for the "I AM" cannot be violated. It is your highest truth."

Just as I AM
The life in me
Presence Divine, in harmony
Through light conceived
By love so real
I AM I AM
That I AM
I AM

Just as I AM
Eternal and free
Creator of my destiny
Return I have to the ONE in me
I AM I AM
That I AM
I AM

Just as I AM
HE beckons me
HIS lambs to guide, in truth to lead
The lesson is to ever be
The I AM That I AM
I AM

10

THE CHURCH IS
ONE FOUNDATION

I seemed to have been in the mood for contemplating songs I had sung in Church during my childhood. The reason being, that as my awareness grew I began to reflect on the lyrics of these songs. I felt that though the titles were meaningful, the lyrics could be updated to reflect a new awareness.

The "Church is One foundation" was the title of one of the songs I pondered upon with the Father.

The Church is more than a physical structure whether it is called Church, Temple, Mosque, Synagogue etc. The foundation is that which is Divine, of God.

The Church is meant to be the foundation of all God's truth, values, virtues, qualities attributes and laws. It represents the body of God which embraces all without distinction or discrimination, as the body of God represents the ONENESS of All.

There is only One God; there is One Body; there is One Church whatever you choose to call that church, and there is One foundation.

The Father has said to me *"You (meaning man on earth) have made the Church, Temples, Mosque and Synagogues a place of worship; yet I say to you that you are the temple; you being the body of God are the temple where God resides. The foundation of the Church starts with you."*

The Church has been institutionalised but God is not an institution and cannot be institutionalised or limited. HE is sacred energy that is limitless in HIS eternalness.

The Father has said to me: *"The body of God is not divided and therefore should you wish your Church to reflect God then there should be no division amongst churches. In God's Kingdom there is no separation and therefore the Church must condone only unity. In the body of God there is no inferiority or superiority; no part is better than the other and none chosen above the other. There is only ONENESS. Each religion has created its own "church" to reflect the dogmas and doctrine of its respective beliefs. In God's Kingdom there is only truth. Truth cannot be believed; it must be known. Truth is the Religion of God and God's truth will not always be confined to what is recorded on paper but must be discovered through mortal experience through the union of the individual with God. The Church is the holder of all truth but the Church I speak off is not the creation of man, but the creation of God through the soul of man. There rests the seat of God's church."*

If the Church is One foundation, all churches should share the same truth if they intend to represent the ONE and ONLY God."

Should each come into the understanding of what this means, then, should you stand in unity in a place of physical orientation, there will be your church. Likewise, should you congregate in the structure labelled Church, there too shall be your church. The Church of God is where you are, should you rest in unity within the understanding and light, of who you are. You must recognise that the Church in reality can never be a physical structure, for the physical holds no reality.

Should you choose to embrace all that is real, then I ask that you see "All" within you and yourself within "All"; you will know that there is only One foundation, for there is only One God who is All.

The Church is One foundation
In wholeness and accord
There is no separation
For each is part of God
HIS body can't be broken
Yet all in HIM is free
United through the God mind
HIS Church will ever be.

The Church is One foundation
One Light, One love in All
Each soul is in dominion
Their birthright to recall

Through resurrected Christ light
Their vision to repair
And knowledge to inspire
God's Church to be revered.

The Church is One foundation
On which each life is built
The brotherhood of mankind
God's purpose to fulfil
HIS Kingdom to establish
On earth through minds and hearts
HIS light ever to burnish
HIS Church ordained to rise.

11

PRAYER—ITS PURPOSE, POWER AND PRICE

Given the diverse cultural and religious practices which exist in our world, peoples' perceptions of prayer vary. I grew up with the understanding that prayer was a petition to an invisible God who existed above and beyond our plane of existence; and after praying we were to wait with faith for the answer.

Through my interactions with the Father and the Masters, my view point on prayer began to change.

I remember Christ Michael saying: *"Let your prayers be for everything and everyone except yourself for in this manner only, can that which you desire and seek come unto you. When you have learnt the secret of the ancients so shall you have learnt the secret of life, for you cannot expect to receive that which you already have."*

During meditation I pondered upon this with God. HE said to me *"Prayer is a commemoration of ONENESS. It is the unification of the finite with the infinite to bring you into remembrance of your ONENESS with ME, and the knowledge that you already have that for which you have asked"*. I got the impression that HE was saying that you are ONE with ME (God) and have the power to give yourself what you desire. HE continued by saying *"It is through prayer and return to ONENESS that I will show you how to unfold for yourself that which you desire."*

Our perspective of prayer is heavily influenced by our religious persuasions or beliefs. We have been conditioned to view prayer in the way we were taught. One thing I have learnt is, as civilisations evolve spiritually and become more advanced, perspectives should indeed shift to a higher understanding. That which man has practiced in error, although unknowingly so, must now be corrected, so that true results can be realised and sustained.

How many through prayer simply list to God all their desires, even imposing a time frame? In so doing we are asking or telling God to serve us, but are we giving any thought as to what we will re-give? I taught in an earlier piece that the Law of Balance is the foundation of the universe, and is the basis of giving and re-giving. I have been taught that this law should underpin all our transactions, activities and relationships, even our relationship with the god within us. When we ask God to give us the things we desire, we are asking HIM to show us HIS love for us by giving us what we want. However, God wants love from us also. How are we going to re-give our love to God? Perhaps, by loving and honouring every life force in God's creation. The first lesson here, is that, when we go to God in prayer we must have the intention of giving something in exchange.

We are all ONE with God because God is within each of us. All that we think, desire, project or create will reflect our nature. If our nature is the nature of God then we should ensure that all that we create is in the image of the god within us. If we ask for things without a thought of how we could re-give, our prayers are selfish, and we are making ourselves into our selfish image. Master St Germain taught, *"God will fulfil your every desire if you will work with God to fulfil it."* I understand this to mean, that we must be prepared to take the necessary action to help our desire come to fruition. The measures we require to take may be pro active practical steps. In doing this, we are re-giving of our time, effort and abilities. There is a saying *"God helps those who help themselves"*. I would say the concept is similar.

Master St Germain also taught *"God will give you what you desire but you must re-give equally by serving God through service to your fellow men."* For example, when a Mother prays for God to lovingly protect her only son who is sent overseas to fight in a war, she must also extend her love equally to the other mothers' sons who have been sent to war. It is only then that she will be in the re-giving. This in my view is moving away from selfish prayer to selfless prayer. However, if this mother prays with great devotion, sincerity and love from her heart, but then turns angrily upon a friend or neighbour, her pray is voided. Remember the Law of ONE. We are all ONE in God and God is all there is. God does not hurt any part of HIMSELF; we must follow this too.

If our prayers are to be answered, we must take positive action, and cause the love that God has given us to be re-given. If you ask God to bless and heal your friend who is ill, you can do your part in helping to bless your friend by seeing whether there is anything you can do to be of assistance, such as ensuring that your friend has meals or visiting him/her.

What about if a business man asks God to bless his business with prosperity? What does the business man have to do? Obviously he will have to do his part by taking the necessary practical steps (advertising etc) to ensure that his business is successful. He cannot simply sit and ask in prayer for what he wants without taking positive action. He has to reach out for his desire. If he does not know what steps he should take, he should invite God to inspire him, so that he understands what needs to be done. Additionally, in the re-giving, he should go out into his business and bless all in it. He should take the necessary steps to make his employees prosper, for when he gives to his employees the love God has given him, it is in fact, God's love being given to them. In so doing his prayers will be answered and his business will be blessed.

If you do not know what you should be re-giving ask God to illuminate your mind by showing you what you can do to be in the re-giving.

When you pray you should not pray in separation from God by appealing to a God outside of yourself. You should commune with the god within you. Let us say you have a problem which you take to God in prayer. You ask God to solve it for you or take it away. You may feel lighter and even comforted, but what you are doing, is asking God to do something for you without working with God to fulfil your desire. Prayer may placate, but I say prayer should empower you. Through inner communion you can ask God to unite HIS God mind with yours and think with you that you may receive an inspired solution, or to help you view the experience from a different perspective, or to give you insight as to how you could have better dealt with the experience or issue. In taking this approach to prayer, you are working with God instead of requiring God to work for you by giving you what you wish for, without any personal input. Asking God to solve the problem or take it away is shirking your responsibility.

I have heard so many people say *"If there is a God there would be no wars"* or *"why does God not stop these wars and stop innocent people from being killed; surely God must not exist?"* So when we pray to God to put an end to the wars and HE doesn't, surely HE is to blame. At least that is what many think. God gave man free will with the hope that man would choose to exercise free will in accordance with the will and nature of God; the nature of God being love and balance. When we pray to God to stop the wars, we are asking God to let us defy HIS Law of Balance without suffering from its effects. We then blame God for our own actions in breaking HIS law.

God will not stop the wars, for HE does not interfere with the exercise of man's fee will. We all contribute to the collective consciousness and must accept some responsibility. I have been told by our celestial brothers that God will intervene if man abuses nuclear weapons, as this has the ability to destroy the "soul's energy" and the very fabric of space. Man has free will which he can use in whatever way he chooses, but he cannot use it in a way to destroy that which he has not created, being the soul energy which comes from God.

I said earlier, that which we create usually reflects our image and nature. We must therefore be careful that when we pray we do not pray to someone or something we created in our own image. An example is: if someone through prayer says: *"Don't punish me O God, but have mercy upon me for I have sinned"*, that person is not praying to a God of love. If one truly knows God, then one will know that, God is love only. That person is praying to a God of anger and fear which he/she has created in his/her own image. In other words he/she is projecting a God which reflects his/her fearful and angry nature. This person's prayer cannot be answered because the person has not prayed to a God of love; the only true living God which exists is the God of Love.

How many of you have heard time and time again *"The Lord giveth and the Lord taketh away."* We have been conditioned to believe this. If God is a God of love and the Law of Balance is simply giving for equal re-giving, for God to take, is a violation of HIS own law. God only gives;

HE never takes that which has not been given. Death is simply rebirth to new life. We are given life and at the end of our incarnation we re-give our life to God that HE may re-give life again.

How should we pray? I was again contemplating this with God. HE said to me *"Your prayer must originate from the soul, born of a desire from the heart. A proliferation of words I do not need; simple heart or soul felt thoughts will communicate your longing and desire to ME. Let your thoughts be the language through which you communicate with ME. As your thoughts register in MY mind, I will speak with you wordlessly through MY mind. MY answer or response you will receive if you could but still your mind to so receive it. I will tell you what you must do in order that your prayer may be fulfilled, but you must hear ME first. Silence is the conduit of MY intelligence and you must be silent to hear. Through prayer you reunite with your god mind which holds all the answers you seek. I do not require when you pray that you kneel or bow to ME in reverence. Reverence must come from a feeling in the heart, for then I know that you are sincere. I wish to encourage man to remove himself from the ancient ways of doing things. He must see himself as ONE with ME. I do not need him to grovel, implore, cajole or negotiate with ME. He belittles the god within himself when he does this. He must simply come in equality, notwithstanding, that he does not feel equal to ME. What I AM he is. Until he can master his finite form and find God freedom, I will work with him in partnership as equals. I will give to him what he seeks if he works with ME, and re-gives equally, the love I have given unto him."*

I asked the Father to describe to me simply what Prayer means to HIM. HE said: *"Prayer is the communion between man and the god within man, that he may be reminded of who he is and discover his power to unfold for himself that which he desires. Prayer should be a way of life—"living in action", where daily one remains in moment to moment communion with the Divine, that one may always be in the re-giving of that which the Divine gives."*

From my communion with God, I discern that HE does not wish us to spend our days on our knees praying or praising HIM. HE desires our life to be a living prayer by continuously working with HIM to re-give the love that HE has given to us, that we may attain HIS presence, and in so doing, realise that we have the power to give ourselves that which we desire.

The **PURPOSE** of prayer is to come into the knowing and feeling of ONENESS with God, that we may understand we have the **POWER** to fulfil our desires, through the **PRICE** of positive action and the re-giving of the love given to us by God.

12

THE CAPTAIN
OF MY SHIP

How many times have we heard that we are the master of our own destiny? We court and create the life we have with the ability to create the life we desire. Yet, there are many who cannot access the master within themselves, or even accept the possibility that they hold the power to assert their inherent mastery to direct the course of their lives.

The Father has said to me that the journey on this physical plane is meant to open our inner eyes to the understanding that we are not alone. HE, the infinite spirit dwells within us. HE says to me: *"If you (meaning all children of God) will allow ME to enter into your consciousness, I can "enable you", and teach you the ways of mastery."*

The ocean of life is vast, and the myriad routes and options ahead can appear daunting. We stand at the helm of our ship, alone at times, whilst other times, in the company of many. When we feel alone we can become confused, and this disables our ability to make prudent choices. We may take advice from others which may not always be sound, and as we navigate to "the call" of others, we surrender our personal sovereignty. We may find ourselves in turbulent waters and unfulfilling places, or in a comfort zone without any possibility of truly experiencing our highest potential. Alternatively, unschooled, we take the wheel of life on our own and often navigate into dangerous situations.

The Father says to me: *"I offer you my services that you may make ME the Captain of your ship. I shall instruct you in the ways of Captaincy that you may learn to mirror ME. You will then be able to take over the ship, which is your life, and navigate with certainty."*

We need not stand alone at the wheel. Often, we cannot see that which is ahead of us, or know with assurance the direction to take. The Father has said to me: *"I AM with you at the helm; I shall plot the co-ordinates perfect for your journey and shall hold your hands steady at the wheel, that you may brave the twists and turns when you encounter them. With ME by your side, you shall gracefully steer your ship through rough waters, and gratefully, sail with elegance when the waters are ambient. You will see your way more clearly through MY eyes, and know with greater certainty, when you allow ME to think with you. I will avert you from mortal danger and will be your LIFEGUARD AND LIFE BOAT if necessary."*

How wondrous to know we need not feel alone on our life's journey; indeed we are not alone. We simply need to allow the Master within us entry. We will then begin to learn how to assume control of ourselves, and eventually navigate the waters of life, knowing the truth and purpose of our journey.

Let us look at our journey on this earth plane as a *"faith voyage of daring adventure out upon the high seas of unexplored truth"* (Christ Michael). It is through the human experience, with the guidance of the Captain of our ship, that we can discover other shores where treasured realities of spirit exist. This discovery will enable our souls to evolve, and create greater synergy between the human mind and the Captain's (God's) mind.

13

A Matter of
Responsibility

Anyone who has the goal of self mastery will know that assumption of total self responsibility is necessary. Mastery of self leads to empowerment of self.

To experience true power requires an attitude of responsibility, firstly towards self. This means, being accountable for one's expressions, actions and creations. As one evolves into a state of empowerment, one will always act responsibly.

Many seek to have power in the physical world. What that entails may vary, depending on one's interpretation or perception of power. However, the power I speak of, is that which all men secretly or unknowingly desire. It is the intrinsic power bequeathed by the birth of his immortal soul. The soul derives its power from its Creator, the Father of All. The soul of man[22] holds the power of its Creator as its inheritance, and man can use that power to do what God can do.

Should man be able to access his soul, he will be able to find the seat of his power. This power is untouched by physical or ego desires, or sense related needs. It is the purest form of energy which in itself has creative properties. It is the only form of power that is real and enduring. This power creates and upholds only the highest truth, and is embraced in the light of knowing. It creates all things that are good and knows only the Law of Balance. Its inherent nature is to be steadfast. It cannot be lost, diminished or stolen. The nature of this power is to naturally empower all who can embrace it.

To epitomise the power of the Spirit (God's spirit within man's mind/ soul) requires an ability to master the physical by overcoming tendencies born of ego thinking. The soul has God potential, being the power of THE ONE LIGHT, which displays its humility through boundless love and joy, tranquillity, peace and goodness. Its power is asserted in the ways of mastery, fairness and balanced creation. Our journey on Earth

---

22   The use of the word man and he is meant to include the female gender.

provides us with an opportunity to allow our soul's power to express itself in and through our lives and work.

The soul's potential is there to be accessed or tapped into, but it has transformative value. Once touched, the potential of the soul will revolutionise your thinking, desires and state of being. Excuses and predilection to error will not be tolerated. Discipline and dedication to the soul's mission becomes an imperative. Responsibility for self becomes responsibility towards all, both in attitude and action. The soul's potential through the spirit of God can immortally spiritualise the human.

The question is, how many are prepared to assume this level of responsibility for self and others; to be a master and a leader in truth, and in the ways of balance, as a preference to the fleeting joys that physical and sensual power ascribes? Many desire the wealth and power held by the elite in the physical world, unknowing that by nature they too are wealthy and powerful; their sovereignty derived from being sons and daughters of God; a title that transcends the short lived power enjoyed in the physical realm.

Divine power which is yours, mandates an attitude of accountability towards the Father within, responsibility for one's thoughts and creations, balance in execution of service to God and all, the ability to discern between right and wrong, choosing the path of impeccability, recognising that there is in truth only ONENESS and ONE will, and choosing that will. This is a heavy responsibility, yet not by any means a burdensome one. He, who can experience the power of his soul, will yearn for more and seek more, until he becomes one with his power. Only then shall he be cloaked in the raiment of his supreme self and find his wings of immortality.

Responsibility is the price of power. It is duty and dedication to truth, self, all and God without distinction. When one is moved by the true power of his soul, fears and lack of confidence in the ability to sustain the discipline of responsibility will gradually dissolve. The conflict between the physical and the spiritual will gradually mitigate until there is none, and each will be able to ease into assuming responsibility for his mortal journey, within the context of his immortality.

If self mastery is the goal, self responsibility is the price, and this involves eternal vigilance over self.

14

Each must find Balance in Perfection of Service

The destination for all remains constant, yet the pathways will of necessity differ. Each soul has contracted to fulfil a purpose which is directed by its chosen mission, and to experience variables during its journey, so that lessons maybe learnt for the enhancement of that soul.

The soul that is allowed dominion through the mortal trajectory, will know its purpose, and determine the route or pathways best suited to its fulfilment.

Though missions may differ and pathways diverse, all must serve their mission in the underlying knowing that their service is ultimately being rendered to God. When we serve our fellow men through love, we serve God, and through that service we are giving love and causing that love to be re-given to God. Love in service, is balanced on giving and equal re-giving.

Though the skills required for serving and fulfilling one's mission may differ from another, there are commonalities derived from the cosmic tool kit which must be applied to all service, regardless of its nature. These are the Godly values and attributes which render perfection in service. Higher knowing or knowledge, tolerance, patience, divine diplomacy, compassion, devotion, discipline, kindness, humility and selflessness, reflect the qualities with which one must be armed in service.

Master St Germain has taught elsewhere that *"Kindness is love in action and humility is love personified."* Christ Michael has taught elsewhere that *"Selflessness is the badge of human greatness and tact is the fulcrum of social leverage."* HE further taught that *"Tolerance is the earmark of a great soul and must ennoble another by judgments correctly rendered."*[23]

Lady Master Nada taught that *"A state of selflessness must be achieved or you cannot fulfil your mission. The natural course of your life is always the preferring*

---

[23] The quotes are from the Phoenix Journals

of the love of God and service to that God incarnate. *To be aware of self and its pleasures, its privileges and preferences and then to make a choice to forego that self, is a step on the path of selflessness.*"[24]

Master Serapis Bey taught that "*Discipline means to withdraw your energy and your attention from that which is matter and direct its flow to that which is higher.*"

As I write this piece Lady Master Nada says to me that "*Devotion is wholehearted engagement with and to a cause; and that devotion carries the vibration of unity as you become one with your cause or mission.*"

My Higher self teaches that "*Patience in service is the ability to hold the hand of others until they are able to stand on their feet through awareness, knowledge and acceptance.*"

We have been given the tools to apply in service, and the "instructor's manual" through various teachings, so that we may come to know and understand the value of each tool. These tools however, are attributes we must possess, which we can draw from and apply as appropriate.

The measure with which we apply these qualities and attributes must always be defined by wisdom and the need to honour truth.

Service rendered in perfection combines the gifts from God, being the qualities that will be skilfully applied to engender effective results.

Lets us say that your mission is to reveal truth of a thing to many; you will ascertain the abilities of your audience in terms of their receptivity to different paradigms and their level of intellectual understanding. You may need to exercise greater patience and tolerance towards those who are not as open, or those who may be resistant to change. More diplomacy or tact may be required. Your ability to endear others to you

---

[24]   The Rainbow Masters

through your conduct, behaviour and presentation of information, may in fact be the catalyst that will persuade another to consider a different perspective, or at the very least to investigate further for themselves. The lesson is that, the point of balance will differ depending on who you are serving and what your service is. Yet, that balance is achieved through the application of the same values and qualities upon which all service is rendered.

Although one must not lose sight of the objective through service, attachment to the outcome should not diminish or detract from service being rendered in balance. Service rendered in balance and perfection will remain so, regardless of the outcome.

From all that I have been taught by my celestial friends, balance within each of us is the home ground; home, being that place where we find perfect balance. It is here that we can experience the Kingdom of God. Christ Michael taught elsewhere *"In MY Father's Kingdom there shall only be those who seek perfection through service. He who would be in my Father's Kingdom must become a server of All."*[25]

Let us seek perfection in service and find our balance in so doing, so that the Kingdom will be established and experienced through us.

---

[25]   Phoenix Journals

15

LISTEN WITH THE MIND AND UNDERSTANDING OF YOUR SPIRIT

A spiritual revolution is taking place within mankind where many are awakening to their true identity. There is an inner recognition of spirit, and the higher mind which encapsulates TRUTH. Many are beginning to understand, that in truth, they are not the physical body even though they are enjoying a physical experience. Their reality lies in the non physical higher mind and soul. The physical body is a projected manifestation so that the soul may progressively evolve through mortal experience.

In order for truth to be known in any situation, one must listen with the mind of spirit, so that, a spiritual understanding is achieved of outer activities. It is this mind which will provide you with validation of truth, of anything that is said to you or placed before you. The higher mind, otherwise referred to as the higher mental body, can be looked upon as your spiritual consciousness which possesses its own senses. It hears, sees and knows truth. The knowledge that can be accessed through this mind or spirit mind is transcendental or cosmic, and offers spiritual insights into the realities eternal in nature, undefined by time and space limitations.

The mind of spirit knows and sees the outer world for the illusion that it is; even as the illusionary play unfolds, the spirit eyes see truth in a situation and know the lessons to be learnt there from.

The spirit eyes see through love in wisdom, and are not shadowed by the raw emotions which guide the human response to another, or an event. It enjoys an expanded view and attends its response with an elevated understanding against the backdrop of truth. It is disparate from the ego mind, which perceives and reacts against the backdrop of itself.

The spirit mind offers exalted consciousness which sees, knows, hears, thinks and responds with wisdom. Should one access the spirit mind and train one's self to hear, see, think and respond with it, then one's response will always be in balance and harmony.

Were you to think with your spirit/god/higher mind, perspectives previously formed through the use of your outer senses, or developed through established programming will be transformed. The more you cultivate a relationship with this mind, in time, it will become your dwelling place, and you will gradually become attuned to its eyes, ears, thinking and knowing.

The first step in your attempt to connect with your higher mind is a willingness to step out of the uniform of the human mind. You must then resolve to embrace your true identity, so that, you may apply its wisdom, knowing, truth, vision and understanding to every situation you encounter in your life; this includes your interaction and interchange with others.

16

LOOK UPON A THING OR HAPPENING WITH WISDOM

This piece can be viewed as an extension of the preceding one.

The Ascended Master Lanto said *"Look upon a thing or happening with wisdom."* I pondered upon this with him and asked him to think with me. We wrote this piece together.

Wisdom is the eye to truth. One can only see truth if one looks through the eye of wisdom. To see or know truth one must attain wisdom. The "lower records" of information being the human mind, often mistaken as the brain, is not the conduit of wisdom. It is the higher mind not in physical momentum that will offer wisdom. Wisdom abides in each and each can think with it.

Wisdom cannot be observed or recorded from what you sense with your outer senses. It must be known and that knowledge can be granted only from the higher intelligence of the mind of God, of which each is a part.

The essence is to attach ourselves to that mind and be a constant channel of divine wisdom until it becomes a part of each of us. It secures us and allows us to filter its truth into our life and daily living.

Why should we look at a thing or happening with wisdom? Simply because, it is the vehicle which allows us to assume and maintain control over our lives. It directs our choices and pathways and offers foresight. It is humbling yet empowering in its abilities. It brings clarity to a situation that would otherwise become muddled with an emotional response. It trains us to see with our "subjective mind", being the higher mind, and removes the burden of judgment against others or self.

Wisdom allows us to see beyond the temporary results of the experience so that we come to know and appreciate the lesson. It bestows deeper and lasting vision that corrects the human perception of a thing or occurrence, and it heals the lower mind. Wisdom is omniversal, not confined to one person but to the ONE consciousness, from which all can draw.

The ego mind often influences our visions and feelings. In this instance we allow the physical structure of the ego to control our understanding, born of that which might be a tainted perception. The ego has no vision per se. It knows only self. It often will see a situation within the context of self. It cannot comprehend the biggest picture. We are not confined to our ego. If we see a thing or occurrence through the ego mind, we see in limitation. We deny ourselves the intelligence of our true mind and are unable to apply that intelligence to various experiences in our lives.

Let us look at a thing or happening with wisdom, and we will transform that which we might have initially perceived as "ugly or distressing" into something of great benefit. It is the lessons learnt through the experience which catalyse our personal and spiritual growth.

I recall Master St Germain teaching elsewhere, "*The incidents in your lives are of secondary importance but your adjustments to these incidents and what you gain is of primary importance.*"[26]

Should we be able to look at these incidents through the eyes of wisdom, which is stored in the echelons of the higher mind, we shall see in truth, grow in spiritual stature and gain control over self, the latter of which is the greatest power of all.

---

[26] Phoenix Journals

17

IMMUNITY OF SPIRIT

There is an inclination shared by all men to preserve and protect that which belongs to them. This includes the physical body which can be seen and felt, and which man has come to know as himself.

We tend to take great care to ensure that our bodies are immunised against disease and illness. There are vaccines specifically prepared to prevent infections and contamination, detrimental to the body's health. The body is preserved first and foremost, as many believe that it is the body which represents life. The body is merely a vehicle by which the soul evolves through mortal experience. We need to attend to the body as well as the spirit within.

Ascended Master Djwhal Khul, taught that, a psychological cause of disease is that which is based on wrong thought.[27] He also taught through Alice Bailey that all disease is the result of inhibited soul life. He says that *"disease appears where there is a lack of alignment between the soul and the form, the life and its expression, the subjective and the objective realities. Consequently, spirit and matter are not freely related to each other."* In other words, there is a lack of balance between the soul and the physical form, the true life of the soul and its human expression, as well as the subjective realities of higher consciousness and the objective reality of the physical world. Many do not know they have a soul, or carry the infinite spirit within themselves.

Seek first to be immunised by spirit, for the spirit has its own immunity through its divinity. A daily spiritual injection will ensure renewal of mind and precipitate healthy perspectives and perceptions. Our choices will become spirit directed, and eventually our physical bodies will become harmonised with spirit and assume its radiance and agelessness.

There may be times when we feel locked in the physical world with all its challenges, and suffocated by dense and heavy vibrations which

---

[27]   See Esoteric Healing—Alice Bailey

disturb the natural balance of our auras. Let us reach within for a spiritual injection. We must allow the spirit within, to tend us with its grace and comforting presence. We must bathe in its energy and see ourselves revitalised and transformed. A spiritual injection can be the prevention as well as the cure; it can prevent us from being sucked into lower energies and lower thinking, which forebodes depressive states. It can also relieve us from the stress and overwhelming emotional conflicts, which can stifle the balance from us.

That which is unseen is that which is real. The spirit is real and must be acknowledged and connected with, that it may tend us on our journey through the physical plane. The spirit is the one true healer. Should we be able to accrete sufficient light from the spirit within, into our physical bodies, our cells will begin to pulsate at a higher frequency. We will find that the thoughts and creations of our mind will be of a "higher dimension", and the physical body will thrive in health.

My Higher self gave me the following visualisation.

"Take a few deep breaths and close your eyes. Visualise a star of light (Your Higher self or celestial soul) above your head. See a tube of light emanating from the star all the way down through your crown into your body, filling your entire body with its light. Focus now on the light moving into every cell, causing the cells in your body to sparkle with light and dance with life. See the lighted cells perfectly formed, healthy and mobile; see them speaking with each other. Allow your consciousness to flow into your body and become immersed in this light. Become the light. See now, the light penetrating the pores of your body and expanding out to fill your outer energy field. Now take your consciousness back to the star of light and imagine yourself as that star, and watch down on your physical body and energy fields. Allow yourself to feel connected to all that you are through that star. Take a few deep breaths and open your eyes."

18

"MAY YOU PASS EVERY TEST"

I was pondering upon the words *"May you Pass every test"* with Master St Germain, and I valued his exhortation that such a salutation may be used in place of *"God Bless you"*.

I compared both, and with the guidance of the Source, Christ Michael and Master St Germain, it became clear to me how empowering the words *"May you pass every test"* truly are. It carries with it a tone of motivation, encouragement and subtle challenge for ones to assume responsibility for the experiences they create in their lives. It enables them to discover their inner strength and power through the God presence individualised within each, and to overcome the perceived negativities resulting or emanating from the experience.

These words do not inspire self pity, but radiate an expectation that each experience should be viewed as an "instruction", with a lesson to be distilled.

Every time we are able to pass the tests and challenges we face in life, we grow in self mastery. With each success, we become even more motivated to sustain the momentum of our desire to overcome all hurdles in life, knowing that with each test we pass we are graduating into higher classes to continue our evolution. Passing the tests is mandatory for our ascension. As we grow in mastery through the ability to assert our true potential to each and every situation; to conquer the lower vibrations through the victory of our light, we are essentially manifesting the god within us and becoming one with the will of the Source, which is to become God in manifest.

When we say *"God Bless you"* to someone, it carries a comforting, supportive and assuring tone. Usually it is said with genuine intent, compassion, kindness and pity. We are placing the onus on the Father to bless the person with his/her desires, or to fulfil a need that the person may lack. Even if we do not think it, we are essentially saying that the person needs God's blessings to help them overcome life's challenges or tests. It is then up to the Father to do the task in separation from the person to whom we have said *"God Bless you"*. This perceived separation, is in effect denying the infinite spirit within the person to whom we have issued the salutation, from achieving HIS full creative potential, by working through and with the person to overcome his/her challenges.

God's blessings are freely given, but if we seek to receive without doing our part to create the outcome we desire, we are abdicating our responsibilities. When we allow the Presence within, to work with us to overcome and create, we are honouring our God potential.

When we say *"May you pass every test"*, there is an underlying tone of confidence that the person has the ability to triumph. That ability comes from the "I AM" within each, and is a recognition of the power of the "I AM". When success is achieved, this is a victory for the person and the "I AM" of the person, in unity, with the ONE. As there is no separation, all being ONE, when we pass the test or tests in our lives, we are in effect creating our blessings. It is a blessing to recognise the "I AM" within and to invite the "I AM" to work with you, that you may be blessed with the eventual outcome you seek. *"May you pass every test"* should be seen as a benediction of empowerment; for you who have recognised the power of the "I AM" within you, know the potential that your brother/sister has for passing every test.

I have endeavoured to teach through my shared personal experiences and the preceding teachings, all of which I have received from more than one celestial source, that:

- Perceived separation from God is an illusion;
- We are all ONE, sharing ONE heartbeat;
- The "I AM" presence of God dwells within each;
- Should we choose to make the "I AM" the Captain of our ship, we shall sail through our experiences in the vast ocean of life with acquired wisdom and higher vision;
- Our true power lies within us, waiting for us to assume responsibility for it; and

- Should we take a daily spiritual injection, we will train ourselves to listen with the ears and understanding of spirit, and view our experiences through knowing and wisdom, which will lead to balanced responses and creations.

The key to passing every test can be found in perseverance, desire and discipline. Like Master St Germain, I believe that we should espouse our inalienable divine right to live in accordance with our highest conception of God, and be free to BE WHO WE TRULY ARE. The mountain may be steep, but should we keep our sights and selves anchored to the pinnacle, we will gladly scale the hurdles ahead, attain victory over our lower selves, and in so doing return to our Source.

May we pass every test and go the distance!

Christ Michael's words of encouragement in the Spiritual March below can provide us with impetus. I channelled this from HIM.

The Spiritual March

Onward children Onward
March toward the height
The pinnacle of glory
Where your spirit shall alight.
Do not fear the battle
That plays out at your side
For the Mighty I AM Presence
Shall keep you in your stride.

Onward children Onward
This I ask of you
Champions of MY vision
Bearers of the Truth.

Onward children Onward
Bear the golden torch

Beacons to the rescue
Ardent for the cause.
March with ME to victory
A new world to behold
MY rod and staff I give to you
Be shepherds to MY fold.

Onward children Onward
This I ask of you
Champions of MY vision
Bearers of the Truth.

19

FULL CIRCLE

As a teenager growing up in the shelter of the countryside, I desired the freedom and excitement of exploring and living in the city. I was very much like many children who wished to spread their wings and experience independence.

I thrived on the excitement of living and working in the city. The lifestyle and variety of leisure activities appealed to me greatly. In my profession it was simply the place to be. There was always something to do and somewhere to go. Life was hectic and complex, and my mind was constantly active. There was little time for rest, reflection and true relaxation.

The city environment was charged with dense energies, and stress was a normal phenomenon, as demands of work tightened its reigns over my time and senses. There are things that go on in the city which would be alien to life and expectations in the countryside.

As the focus in my life shifted to the spiritual, my interests changed. I soon began to hear the noise of the city and felt trapped by the proliferation of skyscraper buildings. I could not bear to be in crowded or noisy places and stopped attending wine bars and clubs, and sought quieter places for socialising.

There was scarcely any form of nature unless one ventured specifically to a park. I started to reflect on all the distractions of city life, which have the power, if one allows it to, to numb one's natural creative potential and talents. It was easy to become a slave to consumerism with the bold adverts and designer labels gnawing at your senses everywhere you turned. One could become easily swallowed up in city life, as all the outside noise made it impossible for one to hear one's own thoughts. The environment in itself does not foster deep thought or candid self reflection, as one tends to get caught up in the hype and business of celebrities, the world of fashion and hedonistic pleasures. City life panders to the outer senses in a way that can become all consuming if one does not know temperance.

I am still living in the city of London, but through meditation I am taken to places where nature abounds. The pure air and natural fragrance of the blossoming flowers and verdant forests, captivate my senses. It is there that I can truly spread my wings and soar in freedom to explore the terrain of my inner self, and discover the true me. I can abide in the tranquillity of my soul and observe the beauty of God's creation.

In this environment the voice of my Higher self guides me with her wisdom, and I engage in profound meaningful conversations with the Father within me. The power and stoicism of the mountains affect me, and the experience of ONENESS with all nature is inevitable. The atmosphere is wholesome and my natural creativity is sparked. Nature speaks to me using its peculiar language, and I respond with loving thoughts and blessings.

The energy is light and welcoming. It fosters and supports me as I immerse myself in its bounty. Time ceases to be when one becomes a part of nature's stillness, which allows one to enjoy the simplicity of the moments. There is time to notice the curve and structure of the tree trunks, the formation of the branches and uniqueness of each leaf. Each flower has a different story to tell, and is willing to share of its life.

As the beauty of nature begins to reflect upon me, I too blend in and come to know my beauty. Nature births an elixir which rejuvenates my auras and spirit. Nature fortifies me and allows me to experience all that is divine, for when I spend time in and with nature, I am with God.

I can see clearly the inky canvas of the night's sky, freckled with starry eyes, which speaks to me in winks and twinkles. The lord of the night, the flamboyant moon rouses the darkened sky with its haloed light. It tells me that, even though darkness is apparent it is not real, for God never leaves HIS children bereft of light; the stars and the moon testify to this truth. As I ponder upon the vast cosmos, I hear the words "*light always penetrates darkness, and can shine out of and through darkness, as much as it stands against it.*" This truth becomes evident as the piercing eyes of the lighted stars and effulgent moon breach darkness' rule.

110

As I awaken from my meditative state, it dawns upon me that we sometimes choose in our lives to explore imperfection, (even though we may not know we are doing this) before we are drawn to return to that place of perfection. I started out my life in the perfection of the countryside and then chose to explore new and exciting horizons. However, it was necessary for me to take this journey, so that I could discover where "my true life" lay. Now, the magnet of nature lures me to return to the place of my origin; that place where freedom truly exist; where the presence of God can be felt and known outwardly; where the one heartbeat is audible; where there is total balance and where the texture of love is refined in its natural pristine state.

During my exploration, I was seeking and searching for fulfilment in love and to experience the wholeness of love. The search has now come full circle; the search is now over, as it is clear that love was with me all the while.

We all start from the point of perfection, but we choose to take a journey away from our Source in perceived separation. We choose to have a dualistic experience. However, during the course of the endless journey, there will come a time when perfection beckons, when we tire of all that is manufactured and illusory, and we feel that which is real calling us home. We will inevitably make the choice to return to the natural state of our origin, and in that decision and process we will find our peace and ourselves.

20

LESSONS FROM NATURE

The Nature of the Sun/Son

This conversation took place on the beach at the Andaman Resort, Langkawi in August 2012.

The Sun: I am an aspect of the ONE; I am pure light; I mirror the energy of the ONE. Always, the ONE speak in symbols. I am but one (symbol). Many desire me but few contemplate me. Now come to me.

Hazel: In your presence all I see is light. There is no other form. I cannot feel your heat. There are many aspects of you; there is breadth and depth unfathomable.

The Sun: I am that—Light. You are spirit withdrawn from matter. Spirit lacks the sense of nature. It can see things in truth and know all things. Spirit need not feel me to KNOW I am real.

The Sun: What do I bring to your world? What is my purpose do you think?

Hazel: I see the fruits of your labour. Through your light you have transformed nature. Without you, a pall of inactivity and sobriety veils all life. When you appear, you glorify the face of natural life as your glowing rays beautify the landscape of matter. The ocean becomes a festival of colour and rejoices in happy waves, as you regale its breadth with fastidious multifaceted rays. Your pale golden accents massage a sheen onto the ocean's face and it radiates an ambience which mirrors your disposition. You have enlivened all things, for even the densely huddled trees which embellish the mountains seem relaxed and poised, simply wearing your smile in silence; polite observers of the Master at work. The golden sand basks in your delight, and you court all natural life with your resilience and stamina. All creatures emerge from their shelters to receive your special brand of therapy.

As you weave your magic smile, joy and peace settles in the heart and minds of all. You are our miracle.

The Sun: I freely give to you that which I am. I am no different from the ONE. I am the Sun yet I am a son, and I am from the ONE, as are you. All that I give to nature, it re-gives in one form or another to other life forms. I too obey the sacred laws and work within the mantra of creation. It is only the ONE/SUN[28]/Son[29] that can give life and bring recognition of the truth. My presence simply reminds you of the beauty of nature through the Sun, (symbol) that you may discern the beauty of your nature through the ONE/SUN/Son, WHO birthed the light within you.

The ONE and the Son is within you by the light of you, destined to transform and beautify the mundane into the realisation that light bequeaths life. I speak not of existence but of value; for your life to have value you must recognise the light within you, being the light that you are. You are to dwell in the "light vibration" and emit its frequency into your outer activity. In this, you experience the vibrancy of life, of being alive.

I am a symbol of light which is life, so that, you seek your inner ONE/SUN/Son to find the life in you, and reap HIS benefits that nature derives from me.

Just as the vegetation needs me to grow and yield fruit/food to feed your physical body, you need the ONE/SUN/Son within you to nurture your mind that you may grow into the remembrance of who you are. You need the sustenance of the inner light (ONE/SUN/Son) to find your inner path,

---

[28] Central Sun
[29] Son of God

just as you need me in your physical world to find your outer coordinates.

Just as you desire the sun to shine upon your body which radiates a feeling of warmth and joviality, so too, you need the inner ONE/SUN/Son to shine through your heart and entire being, for you to dwell in ecstasy.

You seek me for "colour" which pleases the eye, yet, I say seek HIM for the colour of inspiration which pleases and motivates the soul.

You are likened to a foetus, drawing from the life force of its mother until it grows in nature and character, in readiness for independence. You must draw from the nature and character of the ONE/SUN/Son until you grow into likeness of HIM, and can do what HE can do. When you can do what HE can do, I will not be needed, for your inner world will become your world in truth—a world of LIGHT.

Whereas, I work in cycles, the ONE/SUN/Son is constant; you are never without HIM. You must know that symbols are just that; it offers lessons but never substitutes reality. I too, am like the Father, as I appear unfathomable, yet, I am present. When you cannot see me I am still present, albeit elsewhere. Though you may not see HIM, HE is always present.

Only the ONE/SUN/Son can create life, maintain life, renew life, reveal truth, anoint with clarity, enhance the beauty in and of all things, overcome the dimness of fear, darkness, doubt and uncertainty. Only the ONE/SUN/Son can transform your world. I am but a symbol of HIM. You hold the ONE/SUN/Son within you. Seek HIM first and know yourself as LIGHT, and you shall bring to your outer world that which I bring to nature.

"What is Wisdom but your Soul speaking its Truth"
Higher self

21

EXHORTATIONS
OF THE MASTER

During the revolutionary period in my life, unbeknownst to me, I was channelling wisdom from my Higher self, usually in prose or poetry format. She communicated higher thoughts to me, as part of my education, and also to share them with others.

The truth is, during those years, I did not even know I had a Higher self. I just thought that I was being divinely inspired. The most poignant piece she wrote through me was called "Exhortations of the Master". She was and is the Master within me. Seldom do I make distinctions now, for it is my view that the Father, being my Highest self and the Mighty I AM within me, is my aspiration. We are ONE.

Each person is an extension of his/her soul and has a Higher self, and is able if desirous, to communicate with this aspect. I have been told that the Higher self is the person's primary guide.

When I awakened, my Higher self and I began to have regular communication. In fact, she would often tell me what she wanted to speak about. Many nights as I was about to fall asleep she would begin to speak, and I would have to get up to take the message.

I was in awe at the wisdom given, and learnt so much. Her wisdom became a part of my daily life, perspective and practice. During the last four years, I received many teaching messages from her for the benefit of my spiritual growth. She is always available to proffer advice and guidance when needed.

You can achieve similar results by stating your intent to connect for your highest good. I can assure you that with effort and perseverance, you will begin to experience a delightfully revealing energy which will transcend the physical consciousness. Awareness will begin to glow from within as the comfort of your Higher self's presence becomes natural to you. Each person's Higher self will reveal himself/herself in ways most effective to the understanding of the person. I have been taught by one of my earth teachers, Toby Alexander,[30] that our hands have a neurological connection to our Higher selves. He taught me the following method:

Relax by taking a few deep breaths, then extend your left hand with the palm facing downwards. Relax your fingers and ensure they are pointing away from you. Your hand should be extended outward not touching anything at all.

Focus your attention on your left hand, and feel the energy as if you are projecting your consciousness there. Now say aloud "Connecting to my Higher self". You should feel tingling in the fingertips of your left hand. This is indicative of you being connected to your Higher self.

You can then ask a question to which you know the answer is YES. In your left hand, you should feel a valve opening in your palm, and energy moving towards your fingers away from you. This is the energy signature for a "yes" answer.

You can then ask a question to which you know the answer is NO. In your left hand you should feel the energy moving towards your palm and wrists. This is the energy signature for a "no" answer.

Using this method you can obtain "yes and no" guidance from your Higher self until your telepathic abilities develop.

There will come a time when you will not feel separate from your Higher self, and you will assume his/her mind set. However, bear in mind, in the human world the ego can cause great interruption and disturbance to a mind that is not constantly vigilant. I do experience from time to time an ego attack, but I have learnt to quickly go to my Higher self and say "*I relinquish my ego to your light—the light of spirit.*" In this way, harmony in thought and response will prevail.

---

[30] DNAperfection.com. Credit and acknowledgement is given fully to Toby Alexander for the technique of connecting to one's Higher self.

I share with you, "Exhortations of the Master" and Conversations with the Master, so that, you may be inspired to connect with the "Master" within you, and reap the bounty of his/her wisdom, light and divinity.

EXHORTATIONS OF THE MASTER

It matters not the hue that stains mortal skin
It matters only that the spirit's pure and white.
It matters not the creed or race our birth dictates
It matters that all are equal in God's sight.
It matter not the wholeness of the body's form
It matters that the spirit, heart and mind's upright.
It matters not the measure of our length and breadth
It matters that our mould is weighed
by good and grace's might.
It matters not what fabric lines the walls of rigid backs
It matters that the heart is made of gold and clothed in light.
It matters not that birthright casts our lot in life
It matters that we honour our blessings right.
It matters not that fortune seeks its victor's hold
It matters only that the victor shares his prize.
It matters not that poverty's a rampant scourge
It matters that humility rewards the victim's plight.
It matters not the cross we think we bear
It matters that HE who bore the greater
cross will help us win the fight.
It matters not the length of mortal life
It matters that our spirits' immortality was birthed
By HIM who through abundant love created Life.

22

CONVERSATIONS WITH THE MASTER

The Search for Wisdom

Student—Master, I seek wisdom beyond my current understanding. How can I achieve this?

Master—I have two answers to this question.

Student—What's the first answer, Master?

Master—Why do you seek that which is yours? Should you not claim it?

Student—What do you mean?

Master—That which you seek is legated by your soul. It is the light within your soul that you desire, for wisdom is merely the language through which the light within expresses its presence.

Student—How do I find this light?

Master—Through quiet communion with yourself and an expressed desire to claim your birthright.

Student—Do you mean through meditation?

Master—Yes, MY child. It is through meditation that you will hear the silent voice of God within, provide the wisdom and guidance you seek. You must listen to hear.

Master—What is the second way?

Master—Build a bridge that will take you to the other side where the treasure of wisdom awaits.

Student—Master, how long must this bridge be, and can you give me the exact location when I get to the other side?

Master—The length must be in proportion to the breadth of wisdom you seek, and you shall know where it is when you get to the other side.

Student—I do not understand.

Master—It is in the building of the bridge that knowledge and wisdom is gained. The bridge is your life and experiences, which conspire to bring you to a higher understanding of you. It is through your life's journey that opportunities will present themselves for the awakening of the wisdom within. If you can discern this, you will come into the knowing of and recognition, that the receptacle of the treasure I speak of, is you. If you continuously seek it outside of yourself, you shall deny yourself the privilege of self discovery.

Daily advice

Student—Master, what advice can you give me this day?

Master:

Let your eyes see the beauty which abounds
Let your ears hear the wisdom of the wind
Let your tongue utter words of honey dew
Let your heart inspire love in all you do
Let your hands be given in labour of love
Let your feet be guided to higher grounds above
Let your mind harbour thoughts, clean and pure
Let your spirit pray now and ever more.

The Greatest Lesson

Master—Every life force has a purpose and an inner glory, and is precious in the eyes of God. God sees and examines what is in the heart of men/women. HE attends to HIS creation regardless of its/ their humble origins, experience, tragic or unwholesome nature. HE does not discriminate, for the physical is not the basis of that which is real, and HE sees only that which is real. Yet, HE, being the Creator of all things, knows that each life force has its own unique story. HE encourages HIS children to listen and learn from each other's story, and in so doing honour all that is creation.

Student—Master, but what of that tree whose rough ridged bark and empty branches tell a maudlin tale?

Master—That which you see are gifts bestowed by nature's age. The beauty lies, not in the facial expression of its bark, but in the defined vitality of its inner seed, which feeds the spine of every branch, and holds with dignity its stature when barren winds deprive it of its fruitful season. Its inner wisdom knows that fertile winds will pass its way again; it remains prepared to house the lush of leaves in due season. Humans should admire and emulate the tree of life, and aim to mirror the resilience of the physical tree, which remains steadfast and faithful, even during the barren seasons in life. They should allow faith to sustain them during these times, and know with surety, that the pattern of life will change again to restore them, and usher fulfilment.

The Master took the student on a journey.

Master—Look at that waterfall, MY child, and tell me what you see?

Student—Why Master, I see a transparent flow of pure twinkling water feeding the lake at its base, providing a haven for other life. Why is this important, Master?

Master—This waterfall teaches you a lesson. You should aspire to be like it, so that, your natural beauty and wealth which is the pure light within, constantly radiates and flows towards all who are in your path; that you may provide an ambient environment for their growth and sustenance, enabling them to eventually feel prepared and confident to move into oceans of greater experience and learning.

The Road of Life, The Twists and Turns, The Light Within, The Circle of infinity

The Master takes the student on another journey.

Master—Where are we, MY child?

Student—Why Master, we are on what appears to be a very long road with rapid twists and turns. From where I stand the road seems endless. Why have YOU brought me here, Master, and why is the road important?

Master—What appears to be an endless road is the eternalness of your life, the life being the soul within, which is immortal. I want you to see that you are an eternal being.

Student—What do the twists and turns on the road represent?

Master—On the road of your life you shall encounter many experiences, all meant to yield lessons to engender the growth of your soul. Initially, you may perceive some of these experiences as negative, and for a while your journey will appear uncomfortable. What appears to create disturbances along your path provides a breeding ground for the building of your character. You would see that after every twist the path becomes clear again. If you can use the twists and turns on your life's journey to evolve, you shall be able to progress, and you will note that further along your journey the twists are fewer.

Student—Does that mean at that point I will not have experiences to teach me lessons to enable me to evolve further?

Master—No, MY child, there will always be experiences; until you become an enlightened being you will continue to grow. You are the one who creates the twists and turns for the purpose of learning. As you progress spiritually you become closer to mastering your God attributes, and your experiences and responses thereto will be more balanced.

Student—Master, how do I get through the twists and turns?

Master—I will lead you out of the depths of the curves in your life. Close your eyes MY child and follow ME.

Student—How can I see to follow you if my eyes are closed?

Master—How many times have I told you that you will never see ME through your outer eyes, but only through your inward vision? I AM the light within you and can only be accessed through the inner vision of your mind, not your senses. You must seek ME within you; you shall find ME and I shall guide you.

Student—Master, you said that on the journey of my life I must master my God attributes. What does this mean?

Master—The purpose of your life is to reach the topmost pinnacle of human unfoldment. You are meant to find God within, free your God self and gain God mastery by becoming one with HIM, that you may be able to return to the Source from WHOM you were birthed. The point of your beginning is the point of your ending, being God.

Student—Does that mean that the road of my life is circular instead of linear?

Master—That is correct, think of your life as the Circle of Infinity.

Love and Perception

Student—Master, I desire that you live through me. I desire to be all that you are. Will you teach me how to love others as you love?

Master—All that I AM you could be if you choose to. Have I not for these many months been alive within you? Have I not fulfilled within you your need for love? Have I not shown you love when you have achieved, as well as, when you have faltered?

Student—YOU have indeed, Master. I feel very blessed to enjoy this state of knowing communion with you, whereby I am consistently guided by YOUR love and wisdom. I am consciously making an effort to love every life force as you do.

Master—Yes, I see and feel your burning desire. This is what you must do. I ask that for two days we do not speak of this; on the third day we shall revisit your question.

On the third day the student knocked on the Master's door a little "worse for wear".

Master—MY child, how are you this day?

Student—Master, since we last spoke I have not been doing all that well.

Master—Why is that?

Student—I have felt irritable for two days. As a result of this, I experienced annoyance at my brothers and sisters' actions. I really tried to control it, but could not help be irritated by things they said or failed to do. How will I ever learn to love as you do? Why won't you teach me?

Master—MY child, have I not loved you unconditionally through patience, tolerance, empathy, understanding, and compassion?

Student—Yes, you have. I acknowledged this already.

Master—So therefore, have I not taught you how to love?

Student—I suppose so. Why did you send me away for two days with instructions not to speak of this?

Master—I sent you to apply what you have been taught. You know the lessons, but only experience can test your ability to apply the lessons, so that you know whether you have reached the mark of the Master. You felt irritable and that caused a feeling of annoyance with your peers. If you desire to love as the Master, you must first master your emotions, and secondly, you must see every experience as an opportunity to test and apply your God light and love.

Learning is seldom theoretical. I can teach you by example, but I cannot love for you. The more aligned you remain with ME, MY values and virtues, the greater will you experience the fruits of God's love which becomes yours to give, that you may be re-given. You must effort to push through the limitations of human consciousness and taste that cosmic nectar. It is then, that you may freely love through the god within.

Student—I understand now Master. It is certainly not easy to do this.

Master—I have taught you before that when you tire of being the student you will work to become the Master, for it is your God mastery that you must prove in the here and now. It is in this seat of consciousness that you must find balance.

The student thanked the Master and asked that the Master speak of Perceptions.

Master—Man perceives with and through the senses, masterminded by the illustrious ego. To truly know is to perceive through the inward sense, which is divine. It is your personal perceptions that sometimes influence your interpretations of the behaviour, conduct or decisions of others.

I will take the example of your annoyance with the actions/inactions or words of your peers. Those feelings were evoked through your personal perceptions based on your personal preferences, choices, values and actions. If your personal preferences are divinely aligned, they are more of the "subjective God mind". In this case, through divine knowing, your perceptions will be persuaded by an understanding which transcends your emotions. Instead of reacting you will respond through balanced thought. You will realize that your peer is an aspect of you and vice versa, through the ONENESS of All. You will then perhaps conclude one or any of the following:

- You need that person in your life to grow, to understand yourself or simply master your ability to shine your god light and love.
- That person needs you to teach or guide them to where they must be, or merely sow a seed of wisdom, or water the withering love within.
- That person is a reminder to you that each of God's children is unique, and through their unique personalities they are seeking to reunite with God, even if they are not aware of this.

You may also, firmly judge behaviour which is unbalanced and contrary to God's laws. You must dissociate from the behaviour without "hating" the creator of that behaviour.

Most people perceive others as irritating because one or other, or both, are still growing. The experience merely provides the soil for growth. When you can see this, notwithstanding your fleeting feeling of discontent with another, the joy of this revelation will rebalance your thinking. You will assess yourself first before you assess another. As God beings, you must seek after your own perfection before you require it of others.

Master—I wish you to remember that when you perceive through your outer senses you create an impediment or barrier between us, and you are unable to reap the influence of your balanced nature which I AM. I cannot infringe or interfere with your choices. You must ask ME to guide you in your perceptions, so that they will be influenced with the light of divine knowing.

ONENESS—The Benefits

Student—Master, may I enter?

Master—Of course you may MY child, I am always here for you.

Student—Thank you.

Master—What is it MY child? Why are you so forlorn this day?

Student—I don't feel very happy this day Master

Master—Why have you come to ME?

Student—I always feel better when I speak with YOU. It is as if I feel in touch again.

Master—Why do you think that is?

Student—I see YOU as a sanctuary where I can visit to regain my balance and harmony. YOU are always able to make me see things from a broader perspective.

Master—MY child, are we not ONE mind?

Student—Yes.

Master—Do you accept that if we are ONE mind, then you can choose to think and respond to circumstances in your life through the ONE mind?

Student—I suppose so Master?

Master—MY child, why do you think that you feel emotions of unhappiness as often as you do?

Student—Perhaps, I respond too frequently with my senses?

Master—Yes, that is correct.

Student—I am human Master. I must experience emotions.

Master—That is correct, but you allow your emotions to dominate you, and in so doing you create a separation between us and forget MY presence within you. You therefore think with your senses and not your god mind.

Student—That makes sense.

Master—Do you know what being Human means?

Student—Yes, you have taught me before that Human means "Higher Universal" man.

Master—What does that tell you?

Student—It reminds me that I must strive to live within the Mighty presence within me, and allow that Presence to work through me in all I do. It is not easy to always be conscious of this Master?

Master—MY child, it is always your choice, for free will is a divine bestowal. However, when you tire of being the student and wish to become the Master, you will effort to live in a higher state of consciousness that goes beyond your senses. When the discomfort caused by the emotions becomes too great, perhaps, you will choose the easier route. Only then, will you freely and actively choose to live in MY presence and experience a greater ONENESS with ME. When you begin to feel ONENESS with ME, you will find it easier to maintain a state of inner joy and peace.

I bid you to remember, that when you live in conscious knowing of MY presence within, you are exalted, and when by your actions you allow ME to live through you, the I AM within you is exalted.

Patience, Time and Service

Student—Master, I come to you today for guidance. I feel stuck today. I know that I am manifesting what I desire, yet I feel impatient for its materialisation, and feel as if progress in service evades me.

Master—You feel stuck because of your impatience. Your impatience has put a spoke in your ability to discern the progress you are making, and visualise the goal as already materialised. Your impatience has stemmed the natural flow, and breeds doubt into the eventual outcome you seek. What you have projected is already here; its manifestation depends on your ability to sustain the vision and to go with the flow of divine timing.

Were you to allow your impatience to be dissolved in your faith and knowing, you will see with clarity that you have made and are making progress toward the accomplishment of your goal. There are many unseen hands working to assist you. The power of the universal mind within yours is creating transference of energy that will cause materialisation. You, however, must do your part. You live for tomorrow when you should be focussing on the now, and the service you are rendering and can offer in the now.

Desire for greater service is laudable, yet, foundations must be built before greater service can be undertaken. Your vision for tomorrow should remain unclouded whilst you prosper in the knowledge, that as you remain attuned to the divine within, you will find yourself moving with the divine tide. You will enjoy the flow in the present, but with the foresight, that the future you desire is being moulded.

The element of time creates friction within your thinking. You feel time's passage will rob you of your ability to accomplish what you desire in service. You must see yourself as an eternal being operating within the sphere of eternity. Rest in the energy of that which is eternal and release time to the cosmos. Time inhibits your thinking, so be purposeful in your attempt to surrender your attachment to it. Gently meander with the divine flow as the tide takes you to your chosen destination. You may feel confined to the river, but I will remind you that the river is in constant flow, never stagnant. You have in fact entered the estuary where the divine tide lingers to hold you in abeyance, as I equip you with further resources, that you may enter the vast ocean where you shall assume your duties in wholehearted service.

Student—Master, I thank YOU. Once again YOU have assisted me in my return to balanced thinking, and enabled me to see clearly through YOUR eyes. I have released that which is counterproductive to the manifestation of my goals and desires, and I am once again in the cycle of YOUR energy, knowing that YOU are working with me to enable me to be of greater service.

Light workers and Lighthouses

Student—Master, speak to me of Light workers.

Master—You, who are intent on service are indeed workers of light. You are part of the dynamic light system on the planet, meant to make substantial inroads into the darkness, as you prevail your light of higher knowledge and understanding unto the unschooled or untaught, that they may remove themselves from the helplessness of ignorance. The energy of transformation is circulating on the planet at the moment, and within the energetic field of all individuals. Many will feel the pinch of light seeking entrance into their hearts, minds and immortal soul. They will be triggered to search for deeper answers to life. There is currently, much "spring cleaning" taking place at every level of existence on the planet. That which is pure will resurrect, and the dross left behind. New life is beginning to breathe through that which is old and seasoned.

Many will seek and search for an avenue or path which defines their true purpose. As the understanding of how the mass consciousness works, becomes apparent, the human mind will become inclined to service of all, instead of a limited demography. The light workers who are scattered throughout the globe must keep their light quotient high. Their intent in service must be pure, and they must become veritable lighthouses. More so now, guardians of the light are needed to guide others into the lighthouse, where they will be safe from the outer onslaught of weariness, temptation and uncertainty.

Think of a lighthouse stationed near the coast. The lighthouse is sturdy, unshakeable and generous in height and width. During the night, its radiance transforms the coast as it streams forth light as a beacon. This light brings hope to all who are lost or in trouble in the ocean. It serves as a signpost for those floundering, to know that help is close by. It provides a haven and shelter for those seeking to find their way. The lighthouse does not reject those who seek refuge, but its doors are open to all in need. So too, must light workers aim to be; a source of shelter, comfort, guidance and help to those who are lost, floundering, confused, seeking and searching for a way out of the darkness.

Keep your inner flame burning brightly, so that, your outer radiance may, like the lighthouse, be visible to those seeking a way out of confusion, ignorance and darkness. Stand ready and available to share the light of higher understanding, and offer clarity to those seeking truth. Be a lighthouse!

23

HIGHER SELF
TEACHINGS

I Am Called

The humble path beckons me
To tread upon its pliant fields
In the simplicity of my nature.
It asks of me to shrug the tiring pulse of ego,
That stifling cloak which pinches the breath of life
That I may in the freedom of myself
Engage the essence of me.
It moves me to inhale its neutral fragrance
That my senses may captivate the joy of just being.
It bathes me in the pollen of its floral blooms
That the seeds of humility may germinate
Into the energy of auras divine,
Where I stand in the sanctuary of my knowing
And journey through and to the wealth of who I am,
That I may dwell in the stillness of my core
And be that star that leads the sons of God
To find the richness of their being
Without the flutter of banal codes of earthly striving.
Yes, I am called to the altar of humility
Where I kneel to be knighted by its golden sword.
Prepared am I to take this mantle on
To walk in humble tones throughout this life
To serve the greater will,
Yet knowing through the I AM of myself
In the reverie of its silence
That, through the lineage of my birth
I am exalted.

WALK IN THE RHYTHM OF GOD; WALK WITH THE RHYTHM OF GOD

The Law of ONE is the primary context of all existence. It is the singular that underlies the rhythm of God's creation. Co-centricity is the concentrated point from which this rhythm is poised. It is the process of creation which will assist your understanding of God and enable you to appreciate HIS rhythms. What is rhythm, but a sequence of tones which captures the essence of the stillness from which the soul's light emanate.

God's rhythm is sourced from HIS thinking, and derived of combined virtues of sacred intent. The motivation of HIS thoughts is that which creates the effect of HIS ideas. HIS ideas are conceived in the crater of the universal mind, posited in a state of perfect balance. HIS rhythms become the sequence of balanced thought which exist in the harmony of HIS nature, being Love and Joy.

God's rhythm is balance. That which is in balance is in perfect accord. When you can walk in the rhythm of God, even though you walk on the "tight rope" of life, with the vagaries and vicissitudes of the tidal wind threatening to tip you over the edge, you shall remain firmly ensconced in the comfort of HIS steadfast hold. Even if you are swayed by currents of defeat and hopelessness at times, you will know how to reacquire HIS rhythm once you have walked in HIM.

When you walk in the rhythm of God you are steadied by unfailing, abiding love. You will lose the rhythm however, when you allow yourself to become embroiled in the tempers of anarchy created by yourself or others. When this occurs duality becomes the order, and love no longer remains in the sacred vessel of ONENESS, but becomes antagonised in the battlefield of LOVE AND HATE. Your rhythm becomes disturbed and you fall out of tune with God's rhythm.

The kiln of your mind should be the repository of God's Love, so that, you may draw from its strands to weave balanced thoughts and co-creative ideas in harmony with the Divine will. When you walk in the rhythm of God, you shall find perfect synchronicity with HIS eternal will. Your choices and decisions will be in accord with the Universal Mind. You will be purposely led, unfalteringly along a refined path of service, where the divine in you shall prosper. Knowing, Truth, and Wisdom will be your tune; victory the reward, if you can stay the course in God's rhythm.

The Christ walked in your rhythm during HIS auspicious incarnation on earth. In so doing, HE came to understand more fully, HIS creation. HE left a legacy of HIS Father's rhythm for mankind to understand and choose. It is now time for you to walk in HIS rhythm that you may better understand HIS presence within you, the truth of you, the origin of you, the eternalness of you and the reality of you. You must of necessity accustom yourself to HIS vibration. Bliss and love equals balance and peace. You cannot interfere with the matchless rhythm of God, but you can choose to align yours with HIS, and adopt HIS as your own. God's rhythm is the rhythm of life; it is ripe with opportunities which allow the ascending sons to return to Paradise.

When you WALK WITH THE RYTHYM of God, your Godliness shall eminently shine through, and your field of light will be magnified. You shall come to know HIS plans for you, and you shall begin to speak with HIS wisdom. You shall gladly take up HIS torch, and shall know without a doubt when the hour of change is upon you.

SPIRITUAL PROFESSIONALISM

Your entire journey in physical manifestation is aimed at the discovery of self, so that self may unfold as your awareness expands, through the education of your earthly experiences. Some experiences you choose beforehand, and others you create along the journey of mortal life. You seldom perceive the true value of your experiences until they are over and you have achieved a measure of emotional balance and perspective.

As you introspectively assess your experiences, you will understand their role as a facilitator of self discovery. You may discover your inner strength, tenacity and distinctive character as you engage in an analysis of the purpose and meaning of these experiences.

Yet, unearthing these experiential benefits should transcend a mortal understanding, and assume a dynamic perspective bred by the spirit within. You should be able to make the link that the discovery of your "character" or "self" is anchored in spirit. When you can make that link, you will be drawn into conscious activity that leads to a harmonious working with your spirit, that it may through your experiences unfold its virtues, qualities and assets for your greatest good. In allowing your spirit to work in partnership with your ego mind, the latter will eventually assume its rightful place as the servant. It is then, that the spirit within shall blossom, and teach you how to gain spirit mastery and control of self.

When the tendrils of spirit are awakened within, you shall hunger for greater attunement, and as you seek through intent and sincere petition, you will begin to acquire instructions to forge a profound and continuous connection. Every effort shall yield rewards of higher understanding, for never shall your spirit deny you that which you seek in truth. Your spirit will respond with the joy of its presence, the elegance of its balance, the beauty and fullness of its attributes and the wisdom of its knowledge. It desires to unfold and gleam through your experiences, so that, in your physical incarnation you will assume the gloss of spirit. As you effort to sustain your connection, your mastery will be enhanced; and soon your perception of who you are will defy earthly definition, as you feel and think of yourself, as a cosmic being with a cosmic identity.

Your mortal life will begin to reflect cosmic truth and ways, and you will knowingly contribute to the raising of the consciousness of those within your sphere of reality. Spirit is already whole. In order for you to attain wholeness in your incarnation, spirit must be allowed to embolden your existence, meaning that, you must acquire the professionalism of spirit. Spiritual professionalism demands that you live to the standard of spirit, which translates to "being" all that spirit is—whole and balanced. You must always choose the celestial highway, so that, you may avoid the traffic of the human ego which impedes your journey and deters your unfolding.

Aim high in your aspiration to acquire and enjoy the accoutrements of spirit. It is only then, that will you find and live your power, your sovereignty, your humility, your refinement, your divinity, your love, and your "self".

Seek the education that will confer spiritual professionalism, and you shall become master of yourself and a teacher of men. Allow your spirit its freedom from the density of mortal existence that you may broaden your vision and perspective of human experience, and find immortal triumph which will usher you into the next sequence of experience in your journey back to the Source.

Leave the mark of your spirit in your mortal achievements, that those who could see will know, that your acquisitions through earthly endeavours were unquantifiable yet real. When you depart for a higher dimension, the reward of your achieved status as a spiritual professional goes with you; its permanence never to be overridden by the transient rewards of "man created power and status", which will forever remain earth bound.

THE POWER OF LOVE

The Power of Love sourced all Creation. It embraces its creative aptitude and embroiders the fruits of its vision. Its creation is primed by pure imaginings and its purpose perfected by all that is intrinsic to itself. Love is the beauty within all creation, and that beauty is divine, for Love is divine in nature and instinct.

In its origin, Love is very simple, natural yet extraordinary in its empowering capacity. It uses its power to create beauty, harmony and balance. It is the Creator's will that man would know himself as Love, know Love as himself, and that he would see Love in all that abounds. The values and qualities of Love endure infinitely, never to be diminished in the cosmic framework of creation. Yet, through limited knowledge and confines of ego related perceptions and interpretations, many have degraded, blemished and diluted that which is powerful, pure and joyous. Many have de-scaled the frequency of original Love in their mortal application.

Love has become confused, as matter, things and emotions guide and interfere with the ability of many to understand their primal nature. Man's perspective is generated by an amalgam of egocentric and physical needs, which become easily muddled with feelings of the heart. Love is often perceived in the context of romance, sex or familial association. Many seek Love, and although instinctively recognize its value, they cannot seem to comprehend it in its totality and live its nature.

You are all required to be Love, but you cannot be that which you neither know nor understand. To be Love, you must know God as yourself. You can only know God as yourself if you dissociate yourself from the material, outwardly, and seek the ethereal, inwardly. It is intended for you to align yourself with God values and you shall do so when you find "God Love". This brand of Love resonates every virtue you will ever seek to espouse on your journey. The Love of God is your true power. Perfect and pure in origin, its comforting balm is the security you seek in your life. Its creative force and potential is the romantic energy generated by that ONE Love.

True Love completes, fills and harmonizes your inner being, so that, you become a vessel of Love, a carrier of invaluable attributes. You will not "need" another to love you when God's Love fills you. You will become Love personified, and as you give from your vessel, HE with whom you are ONE shall replenish you, for HE dwells within and is never lacking. Your actions, words and works shall vibrate with the frequency of Love.

Love requires no definition. It expresses itself through your creations. The measure of your Love will always be apparent, in and through that which you create. When Love becomes your fulcrum, all of your creations will bespeak its timeless virtues.

Man is only recently discovering the power of Love through his ability to heal, when he uses love fired by pure intent to create wholeness in self or others. However, he is yet to fully realize that Love creates the Whole. That which is ethereal, celestial and universal will always respond to expressions of pure love by further empowering the giver, so that, the giver comes into an even more profound understanding of his power, in ONENESS with the Universe.

It is time for all to come into a higher understanding of the Power of Love, so that, the ascending journey may be made in truth and in the clarity of God's Light, which is one and the same with HIS love. Love need not be adapted, adjusted or culturalized. IT JUST IS. You need to understand and integrate the culture of God's love as you progress. You shall be inclined to willingly do so when you are moved by your inner light, and are able to experience the ecstasy of your union with your Creator. It is through this bonding you will find that which you seek, being the illusive Love. You will realize that the feeling of ecstasy is the primary and real emotion of Love. It is only then that you can know Love and its power, and come into the knowing of your power.

THE SOURCE OF CORRECTION

Your spirit is the eternal energy which creates, only through love, and sees only through light. Its sword is wisdom and its shield is truth. It dwells in the kingdom of its peace and is its own fulcrum. Its potential is incomparable and its imaginings pure. What can your spirit offer you? It is the key, the secret to a wholesome life, the Source of all Correction.

You are here to minister to the soul's unfolding through its light and to serve God's will. I will today teach you about the tool for self preservation.

To protect yourself from erroneous perceptions and judgments against others, LIVE IN SPIRIT. Your spirit dwells in the framework of a higher mind and exists in its own assurance. It needs no weapons to attack or defend, for it is neither vulnerable nor liable to lower vibratory emotions. It is its own understanding, and will render through this understanding, compassion for the plight of those you will perceive as "evil". The spirit knows that those who choose the lower path are merely experimenting with that which is alien to them. The spirit sees them as struggling to accept their divine nature and sovereign power. Evil, or what you call sin, is created by those who choose the longer pathway home.

The spirit sees as God sees. The spirit knows that many will, through the ego, seek to attack that which they cannot comprehend, or that which is foreign to their established patterns of thinking. The spirit does not take offence or react, but responds as the ONE whose footsteps it follows. The spirit will respond with pardon and a blessing of love. The spirit knows that it is All.

The spirit sees the sufferings of its brothers and sisters who choose the lower pathway, notwithstanding, that they may have garnered wealth and power on the material level. The spirit sees how diseased and corrupted the incarnate being becomes, notwithstanding a healthy body. It is bereft of the light of its spirit, and is enveloped in a darkened shield. The souls of these beings have no way out.

Through many incarnations you have become accustomed to familiar settings, based on physical and sensory responses. The ego is a well established aspect which motivates behaviour not aligned with spirit choice. The ego becomes your ruler and dictates your response through unconscious programming. At times, your conscious mind wishes to respond in balance, but you have become so conditioned that you respond through your conditioned mind. Think of yourself as software which was pure at your birth, and through myriad incarnations it became slowly defective due to the infiltration of habits foreign to its nature. It is so infected that it requires purification and re-calibrating to operate at its highest potential again.

The panacea, is reunion with Spirit. In your communion with your Higher self, you will be fed the elixir which will nourish your mind and bring clarity of vision. That which once despoiled your view will be removed, and you will experience vistas anew as you explore the bounty of spirit's offerings.

Your interaction and union with your Higher self engages you in celestial thinking, and by your choice, your efforts and your knowledge of spirit's yield, you will overcome the hurdles of your ego and the world surrounding you, as well as, expedite your return to the Source.

Your spirit will guide you on how to deal with worldly issues, should you place yourself under its tutelage. The spirit is a wise teacher, but will not force or impose itself on the student. It will gently re-introduce you to your power, and teach you how to harness your potential to create instead of mis-create. It will sharpen your mind to tune into higher intelligence and introduce you into renowned celestial circles, so that, you once again become comfortable with "yourself" and your inherent power. It will initiate you, teach you, test you and facilitate your continued journey to enlightenment. There will come a time when you will not be able to differentiate yourself from spirit. It is then you will live totally in spirit, without need for physical consciousness.

You are encouraged to step up your efforts to live in spirit, now. Self discovery and enlightenment can take as long or as short as you choose. It is always your choice, but the choice you make should be measured against the knowledge of that which your spirit can offer to you.

I will ask you to ponder upon the following questions?

How comfortable are you in your mortal incarnation?
How do you feel about yourself and your life?
Are you happy inspite of the world around you?
Are you at peace inspite of worldly creations?
How do you interact with other mortals?
Do you respond with your ego, and if so how does it make you feel?
What is it that is missing in your life?
Are you in control?
What is your purpose in this life?
How do you go about achieving your purpose?
Does your purpose impact on you alone, or on many or all?
What does spirit mean to you, and what role does it play in your life?
Do you live in fear?
Do you thrive on anger, or typically respond with anger to situations contrary to your understanding or preferences? How does being angry make you feel? Does it motivate you to make changes within yourself? Does it steal your peace?
What is your idea of love?
What does being balanced mean to you?

These questions are meant to inspire constructive thought and honest insight, so that, you may determine for yourselves the areas in your lives which you need to address. When you can confront short comings, go then to the "Source of Correction", who will help you to be the Spirit you are.

THE GOAL OF SELF MASTERY

Many tend to be dutiful to limitations imposed by themselves, or by others. Limitations create unnatural barriers which impede the graduation to higher levels of experiencing, knowing and being.

Frequently, many define themselves, their worth and capabilities in the measure of the finite. Many create moulds for themselves and live within its parameters. Fear and unknowing, reticence and insouciance, disbelief and mistruth are what colours the thinking of many, and breaches their right to achieve their highest potential.

Success is interpreted within the remit of what is ordinary, being the material or physical composite. Many compete for what is bound in materiality, and devise herewith, the formulae for personal success. They seek to master the material world through gain, and stately, yet, transient power.

Lack of vision precludes many from seeing the mortal journey on earth plane for what it truly is. The body becomes the life of many, and material things, their world. Conquering in the name of both becomes the ultimate goal. You are spirit incarnate, NOT body. You choose to incarnate to continue your ascending journey, which is a spiritual one. The achievement bears on the fulfilment of spirit, not body. You are meant through the earthly run to re-discover your god mind, and seek inner alignment with truth. Your mortal experience through the physical vehicle of the body is facilitating mastery of yourself. It is a spiritual journey in physical disguise.

What is mastery you may ask? It is the ability to overcome one's lower self by achieving discipline over one's emotions, recognising that in truth there is ONE will and choosing that will.

Mastery of self is spiritual mastery, spiritual freedom in the manifested realm of Godhood, where the alchemy of ONENESS is experienced and Light is all there is.

Although I speak of attaining self mastery, you must know that you never lost that mastery; through perceived separation you temporarily forgot it. As the subtle waves of spirit bring you into deeper remembrance of that which you are, you will eventually recognise the power you bear within, and seek to re-align with that power and reclaim your mastery. The path to mastery requires you to conquer the poisonous machinations of the physical ego mind. Recognise that you do not fight against others. You fight against yourselves as you submit to perceptions and judgments which evoke overwhelming feelings and catalyses reactions counter to spirit. The more you give in to the world the less you honour your spirit.

Few have been able to create a harmonious relationship between the physical ego and the spirit. This fosters polarity which often leads to extremes in behaviour. You are not expected to traverse earthly territory without the ego, but if you seek to live a spiritual life and nurture self mastery, an inevitability to such, is the relegation of the ego through ones control, to its natural role, complementary to the body's need for survival.

Think of yourself as corn on the cob. Each sheath which covers the corn must be peeled away. The peeling of the outer skin brings you closer to the core of that which you are. As the peeling unfolds the density lightens, and all that is left is the brilliance of the golden kernels firmly anchored in its spine. You are that golden light when exposed in your natural state, anchored firmly in the ONE. Why would you wish to wear such onerous clothing when your radiant beauty, bounty, inner charm and reality serve you so much more?

Look at yourselves. How many more sheaths must be peeled away so that you can live in your mastery?

Self mastery is a discipline, a mandatory course in the syllabus in the University of Life. When you eventually graduate you will be recipients of the prestigious **GOM** qualification—Master of Godhood.

INNER PRESENCE

The embers of your retiring soul spark to remind you of its immortal presence. It can energize you with an idea or feeling which takes you to a fleetingly new and sudden understanding. It gives out morsels of timely flickers to draw your attention to its embryonic light. Once you have found the spark, it will brandish and parade its value and power, so that, you may be enticed to fuel it into a fully fledged flame. The inner presence, being your light which is the living flame of you, will begin to unwrap itself and blossom in response to your seeking. It beckons you, so that, it may lovingly show you the way home.

This inner presence is your constant companion, the only dependable source in your life. Through the lighted path it has prepared for you, it is the way to immortal glory. It will introduce you to faculties of higher understanding and help you to transit the bridge between mortal and immortal.

Your inner presence combines all and everything in the ONENESS of its elemental nature. In its essence it is God and it knows all that God knows. It is a fraction, YET, the whole of God's light, God's mind, Creation. There can never be disunity within the realms of that inner conjunct, for this energy is that which is real and capable of separation only through simulated thought, by the very One who is its origin.

It is the ego mind of man that carves a distinction in blissful unawareness. He hoards for himself that which is least, and ostracizes through ignorance that which is all and sovereign. He alienates that which he seeks to discover in his very life i.e. himself. He chooses the finite above the infinite as his ego perception assures him that the finite is his measure. Yet, it is the infinite, intangible energy within him that can inspire, influence and motivate him to powerful awakening and achievement. He needs to take the time to fan the embers of the infinite presence within. Many seek their power in the reflection of matter, and disregard that which is their natural, inbred empowerment.

The inner presence within each is the same; unquenchable, unreserved, buoyant and serenely perfect. It requires pure application of lavish attention, so that, its momentum builds to create a working rhythm with you. The inner presence desires active matrimonial harmony through willing consummation, so that, it may confer balance which becomes the perennial motivating energy in your life. This balance will be mirrored in your perspective and actions.

Your inner presence is the faithful Husband/Wife, Father/Mother who loves without margin, with patient awaiting, and who tolerates imbalanced patterns whilst always seeking to re-direct you on your path. It offers comfort, forgiveness and transmutation without intrusive intent, so that, you may progress through your lessons to fulfilment. It will never foist its power upon you, for it must be claimed never imposed.

There is nothing eccentric about your inner presence. It manifests all that is perfect. It defines you when you can engage your energies in its perfection. You will never define your inner light, for you are an extension of it. If allowed, it will define you through your outer expression of its manifested power.

As your inner presence assumes an increasingly dominant role in your life, your perceptions of you and your power, will transition from ego orientation to celestial disposition. Once the bindings occur you will never wish to experience life without that ethereal presence. This delightful union will unearth, unleash and create miracles. It will provide you with a purpose, to which you can apply and reflect its power and attributes. In this way, as a mortal through immortal connection, you become the beacon, the way, the Presence.

YOU ARE—ABUNDANT

Abundance is your natural state. It is the rhythm allocated to you through the birth of your soul. It is your wealth, your governance.

Your ability to conceive this truth is elusive. It has become natural for you to seek that which is external to yourself in the form of acquisitions which you project as "abundance". What you know as abundance is typically what you can see and own.

You cannot comprehend the subtle truth that you are All, and in that All-ness there is no vestige of paucity or lack.

As you gently meander through the soul's evolutionary cycle, you will gradually come into remembrance and acceptance of your natural form. It is the indigenous part of you that has no ending. During the course of your myriad journeys through the evolutionary worlds of time and space, you will at some point achieve the alchemy of wholeness. It takes men many lifetimes to realise and know that they are All, and experience ONENESS. When your mind merges with the Divine mind, you simply "are". You will need nothing, for you shall have everything.

Until such time, it is advocated that you re-programme your thinking of dearth into one of abundance, by initiating within yourself the knowledge that you cannot be anything but abundant. Your soul was created in perfection, and it is through this perfection that you derive the abundance of your CREATOR.

If you are able to accept this rationale, you will begin to see through the eyes of abundance and think without limitation, as that which is abundant has no limit.

The use of the term abundance in your realm tends to have a material or possessory connotation. This is invariably a very limited view point. Creation itself is abundant in divine energy, yet, rarely in your world is the cosmic view taken of abundance. You cannot know abundance unless you come to know yourself, and experience every facet of you as a divine entity.

You hold the power within you as abundant beings to create abundance in your outer world. You can also create whatever abundance you desire in your personal world. What you create should inevitably reflect you.

Through life's experiences abundant lessons can be learnt from the soul's perspective. The lessons are usually learnt through unpleasant or painful circumstances. Many of these adverse circumstances are meant to yield lessons which will enable the participants in the experience to gravitate closer to the god within. This is a step which harmonises their thinking to that which is closer to their true nature. It is from this point that an understanding of God and themselves will be birthed.

Need is an indicator of lack and lack is an indicator of perceived un-wholeness. A change in perception is mandatory in order to manifest abundance in all areas of your life. All power lies within you, and it is for you to utilise and direct that power in a way that creates abundance. The power of you lies in your mind. It is therefore necessary to re-programme your mind to project thoughts of abundance. If you lack confidence, self esteem, self belief or faith, then your creations cannot yield abundance, and neither will you attract abundance.

You also need to relinquish the programme of poverty consciousness, and become more aligned with the abilities, qualities and essence of Christ consciousness. In a state of Christ consciousness you will only know abundance.

The reality of your 3rd dimensional world is that abundance has been associated with financial gains, or what you term money. Indeed, as a "thing" it can provide material wealth and trappings related thereto. Not everyone has abundance YET everyone is abundant. True abundance does not know lack. It is balanced on the fulcrum of equality. True abundance does not exist in your physical world.

Is there any ill or evil in having or desiring money? The answer is simply NO. It is the use of that money and the means used to acquire it that matters. If money is a staple in your societal structure and necessary for living, to shun it in its entirety would not be wise. In fact you cannot currently survive without it. Most activities revolve around it. How much you desire depends on your personal needs and wants. It is a means to an end not an end in itself. It is a mechanism for physical survival; for the soul to have its journey and experience in your world, money is a necessity at this time.

Many do not appreciate that through past lives, as well as, through genetic coding, they have brought the id of poverty consciousness with them into this incarnation. Many have taken vows of poverty in various life times which have affected their journey, choices and abilities to create and attract abundance in this life time.

You are not POOR beings. You are spiritually wealthy divine souls who lack nothing and embody everything. You often blame others and circumstances for holding you back. No one is responsible for you but you. It is your inability to see abundance on your path that keeps you stuck in a mire of lack and need.

It is indeed not easy to de programme aeons of false programming. However, if you are committed to working on yourselves, you will each be able to source the root of your beliefs and begin the process of healing.

Abundance does not mean excess; it means fullness and All-ness. It is all encompassing. In your abundance, you must always seek to share, and that includes sharing of yourself through service.

Abundance must breed humility in being and humility in sharing. It is not ornate in outlook. It is simply radiant.

When spirituality underpins your life and higher thinking is your level of intelligence, you will embrace your abundant nature without embarrassment. You will attract in abundance, all you seek in your physical world, and what you seek shall always be in balance, and for the sharing or re-giving.

ONENESS AND ALIGNMENT, ONENESS AND ECSTASY

I AM LIGHT, I AM ECSTASY, A Joy to Behold, A Joy to Be. My energy pluralizes as I divide myself to create. I rest in each part, that each may through established connection, attain a state of being, and experience the prized feeling of ONENESS, which is the whole, undivided, cohesive and complete. When you feel MY presence within your form, joy springs like the dawning sun, and suddenly flickers of ecstasy applauds. Your material world becomes marginalised as you begin to be anchored from within by a sustainable energy, undiminished.

The ONENESS you experience is not possessory in nature, for the spirit does not possess the physical and the physical can never possess that which is free. It is simply a fusion of energy which originates from the Source. There is no disconnect, but empowerment, birthed by the union of physical and spiritual.

Your experience of ONENESS, no matter how fleeting, will encourage conscious effort on your part to remain within the precincts of spirit. The knowing of ONENESS underlies your progression as spiritual individuals, and as a civilisation. Your efforts to remain connected with spirit will result in your spirit responding. As you court your spirit, its dormancy is released into a vibrant awakening, willing and desirous to unfold for your benefit to express its mastery in your dimension.

You shall achieve the wisdom that you cannot sustain joy, love, peace, balance and success without the participation of your spirit. Participation is facilitated through cultured connectivity, as you daily invite your Higher self to express itself through you in thought, action, words and being.

You will come into the secret of self sustenance as you remain in alignment. This experience confers assurance, and a higher understanding of your place in the universe and within God's creation. The intelligence of ONENESS exceeds that of your lower mind.

When you experience alignment with your Source and All, an all inclusive feeling of love transcends physical acquaintance. You will begin to look upon your brothers and sisters with whom you have no physical tie or bond, as projections of the ONE, and therefore aspects of you.

It is time to loosen the shackles of short-sightedness and confined thinking, and demand that your ego mind takes its rightful place as servant to Master spirit. This will afford you the opportunity to embark on a relationship which offers moment to moment support, renewal, excitement, wisdom, peace, balance, joy and empowerment. Do not sequester yourself to a life bereft of spirit camaraderie. Though you walk in mortal form, you can learn to speak and understand the language of spirit, your true language. Choose to reside knowingly in your sovereignty, and live the destiny of your soul. The key, is alignment with the ONE.

As I channelled this piece I was inspired to write the following poem titled "My Space".

MY Space

This is my space
Where electricity flows in streaks of lightning
And leaves an afterglow of timelessness.

This is my space
Where all discord evaporates
And ONENESS bred in the wake of divinity
Where solitude speaks its wisdom
And my true education begins.

This is my space
Where the I AM comes alive
And feeds me with the milk of life—Truth
That I may by its sustenance
Chart my course to higher grounds.

This is my space
Where my soul's expressions
Harmonise me to its vibratory grid
Where there's no beginning, no end, just eternity.

This is my space
Where I am moved by my true being
Where my jaundiced vision clears
And the surrealness of spirit's crystalline measure
Reflects the reality of me.

This is my space
Where the lamps which light my path
Entices me to the treasure chest
The bearer of my heritage.

This is my space
Where silence courts
Those gems stored in the pockets of my soul
That I may be touched by iridescence
To be a walking light in this world.

This is my space
Where joy's pulps explode in freedom, succulent
And charismatic energy o'erf lows.

This is my space
The beatitude of my existence
My kingdom, my heaven, my home.

THE DIVINE BEAT OF COURAGE

Courage is a characteristic of wisdom, for the wise knows that courage is the ammunition which combats the insidious fear generated by a needy mortal ego. Courage is therefore born from wisdom conceived from "knowing", which is divine. The soul holds knowledge and wisdom, and so, courage is a characteristic of the soul. All too often it is easy to succumb to fear as you live in alignment with your lower self, whereas effort is required to connect with your true being from which you can access the storehouse of divine attributes.

Courage is a creative force within one's soul, for its personification can create change in one's life. Lack of courage amongst people has relegated them to a state of resigned living, whereby they accept that which they consider as their fate, and fall within the status quo of believing without knowing.

Courage is synonymous with bravery, fearlessness and strength of character. Its existence and endurance is only possible when one can appreciate the context and sub context of its reality.

Humans are sovereign beings by virtue of their indwelling adjusters.[31] They are carriers of divine essence. In many cases they are unknowing receptacles of Light. Through that sovereignty, man has been conferred with qualities of God and Light, being one and the same.

God and Light are the overarching context of man's existence. God's qualities, virtues and attributes are the sub context within which the value and virtue of courage rests. This is a simplistic way of explaining to man, that he may comprehend. In fact there is only ONE, and therefore ONE context which is Light.

Although there is a scientific explanation for Light, the context to which I refer is inexplicable, for God is Light and Light Just IS. Light

---

[31]   This is the Father fragment or spirit of God within each soul.

cannot be explained. When you know God you will come to know the Light, your Light, and you will emanate and be the Light. There will be no need for definitions and explanations, for "Knowing" cannot be explained or justified.

All that is not of God or for God, is against God. God empowers and enlightens. HE never dis-empowers. However, fear, timidity and low self esteem which generate insecurities are against man's sovereign nature, for they dis-empower and steal his control. To find and know courage, and to be courageous to face your experiences and interactions with others, you need to construct the family tree of your soul. When you can see that God is at the helm of that family tree, and that you are a direct descendant through creation, taking an ascending journey back to HIM, you will realise the sovereignty and power you hold within. Instinctively, through a knowing of your ONENESS, you begin to assume HIS qualities.

Words such as courage do not exist in God's language, for HIS language is only that of Light and Love. Yet, it is necessary in your dimension to identify with "courage", as you are governed by perceptions surrounding your existence, and very basic emotions. Love is really the only emotion which should exist. However, the ego of man has created a conundrum meant to wrap his mind in a veritable twist, so that, he experiences all manner of emotions which he considers validated through his earthly experiences. Fear, insecurity and doubt become conditioned responses to many of his experiences. He must then be taught that only courage can counter the effects of these feelings and states of being.

The illusion of creation has also warped the thinking of man's mind as he cannot see that which is illusion from reality, and truth from untruth. So for now, until man grows into himself, he needs courage, which is a weapon within the spiritual armoury, to fight the illusions of negativity which the collective egos spawn.

Looking panoramically at the world today, courage is sorely lacking, as fear of change and truth clutches the minds of man and imprisons him. Man cannot in mass find the determination to break through the barriers of fear. As a result he contents himself with the excuse *"What can I do, I am only one being? How can I affect or effect change? It is safer for me to fit in and be one of them. I have one life to live, let me enjoy it to the fullest. I will do my best for myself and my family and that is what matters"*. Many surrender their beliefs and knowing, of what is spiritually correct, to the machinations of their senses and to that which is socially and politically correct.

For some, hope has become a substitute for courage. Man is always hoping for the best without realising that hope without action is futile. Many leave it to God, not knowing that God will not work for man, but with man. God will do HIS part, but if man fails to take positive action there will be no change in his circumstances.

All must realise that each is born to be co-creator with God. The insouciance which has captured the thinking of many, and falsely leads them to believe that God will deliver them from all their problems without action on their part, is sorely misplaced. The trite saying *"What will be will be"* will never BE. Only you, can co-create with God that which you wish to BE.

It often takes courage, resolve, determination, knowing and trust in one's sovereignty to create what man deems impossible. Courage knows no bounds, for God is boundless. The insulated thinking of many has destroyed their creative aptitude, and they cannot see themselves for who they are, and cannot know themselves as God. As long as you labour under misapprehensions, you shall always need to "find the courage". Courage comes from self belief, and self belief with God awareness is "God belief". Only then will man's resolve and strength endure.

If you cannot find God, you will not know courage. If your "will" is unconnected with God, you will not get very far. In your world, as possessions of money, power and status confer sovereignty, courage seems expendable and unnecessary. These outer trappings do not serve

God or the god within each ensouled being; neither can they help man find his true, enduring and immortal power.

Courage cannot be taught or bought. It must be discovered and accessed within the recesses of man's soul, as man comes into the knowing of God, through his mortal experience. When man can move into that glorious ONENESS, there will be no need for words such as courage, for you shall be as HE is.

Courage beats resonantly as a sound vibration of the Light. Find the Light, your Light, and you shall find your courage.

COMPASSION—A HEAVENLY COMPASS AND PATHWAY OF PASSION

Compassion is an expression of love. It is the heavenly compass that directs you to a deeper understanding of authentic love. It is an accolade to love when expressed with pure intent, without righteous indignation. It draws from the flow of love to empathise, and reminds of the equality in the nature of God's creation.

Compassion is the breath of God upon HIS universe of time and space. It is the filter through which HIS love descends. It is a natural virtue of love.

It breeds patience and tolerance, and effects a higher understanding of diverse personalities and experiences. Compassion should not be attended with pity, but with knowledge. When you know that each experience in life is purposeful, whether it is your experience or that of another, you can offer understanding and support. Offering compassion does not afford you the right to interfere with the experience of others. You can assist them in seeing the experience through higher vision, and to extract the lesson from the experience. You can encourage and assist them in the transmutation of fault, suffering and disadvantage, to freedom, joy, knowledge and truth. To show true compassion requires you to truly understand your brother, and you can only do so if you seek to know him.

Compassion must be an elevated energy which raises your vibration, and the vibration of the person to whom it is offered. It must not depress the vibration through morose expressions, and apologies for plights. Plights and experiences are often created by the very ones to whom you offer compassion, as a device for learning. When you love with compassion you become an example to others.

The love of God within man can diffuse tensions and anger into compassion. This will birth offerings of kindness, empathy, forgiveness and mercy. It must be offered without discrimination. Even those you perceive in darkness deserve your compassion. Is your brother not a part of you? Is his darkness not a reflection of that part of you, not yet in light? I remind you of the ONENESS of all. Will you shun yourself in anger and hatred? Surely, the dark part of you must be returned to light. With knowledge, truth, love, compassion, understanding, patience and desire this will become possible.

Let compassion begin with self. Any aspect of you which is not in harmony with God is imperfect, flawed, and a disease unto itself, and must be shown compassion. Love for self, must be the guiding force which allows you to recognise the manifested result of the disharmony, usually some form of emotional, mental, psychological or physical suffering. Gently seek counsel from the ONE, as to how you can transform that aspect into divine accord. Let passion for harmony and balance catalyse your efforts to effect change.

Many have shown their compassion for the suffering of others, and the perceived injustices meted out to others, through draconian actions, such as hunger strikes and wars. The passion in compassion does not require self sacrifice or combative action.

When passion is directed without balance, more disharmony and mayhem will result. It requires a balanced response fired by love and perseverance to effect change through education of truth to the masses; that the pool of consciousness that comprise your civilisation begin to effect changes at the level of thought which will then impinge on the resulting creation of man.

Let compassion be your nature in living and serving and let it be the tool that you use to initiate change in self and circumstances. The wings of compassion must always be kept in flight through the tail wind of prayer, for through prayer your compassion will be properly directed and perfectly executed.

CLIMBING THE MOUNTAIN OF YOUR SOUL

I bring you to the mountain that you may be inspired. At such heights, rare breaths minister to the seeking soul who aspires to its pinnacle. Through the ascent, the language of light becomes finely attired and the lungs of awareness expand within the aspirant. The Glory of the pinnacle beckons.

I will not give to you the majestic mountains of time and space where you often visit in the realms of your imagination, beholding the wonderment and majesty of a pristine creation. I will lend it to you as an analogy so that you may recognise a spiritual truth.

Many are so bewitched by the mountains that they expend time and energy to physically train, in preparation for the climb. Climbing a mountain requires great physical, mental and emotional stamina.

Invariably, during their journey through challenging terrain, they may stumble, fall and often become bruised. Yet, with the goal always in sight, they persevere. Weariness of body is seldom experienced as the adrenaline pumps within, spurring them to continue their climb to experience greater heights of personal and physical achievement. Often, they will stop to enjoy the panoramic view, the beauty of which channels inspiration to ascend higher and higher, until they could see what others are unable to see.

With every mile they overcome, they experience an inner exhilaration and expansion of energy. They can feel the waft of accomplishment as the pinnacle of the mountain is in sight. They do not rest until they achieve their mortal goal. Mentally and physically they are pushed to the limits, but the joy, peace and glory they experience at the pinnacle, have made the journey with its varied experiences and casualties well worth it.

Why are you drawn to the mountain? Man seeks greatness, achievement of highest potential and peace. The mountain is symbolic of majesty, bears great height and commanding presence and presents a challenge to all, but itself. It offers a haven of solitude to those searching for peace and quiet reverie. Its natural habitat inspires creative thought and dispensation. It is cast in untold beauty which attracts the soul of those drawn to it.

How befitting is the mountain, analogous to the soul of man, yet, disparate; the latter being spiritual and eternal and the former being physical and natural. Man can discover his soul, his character and truth as he climbs the physical mountain, and indulges in the reverence of solitude which allows him to hear the wisdom of his soul, and experience the beauty within himself. He is free in the mountain to walk with his spirit, untouched by the rancour of extraneous certainties.

Yet, the physical mountain speaks to man its own parable. It tells the story for those who can hear. Man's soul is likened to a mountain, willing man to assume the challenge of ascending it by preparing himself, through reflection of spiritual attitude, and the desire for spiritual aptitude.

The mountain of his soul beckons him to take a welcoming journey to discover his truth and reality. Though this journey may be onerous at times, and he may falter in his climb, he will make progress. This will encourage him to keep his eyes on the goal, being the pinnacle of his soul—the God head.

This mountain can be climbed but can never be proved. It is its own greatness, and offers only rewards to those who are courageous to take the journey. It offers higher vision and sound insight. The higher you ascend the more you become enveloped in vibrations anew. You find your song on this journey as your soul creates a harmony that will lure you continuously to higher placement. On this mountain you will experience the joy of being and the ecstasy of your own presence. Your instincts will be honed as you absorb more and more of the soul's ethereal light. You will become transformed. This is your eternal abode where inspiration never fades, where wisdom is never forgotten and truth always shines.

It is the storehouse of balance where harmony can be purchased through the exchange of desire and effort. The mountain of your soul offers certainty and guarantee of eternal existence. When you make this mountain your dwelling place, you shall reside in your power and all fear shall be admonished in the wake of knowing who you are. The pinnacle is at your behest, forever urging, instructing and guiding you through the perfect path for you; that as you journey to Glory, there too, will be Glory in the journey.

GENEROSITY—THE COSMIC GENE

Generosity is cradled in every spirit and birthed by the single Source of love. It is as eternal as the spring from which the soul was conceived. It burns in the immortality of the living flame of life.

Generosity is often mistaken as an "act". It does not find its centre in matter, but is an intangible virtue which, if honoured righteously, perfumes its journey with the bodacious fragrance of kindness which kindles every moment of one's sojourn.

Generosity is attached to nothing except itself. It does not steal the light of recognition, it does not count the costs of giving and it does not harbour vehicular attachments of expected gratitude, reciprocation, atonement, material rewards, or bow to egoistic camaraderie. It comfortably sits with the choir of divine virtues free from the prison of political riddles, societal contortions, egotistical demands and religious catechism.

Generosity creates a silhouette for the soul. Each soul recognises in its cell memory that the thread of light weaved its existence through the deft mind of the Creator. It acknowledges that it is programmed to give by the very mind which gave it life. The light of generosity creeps into the psyche of the soul, and feeds it with the food of gravitational courage that it may see the gift of giving, spiritualised in the celestial pendulum.

Man must know that the thriving and healing potion of generosity can only be accessed through the knowing of himself, and the very Source from which he was created. When he can comprehend the simple mechanics of his soul's birth and know that his life is a gift bestowed that he may replicate his Father's giving, he will then understand his true nature. He will appreciate that the Father gives generously of HIS love, light, patience, understanding, compassion, tolerance and greatness of HIS spirit. Man can then fashion his life to match the generosity of the Father. After all, the Father's spirit is within him.

The Father generously bestowed upon man the gift of free will. HIS only hope is that man would one day choose to align his will with that of the Father.

True generosity of spirit is priceless, effortless and infallible. When you give in the spirit of love you do not deny yourself, but will always be replete with myriad gifts. Your generosity will ennoble your soul, and liberate the souls of others as you nourish them with kindness.

LOVE'S NEST

Love is the natural state of man. Man needs to epitomise Love's clarity and vein of thinking through his mortal actions. He seeks Love's cleavage which frequently evades his grasp. He may to a certain degree feel, experience and partake of the earthly spices braided into love's authenticity, but for the most part the primary rhythm of love's balance is lacking in his interchange with others.

Love has become an object to be acquired through outward seeking instead of the goal of self discovery. Tears are shed and emotions scarred through the search for love, its anchor and stability. Instead of being moved by the natural instinct of Love, many often seek to control it through possession.

The route map to Love leads always within the self of man; there lay its nesting ground. Love is not illusive to man. It is his perception of love which deprives him of the fine comprehension, that Love cannot be created, borrowed, earned, attained, diminished or demoralised.

It is an essence that creates balance. It births the Law of Giving; it takes nothing; violates nothing, yet, is everything. It fertilises man's thinking so that he grows into an attitude of wisdom which teaches him that he is Love. When he is able to gently move into his primacy, illumination begins to take hold, and he begins to personify Love's magnitude. His actions and thoughts will aspire to the virtues of Love. It becomes the handle which he turns to gain him entrance into a higher state.

The Love of man, being the love of God, being God manifest, has transformative value. It can eclipse the scathing emotions which often proliferate through the ego mind. One however, must attend all things with Love. Love may not necessarily alter the state of events, but can influence one's perspective and perception of such events.

What is Love, but the breath of God, the light of HIS thinking, the embodiment of HIS creation, the giving of HIMSELF? When man can see himself as the breath of God, the light of HIS thinking, the embodiment of creation, and as God HIMSELF, he will graduate into the knowledge that Love is his inner compass which will direct him to the refrain of his soul, composed by rhyming notes in heightened scales of ecstasy. He will then be launched into the reality of ONE accord, his immortal identity.

THE ORIGINAL AUTHORITY

Man finds his origin in "God", the intangible, ethereal Source Energy. God created the soul of man and man is an extension of his soul. Man must therefore return to his soul, his author, to find his authority.

Authority is inbuilt through conception, to be discovered and earned through inner recognition, consciousness and awakening. Man's measure or perception of his authority will grow as he grows in awareness of his origin, his light and his immortality. His authority will be found in his sovereign state of being, his I AM presence.

When man discovers the source of his authority he will be equipped to become the author of his destiny. He will learn to use his authority to exercise self control to gain mastery of, and over himself. He will then be equipped to become a leader of men. He will be able to use his new found authority to create, instead of imitating the actions of others.

Secular education limits the ability to intuitively access truth through spiritual cognition. Man is told what authority means. His influences condition his belief that authority must be conferred upon him, or earned through diligence and promotion. His education teaches that authority is something disjointed from his natural state of being, and must be worked for to be achieved. The meaning of authority assumes a temporal disposition, rather than the timeless, eternal status it enjoys through the knowing of one's Higher self.

Man yearns to forge a place for himself in this world, to be "someone", to achieve status and espouse power. However, the scales used to measure achievement are heavily weighted on materialistic gains. He struggles to achieve all that he seeks, and requires validation from others as a form of recognition. He is left in an "ever wanting" state which encourages self pity, as he is demoralised by his inability to achieve social and fiscal authority.

OPEN YOUR INNER EYES, AWAKEN FROM YOUR SLUMBER, MOVE BEYOND YOUR OUTER SENSES WHICH INHIBITS YOUR TRUE VISION. SEE YOURSELF FOR WHO YOU TRULY ARE.

If you can comprehend the measure of your inner authority, you will never again embark on a treasure hunt which requires you to explore dangerous territory, in order to pillage and plunder that which can never truly give you what you seek. The only journey you need to take is the one which transcends the bridge between your mortal senses and your soul/god mind. As you enter the sanctuary of your soul, you will find the crown which awaits you. Accept the offering, and serenely acknowledge that your unequivocal power, authority and wealth lie within you.

THE DISEMPOWERING PERCEPTION

There is no strength or wisdom in perceptions, inordinately formed from personal perspectives and devoid of all facts.

Perceptions often thrive on its emotional counterpart with the consequence of judgements being formed. These judgements may be erroneous in fact. Man must be taught that he is not to render judgement against the soul of another, for this is contrary to the laws of God.

Man is programmed to perceive; a pattern coordinated with and by the alter ego. Perceptions are formed by the minute, often without much thought, prevalently without knowledge, and using the scale of personal preferences and belief. Perception is the antithesis of knowledge. He who perceives cannot know, and he who knows will not perceive, at least not through his outer senses.

Perception is based on belief; knowledge, on accounted timeless facts. Your perceptions often culminate in a conclusion which will need to be defended. Knowledge requires no defence. As perception is linked with the ego, the defence mechanism is often invoked as one takes offense to an attack on one's perception/belief and judgement. Let us view how the ego creates. Ego—Perception—Judgment/Conclusion—Attack——Offence—Defence. Knowledge is not a consequence or factor in this sequence. Knowledge is simple. It knows, and even if it is attacked for want of physical proof, it continues to know and rests in the stillness of its cause; its truth which is its verification. It remains constant, awaiting perception to be effaced and knowledge to be assumed.

Perceptions are "right" only for those who perceive. It thrives in the subset of lower thinking. Knowledge is of the higher mind. When you perceive you see through lowered eyes whose vision is earthbound and blurred. When you "know", you see through the magnifying glass of spirit's eyes whose vision is cosmically clear.

Personal perceptions often create suffering in the perceiver, for perceptions of another can give rise to disharmony. Perceptions can lead to misunderstandings which birth insidious emotions such as hatred, paralysing anger and intolerance. Perceptions are microscopic in nature. They are formed through attention to small details rather than the panorama of possibilities which exist beyond its grasp.

If your goal is to become enlightened, you must journey out of perception into the realm of knowing. This requires you to invest the effort to be vigilant of your thoughts, and creations of the mind. Seek to dwell in the framework of the higher mind and stay aligned with higher thinking. You will then become friends with knowledge. Outer perceptions are powerless, groundless and defenceless. They are unsustainable and lack endurance.

All perceptions are based on the ONE PERCEPTION that you are separate from God, and thus separate from each other. As you embark on the journey of self discovery, and the truth of ONENESS becomes your life experience, your previous perceptions will be corrected. An inner expansion will birth higher perspectives which will empower your perceptions with truth.

THE CALENDAR OF LIFE

The Calendar of life is meant to be progressive as each cycle brings new experiences, all meant to charm the different facets of your soul alive. By the time you reach the last page in the Calendar there should be no distinction between lower self and Higher self.

The Calendar of which I speak is the Calendar of your soul's life, whose longevity is as eternal as the Source from which you were conceived.

Your physical bodies are on loan to provide a seat for your consciousness, so that, you may tend the infinite and ethereal part of you.

Consider the prudence in measuring your progress by reference to your Spiritual Calendar, instead of your linear one. To do so enables you to focus on your spiritual development, and to see each experience with the potential of awakening another aspect of your soul.

The human mind is seldom in harmony with the higher mind. The higher mind is the bedrock and sole repository of all Knowledge from which spiritual truths are built. Knowledge within mind will unfold as much as you effort to awaken to the truth within. Each experience in your earthly life contains a valuable treasure which will be apparent, should you open your inner eyes to discern it. As you discern the lessons from the experience your soul is enriched.

Each of you is eternal. Your existence on earth affords you the ability to discover your soul and to create a home for yourself within its temple. You can enjoy life in spirit whilst housed in the physical body.

Growth is meant to be consistently progressive. Setbacks are merely personal perceptions of an experience which effortlessly impede your conscious soul's journey. Progress is never achieved without diligent application and effort. You each owe responsibility to yourself-your TRUE SELF.

When your experiences throw spokes at you, challenge them with the will of your light, yet, honour them, for they give you an opportunity to choose "soul prominence" over "soul resistance".

There is no coincidence, no curse and no punishment. There are simply soul choices which must be worked out in a lower realm to propel the soul to the next page in the Calendar of its immortal life.

PLURALITY—THE DUALISTIC EFFECT

The reality of ONENESS has been tendered as Truth. This will survive the delusional thinking which has propelled the world into a state of dualistic energy, where many have become entrapped by the illusion of their own creation.

The archetype of the ONE will never be displaced, for even in the temporariness of man's forgetfulness, the ONE remains, to be remembered within the hearts and minds of men in the appropriateness of time. When all men come into remembrance, time will cease to exist. Time offers man a clutch with which to find his way back home. He attaches significance to all that is linear for he cannot comprehend eternity. To contemplate it invokes fear and uncertainty, for it has no form, and thus he blindly holds to his clutch and follows the sequence of his life not knowing that he must end up where he began. That which he calls time will inevitably lead him into timelessness.

I speak today of pluralism within dualism, or plurality within duality. Plurality supports the dualistic imposed structural thinking, and thereby condemns the singularity of the Law of ONE. It engenders the notion that cultures disjointed precepts. It exemplifies individuality and promotes division in thought and being. It is a construct of the ego mind which reveres self to the exclusion of the whole. Plurality further perpetuates the illusion, and standardises man's thinking, so much so, that many lose their ability to know the truth which becomes jeopardised in the multiplicity of belief systems man has developed, to support the illusion.

Plurality polarises and codifies distinction and distinctiveness. It warps the thinking of man as he seeks to find himself through one of the multitudinous offerings conjured through religious doctrine and dogma, polytheism, mythology, philosophy, secularity, political derivatives, fiscal infrastructures and cults, to name a few.

There are so many systems created for man to "try on for size" that he becomes a victim of his search for identity and empowerment. He wades through belief after belief hoping he will find one which fits comfortably. He often becomes a follower of many rather than a leader of ONE. He becomes a product of someone else's thinking and creation rather than his own. As the sects proliferate, pluralism strikes a blow to the efforts of those who truly seek to lead men to a return to ONENESS. Even those who appear to be on the path are often taken in by charlatans of spirituality as well as, would-be sages and gurus. Many with abilities abuse such, in their desire for aggrandisement and recognition.

The variances resulting from plural concepts within the framework referred to above, lead man into a maze of separation, divided thinking and practices. Regardless of his efforts and talk of unity, and in spite of differences, the pull of superiority always wins. Man is searching for his power. When his power as he conceives it within the physical world, becomes threatened, he will fight to retain control at any cost. Man becomes what his ego makes him instead of the powerful and complete being he is.

The world of man becomes a world of many, and the ONE of All and the All of ONE by-passes the consciousness of man. Perhaps, man must learn his lessons through his pluralistic creations within the dualistic context, before he can eventually realise and know the truth of ONE. Man does not realise that he perjures his own spirit when he denies its efficacy. So be it. He will one day emerge from behind his tinted spectacles, and with clarity see and know the truth. Only then will the illusion fall away and the spectrum shrink, so that, the ONE may prevail.

What appears to be the world is an illusion, and therefore man's search for himself within the illusion will always prove elusive. What is real will never appear, for it will always be there, never to be created; existing and being, waiting incognito for man to find and reveal his true name—ONE, Infinity, Eternity, Light.

PASSION—THE SONG OF THE SOUL

Passion is the price of perfection. A derivative of desire, it is the preceding element to achievement. Passion is that which inspires pro-activity and sustains action until the goal is accomplished.

Passion is the creative instinct within the souls of men born from the Creator's culture. Man must find his Passion and direct it towards that which is achievable. If he can see Passion as divine, his direction will be divinely inspired and his creation divine in orientation.

That which man creates with "Divine Passion" resonate light waves. Misdirected passion mis-creates and cauterizes the very flow of light. Darkened shadows will be the pall over that creation.

Passion must not be allowed to rule the gift of reason, which too, is divine. They are complementary to each other and serve to create the highest if they work in harmony. Each must temper the other whilst allowing for freedom of expression. Passion is born out of love whilst reason is born out of wisdom.

Passion speaks its conviction, and glorifies a higher knowing by the resultant fruit it yields. It radiates eternal energy, and is accompanied on its journey to fulfilment by its loyal friend Faith. Faith is the stepping stone of Passion and Passion is the fuel of Faith, for they co-exist symbiotically. When your Passion wanes remember your Faith, and when your Faith wanes remember your Passion. If you are lacking in both you cannot create.

Passion is the song your soul sings to you, so that, you may find your dedication and live its truth. It is the internal combustion which propels you to your highest potential. Passion can achieve that which you deem impossible, for its energy becomes its reality, and refuses to condone limiting thoughts.

When you find your Passion you will find your motivation. Yet, caution must be given lest you forget that true Passion is incorruptible, untouched by earthy necessities, budded only through the divine seed, and bearing only the sustainable. Passion and sensuality must not be combined or confused. Passion is non sensual. It is a proclamation of spiritual intent derived of higher equation, lending itself to a creative impulse. However, once unleashed, Passion romances the soul through the fulfilment of its creations which then glows in the throes of spiritual love.

Passion breeds perseverance and empowers one's belief. It visualises the fruit, goal or result, and reaches for it. It relinquishes chains of myopic thinking, mind imposed impediments, extraneous interference, and dwells in its focus.

Why do I speak of Passion? This is the key to that which all men desire without awareness, eternal life bathed in abundance, requited love, peace and unreserved joy. Man in his infancy misinterprets Passion, and assigns to it physical attributes and material desires, all superficial and transient at the least.

Passion at its simplest, is the energy of the Christ within, calling you home to experience all that you are.

THE CHANGING FACE OF DEBATE

Debate is essentially, engagement with another or others to verbally discuss views on various topics of interest shared between participants. Why have I chosen this topic? There are too many fence sitters in your world, too many peace keepers who seek to justify not having a view or not espousing a cause, for the sake of peace.

Achieving peace in your world is essential, and this can only be effected through change. Maintaining peace at the expense of its achievement is fruitless. It must be achieved before it can be maintained. To achieve a state of peace, be it inner peace or peace in the world, man must realise that change is necessary. There are many who realise and know this, but are not prepared to take up the baton and encourage others to do the same.

Debate ignites excitement, triggers passion, stimulates thought processes, and generates new, unheard, yet, cultured perspectives. It encourages man to open his mind, undertake research, explore new territories, set aside his reticence, apathy or non partisan attachment, and begin to gravitate towards a cause, a case, a belief, a conviction. In this productive process, each can distil a purpose that goes beyond self achievement.

Debate is not meant to create separation of ideas. Its aim should not be to prove that one group's idea is superior to another, or more credible than another. Victory of one over the other should not be the end goal. The objective should not be to sustain egos or prove that one is right and another wrong. It should not incite vitriolic responses and polarise people. Debate should always be entered into with a view to enlightenment. One may not be fully endeared to all the views of another, but may through the process and through the passage of time become enlightened because of the exchange which takes place. Truth should be the centring point of debate. This simply means that it should be the aim of the exercise, the goal.

There are many dogmas, doctrines and theories which many religiously follow which provide security in belief. Yet, seldom do the followers question whether the dogma, the doctrine or the theory holds any truth. If truth is not the goal, how can you find it. If security is the goal, whatever makes you feel secure will be your truth.

The time is here and now for man to be given the truth. This will surely breach his feelings of security, and leave him feeling naked. Truth provides the warmth of knowing. I fear that man will find himself bereft of his comforting beliefs, as they shatter in the light of truth to be given. It is not too late for man to awaken and see what is before him. He must be willing to listen to those who can lead him to open his closed and fear-centred mind. It is not too late for man to see the need for change, and commit to being a part of the revolution that will change the face, heart and soul of your world.

To those who fear, those who cower, those who resign themselves and those who cradle questionable beliefs, I exhort you to release the weight that holds you back from progressing. Show a willingness to engage in discussion with those who seek to genuinely bring light to the world, and seek higher guidance for discernment. These are the moments you must make full use of. Find your passion and courage, and others who share your vision will be led to you that you may form a network that can grow exponentially. You can then engender and create the inevitable changes necessary for your world to progress.

THE WEIGHT OF PROCRASTINATION

Procrastination bears the identity of false promise. In your procrastination you promise yourself to do that which should be done now, at a later time. Seldom does the self promise realise in the original envisaged outcome.

Procrastination may be motivated by genuine intent, but it bears a thread of indignity, as seldom does the procrastinator intend to follow through. Procrastination breeds further procrastination, and a wastage of time ensues as intentions become eschewed. Procrastination has become a habit, a programme which the subconscious observes.

The flavour of that which should be done grows stale in the wake of your procrastination. As you procrastinate feelings of guilt and embarrassment are often experienced.

There may at times be good reasons for procrastinating, yet, in truth, if you are to assess your life, you shall see that in most cases you postpone that which creates a sense of discomfort, or that which requires effort you are not yet ready to invest.

The ego drive wishes to protect your comfort levels and ensure the feeling of security. It will therefore discourage you from attempting what you must, should that very effort cause or create discomfort, or expose you to the possibility of failure or un-fulfilment. Fear becomes a motivating factor in procrastination.

How many procrastinate out of fear, complacency, reticence or plain laziness? In procrastinating you create and limit the boundaries of achievement and growth. Procrastination sows seeds of inner discontent, as it shall be a constant reminder of what you have not done.

Your mortal journey is meant to be progressive, meaning, a progressive ascent within yourself. Your outer experiences are meant to gravitate you inwardly, so that, your true journey may begin. It is your outer perception of your experiences that in most cases impedes your very exploratory interest, as you are moved only by the outer world.

The experiences and encounters you face conspire to subtly or overtly direct you towards your inner resource. In the majority, the ego halts you in your tracks and diverts your course. The chimes of your Higher self go unheeded, and once again you miss the chance to grow. This syndrome is what I label "unconscious reciprocal deference" which in its essence is procrastination. Let me explain. As your unconscious mind responds to the outer equation of the experience, you are abruptly stopped, and what could have presented an awakening opportunity, meaning your awakening to the glorious inner sense, is put off or deferred. You have in essence matched the rhythm of your unconscious mind, as you mirror it in deferring your obligation and opportunity to discover your greater asset. Do you see that procrastination need not always be a conscious choice?

The bottom line is that many in your world subconsciously defer their own ascension because the guardian, being their ego mind, relative to the subconscious, directs them to do so as the physical vies for supremacy. This type of procrastination postpones the achievement or gradual attainment of the purpose of man's journey.

Contemplate with your Higher self that which you could productively attempt, which can assist in upward or inward movement for your greatest good. When you receive direction take the necessary steps to achieve the goal.

Every moment is a precious gift that should be spent on furthering your purpose, and growing your inner awareness. In truth, there is only eternity and that in itself affords you the ability to procrastinate. Yet, is this a choice that you truly wish to make in exchange for temporary yet false security and contentment?

Procrastination is an ailment which culls the desire within to experience more, and be that which you really are. Those who are awakened to their higher mind should be less inclined to dawdle in their journey, for as higher knowledge is gained, the impetus increases to achieve the ultimate goal.

In the perfection of your soul you will always be, yet it is only in the striving, effort and work through your physical experience, that in your seat of consciousness, you will afford yourself the opportunity to taste that perfection. Procrastination keeps most mortals from awakening to their own perfection.

24

THE CREATOR OF ALL THAT IS

KNOWLEDGE IS THE BEGINNING OF WISDOM

I AM the Source of all knowledge. I AM the repository of the golden chalice, the keeper of the knowledge needed for mankind to sustain on their evolutionary journey back to the Source.

The lessons learnt through the experiences in mortal incarnation provide the conduit to acquire this knowledge. Each experience is rendered that man becomes re-acquainted with his Source, by seeking illumination for the imponderables of the experience, and a higher understanding of its creation. Man needs to appreciate why the experience was created, so that, he can overcome the liability and understand himself more.

I AM poised in the midst of the experience as the goal of the lesson. Yet, many are unable to see as far ahead as the goal when their eyes are cast on the immediate consequences of the experience. That which is immediate always captures man's attention. He seeks understanding through analysis and supposition. He remains perplexed and confused in his inability to truly comprehend. Each experience bears a lesson upon which knowledge is hinged, and if man can come into that knowledge, he will be taking baby steps towards his ultimate graduation. I AM the ONE WHO can anoint man with that knowledge.

All knowledge is sacred. It is distant, yet, near, capitalised in your presence. The acquisition of knowledge is a choice. You must deliberately and by design seek it. From each cycle of life's experiences, you must ask of the lessons *"what knowledge can I gain that will take me to a place of higher understanding, and enable me to graduate from this experience richer than before?"* Knowledge is equated to higher understanding.

What man refers to as knowledge is seldom more than information garnered from various sources. When you have knowledge of something, you know it, and it is indisputable. Knowledge is not subjective, in the sense that it is peculiar to one or some persons. Knowledge is universal and distinct in its feature. Knowledge conveys certainty in understanding. It is not opinion based but provable. Knowledge cannot be held but known.

The proof may not always lie in the explanation, but in discovery, through an inherent knowing when you can tap into the ultimate Source of the resource. Information can become knowledge if validated by the Source, as truth. Where knowledge resides, doubt is absent. Those who are in the knowing are not excited by fear but remain steadfast in the Cause. Inimitable faith is that which will continuously open the doors to higher knowledge. This is because faith is open to truth, and truth is founded on the assurance of knowledge.

Divine knowledge is cosmic. All creation is cosmic in origin and therefore all knowledge has a cosmic base. If you seek to **know** a thing you are seeking a cosmic understanding. Man has assigned a limited understanding to the word knowledge. I AM teaching you that you are cosmic in origin, and you must therefore in the interest of your graduation to higher frequency, endorse a higher understanding to the word.

Higher knowledge is a necessity for any civilisation to mature and evolve in alignment with Divine will. Man must direct his efforts to achieving this knowledge. He must chart his course to the discovery of what is needed for a fulfilling life. I can dispense that knowledge to him. I can bestow upon him the knowledge of God in a most intimate way if only he would seek ME. It is through seeking that he will find his truth, the wisdom that comes with knowing ME. I will be the fountain from which he can drink tirelessly, that he may come into the knowledge to generate and regenerate an understanding of himself and his journey.

I AM the Source of all knowledge.

I do not offer you experiments or broken puzzles to piece together before you come into understanding. I offer you truth, whole hearted, pure and pertinent, so that your purpose on earth may be clear. When you partake of divine knowledge you will forever dwell in the plane of inspiration which allows you to hear the voice of wisdom through your higher mind. The voice of God can be heard within you, if you ask and render your mind attune to a frequency un-besmirched by lower frequency. Perseverance is the key.

Remember that the opposite of knowledge is ignorance. Knowledge is light and ignorance is darkness. Yet, ignorance has nothing to do with being uneducated. Ignorance is lack of knowing of the truth, by choice or design.

A knowing man can be uneducated in worldly terms, but knowledgeable of himself and his Source, wise in his demeanour and conduct and aligned with higher truth.

A knowing man may be impecunious in material wealth but inordinately wealthy spiritually.

A knowing man may be poorly travelled and experienced in the places of your world, but is well travelled and coursed in the inner terrain of his god mind.

A knowing man is not curtailed by beliefs, but expanded in his search for higher truth.

A knowing man is humble in his knowledge, sharing what he knows with his fellow men, and showing them the way and path to true knowledge.

A knowing man is a wise man, for his knowledge is the beginning of his wisdom. His wisdom becomes his radiance, which captures the attention of others who become drawn to that which they search for themselves.

What does it profit a man to derive worldly benefits from intellectual and material pursuits if it fails to bestow upon him inner peace, enduring joy, and most importantly, knowledge of his true purpose which lies in self discovery? Self discovery is an inner journey that outer experiences prompt.

The knowledge that I offer to you will bring certainty in understanding, and provide you with the foundation from which you can grow. I AM not concerned with the physical but with the spiritual, for you are first and foremost a spiritual being. Knowledge is your inheritance, your superlative power. Knowledge leads to enlightenment and illumination of your inner self.

Knowledge is the soul's privilege of being birthed by ME. It is the recipe for wisdom which is the charm of your immortal soul. Wisdom is your cushion that enables you to remain in comfort amidst the exigencies of your outer world, for wisdom is the interpreter of the outer experience in keeping with higher understanding. Wisdom is a divine attribute available to all who seek or possess it, and must be used to fashion an existence that is founded on moral fortitude and divine character.

Your journeys through time and space may be an adventure but there is a specific purpose behind it. You require knowledge to glean what that purpose is. You require knowledge to understand the poetry of your origin and the mechanics of creation. You cannot know why, when or how without knowledge. Only I can give you that knowledge or validate the truth or untruth of what you may believe.

Knowledge is its own comfort. It is serene and restful. It is not blatant or arrogant. It is not condescending of beliefs and cannot be attacked, only questioned. It is rare and original, full of beauty and truth. It cannot be moulded to fit into one's understanding but must be known through divine encounter as your mind merges with MINE.

SPIRITUAL MARKSMANSHIP

The achievement of mastery in your world is governed and influenced by societal structures and expectations. There are limits imposed to the definition and understanding of success. You, being God's children, are moulded by what others have created for you. Class division maps out abilities and opportunities for success.

The mundane practices prevail in favour of the esoteric. True vision which evidences itself through creative measures is seldom honoured, for prestige seems to be lacking in such. Very few are able to bring their vision to the light of understanding of others. The joy in creativity has dwindled and the essence of the soul given short shrift. Men are admired less for their creative talents and more for their status as manufactured celebrities in a world oriented by material goals. Power becomes synonymous with success, and the dollar sign becomes the template by which man measures his achievement.

Man marches to the beat of the temporal drum which imposes a framework within which achievement must occur. Man is expected to achieve certain milestones by given times in his mortal life. The inability of some to achieve these milestones often leads to depressive states of mind and inferior thinking.

Many are subject to the will, demands and expectations foisted upon them. Their lives become a physical one, blended with emotional tyranny which plagues them as their neighbour is able to "acquire" physical and material mastery.

Yet, amongst the majority, are pockets of people who persevere with the higher vision awakened within them through their ability to connect with their Source. These are the protagonist of higher thinking. They are the ones who see beyond the linear table; know that life is eternal and that every experience is meant to be a spiritual one. They come to recognise that their mortal journey affords them the opportunity to fine

197

tune their spiritual skills in a worldly environment, and this becomes the goal.

The efficacy of spiritual living is honoured by those who never lose sight of their purpose. They know that through their sojourn on earth, they are provided with renewed opportunities to scale mortal limitations, and find their prowess through spirit. They learn to overcome the distractions of the world and remain focussed on their mission. They understand that this plane is a transition to higher dimensions.

The protocols they create for themselves are for the mastery of the soul. Like an archer who primes his bow and measures his aim, they remain focussed on the "I AM", for it is the "I AM" that they must achieve through the conquering of the "I". The archer does not succumb to self pity, but through the resilient spirit that he is, he refocuses if he misses the mark. Missing the mark tells him that he is not yet quite ready, and must of necessity continue to persevere in the honing of his skills.

In the process of preparing for success and victory, discomfort, doubt and pain maybe necessary attendants. Yet, the spiritual being shall not wane in his efforts and belief, for he knows that what he must achieve is freedom of his authentic self.

Each of you has a responsibility to yourself to achieve your fullest God potential. You are present to serve the God incarnate. You will be free when you so desire to be free, for freedom is an inner state of being. Only an enlightened man can be free. If you do not feel free then you are not yet enlightened. That simply means that you must increase your efforts. Excuses and blame are derivatives of lower thinking. Higher thinkers take responsibility and action.

The acquisition of material wealth is peripheral to the acquisition of spiritual prowess. Create your template for success, assume control over your choices, set the pace for your achievement, bind yourself to spirit, not the desires of others. Set your aim, maintain your focus, re-evaluate your skills, and take steps to enhance them. Be honest with yourself; be proactive and attune your talents to a cause worthy of achievement.

When the road seems long or perplexity overcomes, inject fresh energy; seek a new perspective and become that spiritual marksman who stands in his spiritual shoes and courageously takes responsibility for his success.

A "HOLY" CONTEMPLATION

The destiny of that which is Whole is Holy. Wholeness, All and Completeness signify and are emblematic of Holy. In your realm Holy is the word prescribed and associated with God, yet, it must be placed in its proper context which brings understanding of its nature.

That which you refer to as Holy is not outside of your being, to be glorified and worshiped ad infinitum. That which is Holy is to be recognised within you through the Wholeness of God's presence. The focus on Holy must change to Whole, for it is only through the identification with the WHOLE that the pedestal upon which Holiness rest will shine through with divine perspective.

Indeed, I AM Holy, through the representation of MY Wholeness, and Holy is but an aspect of the aura I radiate. Those who aspire to the glory of God must stand on the mountain; that higher altitude that allows for panoramic vision, that you may start to see the substance of ME in Wholeness of the form I take through MY creation. I AM, formless otherwise. It is the Wholeness of sight that will enable you to understand that you can only be Holy when you are Whole. Anything else is an aberration in understanding.

I shall address the period in your calendar which you refer to as "Holy week" through the celebration of Easter tide, the culmination of the crucifixion to the resurrection of MY beloved Son Michael[32].

Why have you assigned this week as Holy, apart from any other week in your calendar? Why do you see the crucifixion and resurrection as Holy events or acts? Why is the focus on the acts rather than the lessons? Why do you relive the erroneous belief year after year that MY Son died for your mortal sins? You are through this remembrance reliving your guilt, and holding on to the notion of sin which man created in the

---

[32] Jesus Christ

abstract, the very two things which MY beloved Son sought to dispel
from your thinking and beliefs. How could Michael have died for your
sins when HE did not recognise sin? How could HE have died when
it is impossible for HIM to die? You have made death into a maudlin
affair, and recall these times with great emotional evocation.

Michael in HIS bestowal on Urantia[33], HIS very own creation, came
to teach of the nature and essence of God (ME—the I AM) and the
ONENESS of All. He came to teach that the spirit is the life, and
through baptism, this represented renewal through the choice of
spirit, being the spirit of God, the life within each. HE endeavored to
bring reality in a world that was besmirched with the unreality of sin,
mortality and banal affairs. HE came to teach the Truth of God, and
the eternalness of God's Kingdom through the indicator of immortality
of sprit. HE recognised life only.

Love and Life are synonymous in MY Kingdom. Instead of seeing the
crucifixion as death, see it as symbolic of Love. Do not focus on the
event of death or what transpired before HIS mortal passing, but focus
on HIS love and HIS lessons of Love, remembering the incapability of
HIS or your death.

Let the emphasis on this time be one of Wholeness. If I AM the Cause
then so too is MY Son. HE is All that I AM, and you are all that HE
IS. When you can focus on your Wholeness through HIM and through
ME, you will understand the nuances of Holy. It is through Wholeness
that you will attain a state of Holiness.

You see the resurrection as HIS promise of eternal life, yet, the
resurrection has a deeper meaning. It represents the resurrection of
spirit within man, so that, he may know that he is spirit personified,
eternal and whole in the image of HE who created.

---

[33] Earth

The lesson is that man must through the renewal and awakening of the spirit within him, identify himself with and as the Whole. It is only then that he can assume the mantle of Holiness. The resurrection signifies the awakening of spirit and life within, that the Paradise goal may be fulfilled through the life journeys of mortal will creatures. Man must cease in his thinking and belief that the resurrection represents an after death affair or state. Michael's resurrection was a return to HIS Source on completion of HIS bestowal. Your resurrection will be the coming alive of the spirit of God within you, so that, you envision your eternalness in your current seat of awareness, and know with certainly that you cannot ever die and need not experience mortal passing to know of your immortality.

Allow the significance of this time to assume a brighter and fuller glow as Truth embodies your awareness. Let this time of celebration be a time to remember and emulate Wholeness, for in your recognition of Wholeness you will truly celebrate the Holiness of All.

Michael, by HIS life in body and life in ME is WHOLE, PERFECT AND HOLY. Be ye like unto HIM and ye will be like unto ME.

Michael is my beloved Son and HE pleases ME greatly. In the communion between MY Son and ME there is no need for words, for HE is ONE with ME in perfection, as HE is to you. Worship ME through HIM by your choosing of MY Will, aligning with MY Will and actioning of MY Will through your works.

Blessings flow from the mount of Paradise to the grave from which all finite creatures must journey through life in spirit to attain perfection. So It is.

I AM THE PLACE WHERE YOU BEGIN AND I AM THE PLACE WHERE YOU SHALL END

The wonders of your existence find its origin in the mind of God. The chords of love strummed in harmony, produced by a balancing scale emitting frequencies of light is your very CAUSE. You were conceived in MY imagination as an idea, and I gave life to you through the breath of light which extended from MY thinking. I thought you into being. I created the soul within, the verity of you. I AM the place where you began. I know the mechanics of your creation, the very mechanics which I have legated to you that you too may create.

You, the physical being is an extension of your immortal soul. You have chosen to take myriad journeys through time and space in mortal clothing. You clothed your light in flesh, so that, you might eventually find that light again. It is through your journey that you shall re-discover the origin of life, return your thoughts to the Creator's will and begin to manifest HIS supreme will through your thoughts, actions and creations. It is only then that you will be able to engage in creative and co-creative endeavours.

As you awaken to MY infinite presence within you, a dawning of new and exciting knowledge shall transgress the dullness of doubt and ignorance, and you shall brave the world with fresh perspectives born of higher understanding. The place where you begin, being the mind of God will become your perpetual dwelling place. You shall be restored in the power and authority of the CAUSE.

I have bequeathed this sanctuary to you. It holds the wealth of my wisdom, knowledge and truth. Wisdom is the nature of God and the nature of man. However, many cannot comprehend that wisdom is necessary in the mortal journey for the birthing and fashioning of a civilisation grounded in Godliness. That which is physical cannot conceive wisdom. Mortal creations based only on physical desires and material aspirations cannot yield the fruit of wisdom. Wisdom derived from knowledge creates truth, being the foundation element of a sustainable civilisation. Wisdom cannot be replaced by intellectual comprehension which is derived from what you observe, perceive, record and recall. Wisdom is beyond analysis; it was created, and must be known through contemplation with the God mind. You can be taught that which is wise, but you can only know it through ME.

I cannot offer wisdom and truth to those who are closed to ME, those who refute MY existence or deny MY presence within them. Those who do not believe in ME, being the highest authority in Creation, cannot believe in any form of esoteric existence, for I created all things. Sadly, you will never be able to truly believe in yourself, for how can you believe in that which you do not know or understand? Your idea of what you believe is jaundiced in the wake of unknowingness. You deny yourself truth and being, when you deny ME.

Man forgets easily that it is I, WHO provided the planet for which you are to experience physical life. Man did not create the planet; he simply chose to retire to the planet momentarily to enjoy a physical experience intended for the enlightenment of his soul. This intent has eluded many who choose to have a purely physical existence. A physical existence without spiritual understanding becomes a void. It is emptied of purpose and bereft of the treasures of life.

You are the fruit which I bore and desire to harvest. Yet, through personal choice many of you are still not matured. You wish to preserve your youth and remain fresh in a vibrant body. You know that body as you.

You are though, possessed of a part of ME which you have buried beneath desires anomalous to spirit. You see yourself as flesh and blood when you are spirit and light.

I do not ask that you forget the physical body you inhabit, only that you know the purpose of the physical journey. It is not for the body but for the spirit. Your management of the body is directed for the benefit of the spirit. During the course of mortal sojourn you shall endure experiences which shall uncover the strength of spirit, and you shall grow into its light through the unfolding.

Seek your origin and it shall be revealed to you. The indwelling spirit[34] shall open your inner eyes, so that, you will see clearly. You shall then be privileged to the priceless part of you. Your human mind does not wish to accept the truth of its inherent prowess. This however, is inevitable, and whether you choose to be open to accept your inheritance now or much later on, it is up to you. If you persist throughout your incarnations to resist the truth of your origin, and breach the laws of creation and God, you shall effectively relinquish your soul to the death of life as it loses its immortal status. The salvation of your soul which affords immortal life lies not with ME unless you choose ME. Salvation is a gift to those who choose to enter the spiritual Kingdom and abide within the Kingdom.

I AM the place where you shall end for I AM the goal of life. Should you be privileged through your own choosing to aspire to ME, you shall return to ME through ascent, in the measure of invested effort and the passage of time. Should you delete ME knowingly from your consciousness and deliberately and persistently through your incarnated experiences choose against ME, there will be no life for you.

One of my laws is that I shall not compel MY children to return to the place of their birth where eternity is what I willed to them.

I AM THE PLACE WHERE YOU BEGIN; AND
I AM THE PLACE WHERE YOU SHALL END if you choose and endeavour to.

---

[34] The spirit of God within each.

CUSTODIANS OF MY LIGHT

I AM and therefore you are. You cannot be without ME. You are not without ME or apart from ME, save in your perception. I AM not the hidden part of you. I AM simply the invisible part, that which holds the seed of your power. I AM, that which gives you Light and creates light through you. You are therefore all light. The light which I speak of bears no resemblance to the light created in your outer world through mechanics. I cannot be switched on or off. I AM forever Light. I do not malfunction or become defective. MY radiance is everlasting. There is nothing that can dim ME. I resonate at the highest frequency.

I bestowed MYSELF to you through your creation. I AM within you. The light of life is within you. I speak of the light of the soul which bears the emblem of your Creator. The Creator marks HIS creation just as you may mark your possessions, so that, you may know what belongs to you. You belong to ME as I created you, and therefore you bear MY signature, being the Light of Creation. I know you by your light, which is MY own.

Light is the Life of your immortal soul. You are not disconnected from your soul. You are the soul. The body is simply a mass of energy used by the soul to chart experiences, so that, it can assert its mastery and innate power through the human form as it remembers who it is through a mortal experience. However, the soul's power is not dominant unless the human trajectory allows for and accommodates that higher association. You need only experience an offering of the soul to make your decision.

Many, who wholeheartedly embrace the offerings of the soul as an instinctive knowing, are drawn to the higher rays. There are many who cannot comprehend that which is not visual, and therefore reject its existence and presence. Many fear the power of their soul, as it would redefine their thinking and demand changes to their comportment. This inherent fear has become a widespread malady.

Those who do not know of the existence of their soul, are motored by the lower mind, the ego mind. This is the distinct portion responsible for your thoughts, reactions and creations. Once you are in the harness of this mind, this becomes your realm of comfort. You and not your ego must make the decision to come into higher understanding of who you are. You are not your ego. Its life is short lived, as is your mortal life. If you allow it to make your decisions, it will serve only your physical dynamic in your physical world. If you can but for a moment set aside the ego, you may benefit from the revelations of your soul. Comfort and reassurance will replace the bridge between you and your soul, for these are the resulting effects of the soul's interaction.

Fear does not exist in the soul, only light and love and higher knowledge. Should you allow the soul entrance, you will quickly discern the difference between the soul mind [35] and the ego mind.

Allowing your soul entrance allows MY light to work within you and through you. Light transmutes and transforms all that is dark if only it is allowed entrance. You will come to know the power of your light when you acknowledge it within yourself, and allow its expression through you. It is then that you will assume control of and over your life.

When you come into your light you have in fact come into MY light, and with effort and time investment, you will begin to know ME as yourself. Illumination is a gradual process. Until you can think, know, feel and behave in ONENESS, we will work in partnership, so that, MY light within you is allowed more and more expression as you graduate in frequency. As your light quotient increases, there will in time be no need for the vehicle of the physical body for you to continue your journey.

You are custodians of MY light. How you treat that light is really your choice. Some ignore it totally; others pay it short shrift, whilst few

---

[35]   The spirit of the Creator dwells in the soul/mind of man.

fully embrace it and work in harmony with it for their highest good. These are the ones who use MY light in service to others. They know that light is never to be hidden but to be shared. They recognise the ONENESS in all things and seek to help others find their inner light and shine it forth in the world. You must comprehend that your outer world is a reflection of your inner world. If your inner world is dark then your outer world shall also be dark.

Seek always to keep your inner world in light, which spells harmony, and your outer world will be so mirrored. Your light is the precious jewel gifted to you upon your birth. You were meant to keep that jewel shining in its original incandescence and wear it as a powerful garment. It was never meant to be buried under worldly things and be forgotten. Many seek grand jewels to wear on their bodies, and wealth that will provide extravagant living. They proudly display outer remnants of wealth which shine without any significance or value. It is temporal and banal. It cannot empower YOU, but it empowers only your ego that simply cannot be satiated. These outer effects will earn you no spiritual glory or everlasting joy. It retards your growth as you become more and more consumed by your need for material effects. These things do not in truth exist. They are things that will be cast aside when you leave this dimension of experience. I AM, not saying that you should not create abundance in your life, but be weary that you know the difference between abundance and avarice.

To those of you who have courageously chosen the light, you must be steadily vigilant lest you become distracted by the world around you. As custodians of MY Light you must make the decisions that are in the highest interest of that Light, for it is only then that MY light can work for you. Should you lose your footing and fall apart, then, who is to tend to the light? It is your divine responsibility to tend that light until you become one with that Light, and know yourself only as LIGHT.

I know only too well how easy it is to fall prey to a diseased world, where the malaise spreads and disconnect results between you and that Light. It is for you to see this and know it, and take every step possible to preserve the Light. It is truly this Light that will become your vehicle for escape from the outer world, where unreality, suffering and grief abounds.

If you tend to this Light, this Light will tend to you. This Light will preserve your sanity, and enable you to transcend the lower vibrations as it propels you to higher understanding and frequency. This Light will resurrect you time and time again if needed. As you come to know this Light every choice will be influenced by this Light. It does not mean that the world around you ceases to exist or that the problems go away. It simply means that you will be able to see it through the magnifying Light, which shows truth and purpose in the experience.

I AM THE LIGHT WITHIN YOU AND I AM THE LIGHT IN YOUR WORLD. I ADMONISH THAT THIS LIGHT IS TO BE REVERED THROUGH ACKNOWLEDGEMNT, FOLLOWED BY WILLING APPLICATION. HOW WILL YOU CARE FOR THIS LIGHT? THE EFFORT OF PRESERVING AND PROTECTING THIS LIGHT CANNOT BE MEASURED. THE CHOICE YOU MAKE WILL IMPACT THE WORLD YOU CREATE. WHAT IS YOUR VISION FOR YOUR WORLD?

THE NEW RELIGION

The religions in your world are man-made. They are premised on age old renditions of those who came before as divine emissaries to teach and reveal the word of God. God sent many of HIS ones to bring enlightenment through the spoken word, yet, seldom were the teachings recorded accurately. They have been tampered with by those responsible for its translations and dissemination. The words are barely recognisable to the ones who gave them initially. Always was the word given in a way to inspire understanding, yet, seldom were they understood. God therefore continues to send his messengers to repeat the word, and to render further truths through various projections, so that, man might gain understanding in the measure of his ability to grasp the truth.

Throughout the ages men of authority distilled doctrines from what was taught, and converted them into teachings to be religiously followed by those who became followers. The various religions have become manifestations of beliefs and doctrines crystallised in records, which do not bear the original thoughts or natural words, but condensed and re interpreted versions.

Man-made religions are "tradition based", finding their credibility in those who hold themselves out as authority for the beliefs and teachings espoused by the religion. They are sectarian in nature and appeal to the minds of men through the use of symbols, ceremony and established creeds.

Those who subscribe to the religions of tradition find security in the chosen system of beliefs, which provides directives for living. Religion plays a supportive and crucial role in their lives. Their human experience is underpinned by the dated beliefs and doctrines taught to them. Religion has become a safety net for many who wholeheartedly accept the teachings as truth, without any personal input or experience of what they follow.

There is truth in some of the teachings espoused by each religion. You may even find some common ground amongst them, yet, they do not represent the whole truth. God often spoke to the readiness of the mind of the receivers. As messenger after messenger was sent, greater truths were revealed to accord with the receptivity of man and his abilities to comprehend; and what was taught before was projected in new and revealing ways.

The reality is that traditional religion has capsulated truth of what is recalled, and projects it as a Gospel. I say to you that the gospel as given is incomplete and erroneous in many ways. Those who seek truth will not find it wholeheartedly in the realms of traditional religion, but must seek it elsewhere. Man's understanding of religion has become an inherited one, as he assents to what is placed before him as a bestowal of truth.

Those born into religious families will be conditioned by the precepts of that particular religion, without a choice. Those who are independent minded will grow in awareness and be led to seek beyond the mainstream to find their truth.

What really is religion? Your religion should be your way of life. Where does life exist? Is it not in the spirit, which is eternal? If religion is a way of life and there exist life only in spirit, then should not man's religion be the way of spirit, instead of a proliferation of sects espousing various dogmas without knowledge of truth of spirit?

If man is to find God through "a religion" and God is pure spirit, then surely the way to God is through the knowledge and experience of spirit. Religion should be a way of life founded on spiritual truths, discovered by each individual on his/her mortal journey. The revelations of spirit through the temporal experience enable man to discover and know the presence of God within himself, as part of him. The religion of spirit will reveal to man his ONENESS with God, whilst the traditional religion teaches of a God who is over, beyond and above his children.

A new religion has been dawning for some time now, and many have found their religion in spirit. In so doing they have discovered God within themselves. They are choosing to exercise their free will choice to manifest the presence of God.

It is the discovery of God within and the choice to manifest HIM that will initiate the career of the ascending mortal. The spirit of God within inspires man to a higher understanding, and will provide insight into realities of the life and ways of spirit. Man is then able to express God's ways through his living, as the fruits of the spirit become the values by which his life is moulded. He will grow into his moral worthiness as he embraces the light of God within himself. He will be motivated by love instead of by guilt and fear, to uphold the values of God.

The religion of spirit is revelatory in character. One of its greatest revelations is the existence of God's love in man's immortal soul. Man will come to know God's love and will know love as God and God as love. Eventually he will know God as himself and himself as love. He will in his search for truth, discover that love is all there is, and God being love, means that God is all there is. In that knowing there will flow awareness that man and God are ONE. In spite of what man's senses perceive, man will discover that there is no separation. As he begins to know God and feel HIS presence within himself, he will eventually know the wholeness of love and he will develop the ability to manifest God's love.

Inherited or traditional religion may teach about love and even provide directives on how man should love, but this will be no more than an intellectual understanding based on mind awareness, rather than spirit awareness. To know, to understand, to experience, to have, to hold, to retain, to live and to express love, you must feel unified with God's love that dwells within. It is only through the experiences you have on your mortal journey that this unfolding can occur.

True religion therefore, cannot be taught but must be discovered through the mortal experience, combined with the motivation to seek truth. It is only then that man will come into remembrance of who he is. As this awareness dawns within him, he becomes bonded to the experience. He will know truth, and remain unmoved by what others tell him is truth, whether or not it be so.

The religion of spirit will always work through inner discovery. This perpetuates a feeling of certainty, and allows for that feeling of security that within you lies all you seek.

The religions of your times are outdated and static in many ways. It pre-empts the fresh winds from passing through the minds of its followers, that real discoveries and revelations of spirit may be enjoyed. It numbs the minds of followers and curtails their freedom to question and explore beyond the projected "Gospel". It holds on to what has been rewritten from generation to generation as truth. It seeks to convert and dominate through authority rather than liberate. It keeps its followers stuck in paradigms and practices that do not field spiritual growth. It breeds differences between sects, and superiority of one's belief or doctrines over another. It teaches love and tolerance, yet, is marked by division and disunity.

It deals in the finite without an appreciation that God in HIS infiniteness cannot be limited by words on paper, and cannot be experienced through the written word. The existence of God, the goodness of God and the reality of God cannot be derived from what someone else tells you or what is recorded. It is to be discovered through myriad, vibrant mortal experiences. Indeed, man must intellectually comprehend God's processes and the science of creation, but to know God in spirit man must experience HIS energy from within. Man cannot experience God through his outer senses, but through his inner faculties that bear knowing.

The religion of spirit offers freedom, the ability to retain one's sovereignty, control over one's life, impetus to seek truth of God and self, and the ecstasy in discovering the depth and breadth of spirit's knowledge.

A religion based on spirit will unify the hearts of men through the love of God, and provide the knowing that God is individualised within each, and therefore each has identical God presence within. It does not dictate or decide what one should believe, for it thrives on progressive revelations. It allows for experiential insights whilst it leads to a shared or common understanding of the ONENESS and brotherhood of all, the sole destiny of the ascending mortal, the reality of the ONE will, a determination to accede to that will, and the realisation of self through service.

The barriers that have long held MY children in bondage will be dissolved in the wake of the ascension, for it is through this process that the spirit presence within each will find its resurrection. The spirit of truth within each of you will be awakened, and in this you will find your new religion.

A FATHER'S PLEA

I come in this solitary moment to introduce MYSELF to those who do not know ME, to those who know of ME, to those who view me in a religious context, and to reinforce MY presence within those who do know ME.

Times of great change loom auspiciously upon your earth plane and you of the human civilisation must come into the knowing of MY presence.

I AM the ONE you call GOD, Creator, Source, Universal Deity, Foremost intelligence, Ultimate determiner, Final Judge and Adjudicator. The variation in title does not matter, for I AM ONE and the same. I will simply refer to MYSELF as the Universal Father of All creation.

Titles and names create distinctions and cause separation in one's understanding, as one seeks a God of his/her culture. Know that God is ONE, All is ONE and ONE is All. It is when you come to understand this simple truth that profound awareness will dawn.

I come to affirm your status as sons and daughters of the light. It is imperative that you perceive yourself in light. Light is the quintessential you. That which darkens your world does not define you. Your body does not define you. Your earthly status does not define you. It is I, the Creator of All, who defines you.

I cannot be seen, yet, I exist. I can be known and experienced from within, and that is the most credible form of sight. Knowing is your proof, feeling, your rule of measure. The nature of ME is the nature of you, and you must therefore call upon your understanding of ME to know yourself.

I have many times delivered the same message in different ways through different ones, and I shall continue to do this until your immortal soul is allowed to influence your human mind to minister truth. Why do I endeavour with constancy and consistency to bring you truth? It is quite simple. You are MINE, and I desire you to return home to ME. The route you take is of course your choice, but I desire to see you placed on the path of knowing.

Which father will leave his children unattended, without care or supreme love? I cannot continue to see you suffer and not endeavour to lead you out of turmoil. It is love which engenders MY effort. I can see what beholds your world presently. I know what is transpiring and what will fall upon thee. I come to assist the confused, to bring clarity, so that, those who may doubt will accept ME once and for all.

I AM the living essence of truth within you. You can only find your truth there. I issue an invitation to you. Turn to ME. Even if you never have before, call upon ME, not in challenge, but in need and love. I shall respond. What other choice do you have? This is my bid to draw you into the fold using only truth and a promise of a brighter future. The purpose of your life at this very moment should be to discover ME, as the winds of change carry yet another cycle to completion that the new and exciting tomorrow may be yielded for your earth.

Many are now walking a tightrope with little balance. Will you not join the bandwagon of lighted beings, and begin the most wondrous exploration of a new plane filled with knowledge and excitement for grander and purposeful living?

The canopy of change has now descended. You need only look around your world to witness the great confusion and collapse materialising. Will you continue to deny what you face or what it portends for your world? Who is your likely salvation now? When all is crumbling around you, who will you call upon? Can you save yourselves? From my vantage point I will offer a negative response.

That which you face on your earth is beyond your control, and that which is taking place cosmically, fortuitously, is also beyond your control. I wish to tell you MY plans for you but how many will hear and believe? How many of MY ones have you castigated and deemed mental? They are the ones who are sane my beloved children. The "mental" ones are the knowing ones; the ones who know MY truth and serve it. It would serve you well to rethink what you have heard from the "voices" of God. Those who bring truth are MY voice.

I take the bolder approach that you may hear without fear. Can you not hear the appeal through these MY words? The Father comes here and now to woo you back home. Will you hear and answer? For generations I have sent MY beloved sons to effort with you of earth plane. Now I come MYSELF. Will you still reject the ONE you say you love? Must I descend from the clouds for you to believe? I do not live up to false conceptions or beliefs, for I serve Truth, which I AM. I can only urge you to seek truth by listening to the voice within. You will not see ME, but you will know ME if you know truth, for I am already here.

> *Will you not take MY hand in love*
> *That I may raise you up to ME*
> *To pastures new where peace abounds*
> *Where freedom kindles light within*
> *No measure to your growth imposed*
> *No darkness there to woo and woe*
> *This is MY light I give to you*
> *The promise of a world anew*
> *Is now at hand to be revealed.*
> *Creation's called and she must leave*[36]
> *Her clothes to change in light of green*
> *Will you not take MY hand in love*
> *For only I can bring you to that place*
> *Where life shall blossom, love prevail*
> *This is MY humble plea to you*
> *Take MY hand, leave behind the life of pain*
> *You shall feel that gentle beat of divine understanding*
> *And you shall know that I AM, your resurrection*

---

[36] This is reference to the Earth—the old is being transformed into the new.

I AM THE CREATOR OF ALL THAT IS—MY SON WHO YOU KNOW AS THE CHRIST IS ONE WITH ME. THERE IS NO DISTINCTION. YOU ARE ONE WITH ME FOR I CREATED YOU.

25

CHRIST MICHAEL

Awaken MY children
Lift the blinds which cloak your sleeping eyes
And see the sparkling SOURCE reposed,
in the crèche of your very being.
Let the wax of torpor melt in the fire of your faith
And drink the milk of wisdom offered from the fountain of your soul.

Awaken MY children
Peel away the scales which bind your deafened ears
And hear the echo of that inner voice reveal,
the mystery of your very being.
Let the sterling knife of knowing carve the weight of disbelief
That your conscious mind may be attuned, to
the rhyming sounds of your souls' truth.

THE EPISTLE[37]

In the circumspection of your thoughts, I parade, to counter that which holds you to brazen ideologies and thoughts which dance in negative symmetry.

I see the colour of your hurts as they recede into the conscious affairs of what could be a dutiful heart. They raid its quiet province with dubious missiles, blind your vision and take you to a place of deep forgetfulness. You retreat from the castle, the throne of your destiny, and deny the life within you its very breath, the primal penalty of a grieving spirit, unfulfilled.

Your sprit belongs to ME and I come to restore you, to chart the path of your resurrection. Cast aside impervious wills. Render to ME the burdens of your timid heart and find release, through freedom of your discontent, as the poultice of MY love begins to heal the plague of weary indifference. Renew through baptism in the plenary circle of light and feel its bounty water the carcass of your ailing mind. Call in the radical, the changing couture to re clothe your thoughts that your journey may start anew.

Hear the voice which speaks in wisdom from the centering space of your reconstituted mind. Be the miner of your soul and free the fuel that shall fire the vibrant youth of your eternal mind. Let your thinking go to the highlands of the inner mind and fill the cup of your desirous soul with the energy of glee.

Perchance, you feel the flutter of imbalance, seek again the reverie of your eternal Presence, the ME of you, and draw the healthy breaths I offer to regain the template of balance.

---

[37]   The Father's message of guidance and encouragement to HIS children. I channelled this whilst in a state of trance.

Lend the care of your resilient heart to tend and mind the solitude of man. Curse not the moments of your learning life, when human toil is required and tears impale the dainty feelings of your heart. Bear witness to the longings of your soul. See the alluring jewel in the hoard of earthly offerings, and use the value which abides to create your ministry of hope. Your faith will field the chronic happenings, and you shall overcome the sufferings, whose shallow soil can birth no lasting fruit.

Come hither to the glades, and breathe the calming perfume of potions brewed especially for you. When its honeysuckle fragrance locks into the vestal vineyard of your holy mind, you shall awaken, and knowledge you shall bear to ease your comprehension of things that cause perplexity and grimness of mood.

Conjecture will become remiss, as the handle of understanding grasps what once was a feeble mind, and strength of spirit joins you to triumph over life. It is then that the trend of your power shall find its identity, and knowledge assumed of your inherent nobility.

I speak in tongues of spirit, the ancient precepts, that the nature of the revelations shall avert the crisis of your thinking, and the beam of heavenly light fill your eyes that you may see in truth all that you behold.

TO MY LIGHT WORKERS

Stand in the mirror of MY being and attune yourselves to the chords of MY energy, as I lead you through this wilderness to the path of life and light. MY hand I shall never take from you, so do not shun the help I give, for you shall need MY guiding hand in the tumultuous days to come.

MY little ones I entrust to you, that you may bring enlightenment to minds not yet fully learned in all MY ways. You will tend to them with loving care and help them nurture their inner light, so that, they may learn to raise the brightness within the lantern of their minds, and themselves become beacons to serve in kind.

Walk in the haloed footsteps of the Christ, that with unassuming grace you may impart the wisdom of HIS truth. Croutons of light I give to you, so that, with the poise of patience you shall release this light, that MY little ones shall reap its inspiration and know the ONENESS of all things in ME.

Step into the pool of MY love and feel its tender tendrils bathe your soul. As its warmth enfolds you, know that you are absorbed in the aura of MY energy, that you may be replete with the pureness of MY love, prepared again to give MY little ones that which I have given you.

Go forth in the wealth of knowing that your path is ever clear and ably lit by the glow of your immortal soul, illumined by the serenity of MY creative Presence. Know that there is no difference between US as you capture that glorious vision of unifying light, that which WE are.

MY love I give to you.

THE NATURE OF TIMING—"MY HOUR HAS NOT YET COME"—"MY HOUR HAS COME"

These words were scripted as words I repeated several times during my earthy incarnation. Indeed, it was all about timing then and it is all about timing now. MY reference to time is not in respect of temporal existence measured by days, but simply readiness, in terms of appropriate events and frameworks in place, for the unfolding of the master plan. Timing is therefore referenced to preparedness.

Time as you know it is fickle. It bespeaks of rigid adherence to notions and expectations which may or may not materialise. The divine plan is not governed by time but by other grander elements, many of which you will not comprehend. A synergy must exist in the energy spanning the universe of time and space, and I will know when that time is here. Certainly however, your planet is in the throes of momentous times of change.

I want to emphasise the need during these changeable times for each child to consider whether his or her time has come, and what the implications are for you in this respect. Deep in the consciousness of each one is a light that will burn with desire so brightly when the time has come, that it will be a hunger too great to be left unsatisfied. If you remain in communion with the Source or with ME, you will be in no doubt as to the certainty of this eventuality when it occurs. Every part of you will literally scream-my time has come; for what you may ask? Simply to serve the Divine will in a way that suits your skills, talents and abilities. You will simply know.

Service has many dimensions to it and God does not compare how one serves in comparison to another. The concern lies in the motivation of that service. God accepts that the path and endowments of each differ.

Every moment in your life is precious and must not be wasted. This is your life. You must make of it, and with it as you choose, but preferably in accordance with the greater will. You cannot abandon life; you live life, you enjoy the blessings in your life and you create the reality you seek in your individual world.

I walked this earth also as man and I endured many experiences. I too, was eager to start my mission or ministry. Yet, the will of MY Father took precedence. HE knew what I had to accomplish before I was ready to complete the task at hand and return to assume Sovereignty of Nebadon. I was always in communion that I would know when the time had come for ME. The years preceding that were spent in humble acknowledgement that I needed to grow and learn from MY experiences, and face life head on and full on. I engaged in a humble yet fulfilling livelihood. I partook of physical work which kept MY body fit and mind active. I also took the opportunity to engage in a private ministry, without ceremony. I helped where and when the opportunities presented themselves. I remained committed to the guidance of those who sought it from ME.

I did not hide away from the world. I was inclined to know the peoples of the world and to understand humanity if I were to determine the way to help them understand MY Father's Kingdom. I had to understand their motivations, expectations and desires. I did not turn away anyone, yet, was careful and wise in MY dealings with all.

The journey on earth never promised to be an easy one, but you cannot run away from it because it does not suit your purpose or because it becomes exhausting to deal with. If your hour has not yet come, then I suggest that you evaluate your life and find your passion, and determine how best you can prepare yourself to further develop your passion. Stay attuned to MY energy within you and I shall lead you to make a healthy contribution. I urge you MY children to enjoy your experience.

To those of you who know that your hour has come, you must resolutely acknowledge it and take up the baton of truth and begin to live your purpose. Readiness is a signal of spiritual preparedness and confidence to assume greater responsibility in MY name. It requires total relinquishment and surrender to spirit. You must not only desire and have the motivations to serve, but also be disciplined in your efforts. I have precious few who are firmly committed, and I need those of you for whom the bell has sounded to seek counsel as to how you can go about MY business fearlessly. Many of you have come for this very purpose, so do not ignore the call.

This is a time when your faith will be put to the test. I have never and will never forsake MY faithful. If you seek ME I will guide your path and show you the way to a fulfilling life. I will sustain you when you choose the divine pathway.

When your hour has come, you will do as I did and seek total communion with the Source, that you may be given instructions and directions in service. I will give to you the wherewithal, so that, you may satisfy MY plans for you.

Life cannot be viewed as a burden but as a blessing, and you are here to find the pleasure of God in all things and be a beacon of light and joy. You are to be the exemplars today that will lead the blind out of bondage. Strengthen yourselves in MY armour. You are the courageous ones who are streamlined in MY energy. If you cannot sustain now how will you sustain when the going really gets tough.

I AM here to work with you, to help you rescue your world from the clutches of darkness. It is thus imperative that you shine your light as brightly as you can, for this is much needed now, in a world that has grown very tired and has become weak under the governance of the dark.

I AM your Father, ONE with the Paradise Father, whose will shall be done. Perfection is the order of Paradise and this "Divine Plan"[38]

---

[38] The plan for the ascension or resurrection of the planet.

shall be executed with precision and perfection. Time cannot purchase perfection if readiness is not achieved.

REMEMBER WHO YOU ARE

These are MY words to you that you may know; you are that which I AM. How the tendency is to forget, with excuse that your earthly lives create division in your thoughts, that you must separate the world you live in from the world you are from. In your minds you continue to live in a world which separates your earthly existence from your spiritual one, when in truth there should be unification. I need each of you to bring the Kingdom of God on earth and that can only be accomplished if you experience that Kingdom within you. You shall then appreciate that there is truly no separation and the infinite spirit resides where you do.

I AM within you and with you and that is truly the end. I do not float above you like some ethereal distant being. I AM your centre, your very core. You keep creating an artificial distinction between what you call your 3D life and where you would like to be. Can you not bring where you would like to be in the present, through the I AM within? I speak not in terms of finite coordinates but in terms of your personal evolution. Your experiences can never hinder your growth; only nurture it if you allow them to. I AM ever with you and if you choose you can know ME as yourself. I AM in fact your constant companion,[39] and when you can see from within you shall see and know MY presence. Is it not prudent that you programme your minds to be consciously aware of this?

MY children, I shall remind you as many times as I deem necessary, for you must be the ones to live ME, so that, you can effectively teach others how to accomplish what you all think is a monumental task. Is it really a task to effort to be ME? Should it not be a relief to be ME? If you can perceive the being of ME in this way then your efforts shall be made with joy and knowing, and not censured for the laborious task that you sometimes deem it to be.

---

[39] Michael of Nebadon (Jesus Christ) poured out HIS spirit upon flesh during the Pentecost. HE is the Spirit of Truth within each of us.

If you could but remember who you are and seek in your moments to be yourselves, your lives will graduate moment to moment in the sweet pleasure of MY presence, and there will be little possibility for you to forget. You will experience an automatic desire to harness MY energy from within, and you will progress your earthly tasks in and with delight and grace.

No task will be insurmountable if you will only recall the power that you are. To remember who you are you must know ME, and effort to keep the light of communion burning brightly lest it dims for want of perseverance. What you perceive as battles are MY battles as I AM within you. If you rely on the rays of light within to provide guidance and assistance you shall receive that which you need to overcome your life's battles and crises.

I desire that you live in the NOW. What will it profit you to seek that which is to come when you must first overcome that which is before you? I AM referring to the impediments within each, which preclude you from breaking through the barriers of a limited consciousness that you may experience higher consciousness. How can you deal with what impends if you cannot be who you are in the present?

MY children, like a Father would, it is MY duty to push you to attain your fullest potential. I appreciate that in your incarnation there are many experiences beyond your liking. However, if you can, through the power within, address these experiences in light, the division which you create in your living will fall away. Surely, the task at hand requires that you reach for the light within which is your impenetrable armour.

I AM asking that you use your hours to bind yourselves to the light within, and consciously apply that light every moment. In so doing you shall effectively programme yourself to live in the awareness that you are a light and that light is all powerful, unquenchable and victorious in all things. If you desire to reap the benefits of the fullness of your light you shall, and your efforts will be a labour of love and not a burden.

You must abandon the excuses, for they do not fit into the trajectory of MY being, and neither do they fit into yours. Excuses create your discomfort. It is very simple. If you desire to be like ME you can. The Father within each shall lead you every moment if you ask. The saying that you are God must follow with the doing, that your actions and words may be aligned, and your life be a living well of goodness which springeth from the Source within.

It is in the here and now that you must find your balance. Don't you see, notwithstanding the impediments you face, it is this environment which will truly offer you the opportunity to find your god light, and "BE" or manifest through your living, God?

In every experience you encounter you should see an opportunity to shine your god light. Strive to mitigate the effects of your less than harmonious ego, and start seeing ME in all things. When you can do so you will be reminded every moment of who you are, for every life force reflects ME.

Will you remember who you are that you may be the life which strums the chords of immortality, and show through your living, where God resides, that others may be moved to find the god within and start their journey to be who they are?

When you remember who you are and walk in the light of your sovereignty I feel it, and the joy that I experience is beyond expression, for then I know that MY little ones are well and truly on their way home. I offer these words to encourage you so please accept them in the spirit of the offering.

WHAT IT MEANS TO WEAR THE MANTLE OF CHRIST

The term mantle has several meanings in your language. The mantle I refer to is the piece of clothing or garment worn over other clothing. However, I bring a higher understanding that you may appreciate the nature of this piece. The Mantle of Christ is a symbol. In itself it represents a resurgence of divine energy to be manifested in physical form. A metaphor divinely inspired by the natural instinct of children to reflect the character of their Father.

What creates the symbolic mantle and its nature? The nature of Christ is imaged in the Mantle of Christ. I shall discourse on this shortly, but first you must consider what qualifies you to wear this mantle. In humility and trust open your hands, heart and mind to the Father that HE may fill you with righteous knowing. You have heard before that to enter the Kingdom you must become like a child again. To achieve the disciplines of higher consciousness you must become like a child again and remain as a child would, totally open and believing that the Father knows best and will guide you always on the pathway to success. The Father does not wish HIS children to assume the Father's personality, merely HIS divine character. Were you to choose to wear the symbolic mantle, you must redeem yourself in the light of the Father and attain HIS characteristics.

When you choose the mantle of Christ it must be worn with honour and solemnity. To further elaborate on the mantle, I clarify that it is not an actual piece of clothing, but a seasoned light which embarks from the Paradise Father. Consider this mantle to be a vest of virtues, a mosaic of divine qualities and impersonal attributes purely centred in its essential Source. It bears an incomparable radiance, is simple in texture, yet, enriched by its energetic display of balance, and empowered through the authentic certainty with which it is portrayed. Its beauteous tapestry weaves the fruits of the spirit as precious stones in the crown of the Father's eternalness.

The mantle is the Christ construct or a thought construct of the Christ consciousness which all men must eventually attain. The availability of this mantle is determined by the progress of one's spiritual growth. One will know when he is ready to assume the much coveted mantle. I say coveted, as those who are on a spiritual path will know that the goal is always ONENESS with God and return to the Source. Readiness to assume the mantle will hinge on preparedness and the ability to become spiritually groomed for this honour.

Before man can think of the Mantle, man is required to shed the old ways of thinking through his dominant ego mind, and seek to relinquish to the light of his spirit that which does not serve his soul's evolution. He, who chooses the mantle, aspires to the greatness of his soul. He seeks the consciousness of Christ. Man is motivated to choose the mantle when he intends to live within the Christ light, and to effectuate the truth of God through service.

When one is ready to adorn the Mantle, he is holding himself out to the world as a spiritual gladiator who embarks on the battlefield of life to do God's work. He is armed with divine truth which has become enshrined in his mortal heart. He wields the sword of wisdom and offers the hand of compassion, mercy, forgiveness and love to his enemies in battle, as he intelligently recognises the light of God in all men. He has long left his prejudices and fear behind in the healing light of his spirit, and he goes forward as a true representative of God.

The abstruse concept of Mantle is decorative as it is embellished with the virtuous light of the Divine. There is however, no ceremony attached to the Mantle. Those who choose to wear it carry the responsibility of a renowned state of being, and must live in accordance with their assumed and expected responsibilities.

The Mantle of Christ must be worn effectively in alignment with the Christ within. It requires determination and deep spiritual insight, a predilection for perfection in service, complete dedication and uncompromising loyalty to the Father's will.

Some may say that it is a heavy burden. Man may be doubtful as to his ability to assume what appears to be a weighty construct. Yet, all men will in time choose the divine mantle, for all men are sons of God and carry the Christ light within. The Christ light cannot forever be buried under the weight and density of the flesh, and the limitations of human understanding. It craves freedom. It is, of course, your individual choice as to when you set yourself free, for the Father will never interfere with your free will. I will say however, that the pain and suffering of awaiting your freedom lies with you as you must choose the hour of your freedom. I cannot free you. I can only give to you the tools, being the lessons. I have bequeathed these to you from generations past to present in many ways through many ones.

Many, in the past, have taken on the mantle with great love and spiritual intent, but with an inability to understand the greater truth. However, today, the possibilities for illumination are greater and many are with courage choosing the Mantle, and seeking guidance from the Christ within. They are discharging obligations assumed in the light of spirit.

There is a greater recognition asserting itself in the hearts and mind of men during these precipitous times, that perhaps, the better way is the way of the light. A greater alignment is taking place within individuals which now motivates them to pursue their divine purpose.

The term Christ is not a title or a name, but an ordination bestowed upon those who choose the will of the Paradise Father and achieve ONENESS with HIM.[40] You will choose HIS will when you come to know HIM as the living spirit of divinity within you. Who amongst you do not wish to know the truth of your origin and nature? You spend your life seeking truth and explore myriad possibilities of self

---

[40] Many say that they are ONE with God. That is the reality, but it is through the mortal journey that one must allow the god within to unfold HIS presence until there is only ONE in your awareness.

discovery. Yet, all you need to do is to look within and call upon the spirit of truth which I destined to you. An ardent seeker will always receive a response.

Cultivating an intimate relationship with the spirit of God within, will be the most rewarding and fulfilling relationship you will ever experience in any lifetime. Discovery of God within is the beginning of self discovery, which will inevitably propel you toward your homeland, Paradise.

The Mantle of Christ is your true nature, the epitome of all God represents. Wearing the mantle affords you opportunities to assert your mastery. It is in essence the light of God. When you wear this Mantle, it covers nothing as a mantle of clothing will. In fact, it reveals All—being the god within you.

"I AM THE WAY, THE TRUTH AND THE LIFE. NO MAN COMMETH UNTO THE FATHER BUT BY ME"

This was a pivotal piece of teaching bequeathed by the Master, Jesus, when He walked your earth plane, yet, how many truly understood its meaning. Man was not sufficiently ready to receive this truth then, and is scarcely ready to receive it now. Yet, it is significant that during these auspicious times when the planet is about to enter a new cycle of life, where dimensions anew are to be experienced and earned, man must awaken to a higher understanding of himself. He can only do so if he understands ME.

Milestones have been achieved by mortals in terms of advancement, yet, spiritually they fail to attune themselves to a great truth that if understood could change the tenor of their existence and path of soul evolution. I come again this day to effort to explain this simple yet understated Truth.

I AM the Way means that I AM your ticket to a new destination. The ticket is only dispensed when a choice is knowingly made. You must choose ME through belief and active seeking, and you will be given directions that will enable you to plot the coordinates that shall keep you on the path as you create an enduring alliance with ME.

When you are able to make this choice you will clearly see that I AM the Way out of the illusion of mortality into the reality of immortality.

We have primarily established that I AM the Way to eternal life. Yet, eternal life can only be guaranteed for those who can find and free their inner god presence. It is I WHO shall direct you on the course you must adopt to achieve this feat. You must firstly, know ME before you can know yourself, and be inclined to liberate that which is divine within you.

I would like to explore with you a different perspective of what it means when I say "I AM the Way". The "Way" cannot be separated from the "Light" as the light brings clarity of purpose and engenders a clear path to the destiny of choice. The "Way" and the "Light" go hand in hand. I say that the Way is the Light and I AM the Way and therefore the Light.

Yet, I shall offer you another perspective of the "Way". Did I not birth MY creation from love, being the reason and root cause? Did I not create by way of electric light waves of motion from the stillness of MY mind? Is it therefore not true to say that stillness motivated by love to create by light is the "Way"? Can you therefore not see that the "Way" is Love and Light, and that when you choose ME you choose Love and Light? If Love and Light are the foundation of your earthly journey you will have found the "Way".

Did I not think MY creation into being? Am I therefore not within MY creation? Isn't the ultimate goal to return to Source? If I AM MY creation and within MY creation then the only way back to the Source is through ME. Does this make sense to those who need to rationalize ME?

I AM the Way, I AM the Light and I AM the Love manifested in MY creation. I created from a point of stillness through Light motion. Does this not mean that if you choose the "Way", you too can create all which you desire to create? The "Way" enables you to reflect and be all that the "Way" is, for are you not also the "Way" through ONENESS with ME? You shall become the "Way" when you find and know ME.

I AM the Truth. Man fights amongst himself seeking to have his truth rendered superior to another. Yet, hardly do men know what Truth is. You cannot know Truth unless you know ME-The "Way". The "Way" shall always lead to the Truth. Man has belittled the Truth by tainting it with his personal agendas. The Truth is never influenced. It is impartial. It is inexplicable and beyond rationalization. The Truth must be known and that knowledge comes from knowing ME. Man's truth is mostly generated by that which is external, seldom reconcilable with his inner knowing and void of inner validation.

The TRUTH JUST IS AND IS JUST. That which is Truth knows only balance. It is as still, steadfast and immutable as the Creator. There lies no mystery or magic in Truth. I can say no more except to remind you that Truth emanates from within you because its origin is divine.

When you choose the "Way", you choose the Truth and it is the Truth when known and accepted that shall lead you to attain the divine promise of eternal life. You shall then accept without hesitation that I AM THE LIFE, that which is eternal; and so you shall be also when you can know this.

The life I speak of is immortal life. Life resides only in the spirit, not the flesh. The spirit is All. Its longevity is guaranteed by the promise of eternal life. Yet, eternal life is always a choice as much as a gift/promise. I will never force my children to choose ME; they must freely make this choice.

I wish to emphasize that even in your sphere of reality which is earth plane, you are eternal. Mortal death is merely a transition to allow the soul to take stock in order to determine the next level of experience needed along its ascending path.

You must understand that your life on earth does not give you the freedom to do that which you please without being accountable or responsible. You do not, contrary to popular belief have one life to live. When you can understand that I AM the Life and so too are you, then you will realize what you do will always impact on the evolution of your immortal soul.

What do I mean when I say "No man commeth unto the Father but by ME"? The ultimate goal as I reminded you earlier is the return to the Source of All. Yet, those created by ME can only return to the Source by ME, for I AM THE WAY.[41]

---

[41]   During the myriad incarnations on earth or through the ascending journey through time and space, there will come a time when Christ Michael's existence will become apparent to many. Every mortal has to merge with his/her Christ self before merging with their "I AM" presence.

You cannot bypass ME to get to the Source for I AND MY FATHER ARE ONE.

You cannot fudge your way to the Source without ME for I AND MY FATHER ARE ONE.

You cannot cajole your way to the Source without ME for I AND MY FATHER ARE ONE.

You cannot say that Christ Michael does not exist and seek to make your way back to the Source for I AND MY FATHER ARE ONE.

You cannot believe in the Source and not in ME for I AND MY FATHER ARE ONE.

You cannot know of ME, denounce ME and choose the Source for I AND MY FATHER ARE ONE.

When you know ME, see ME and hear ME, you will see, hear and know the Father, the Source—the Centre of All. I AND MY FATHER ARE ONE. You must become ONE WITH ME for I AM the Way to the Source.

PEACE—BE QUIET

The peril to peace lies not without, but within your inner resource, your mind. Peace proliferates in the higher breed of mind where it dwells casually, awaiting recourse by patrons called to reclaim ownership of their property.

The higher mind is an institution which offers instruction on reality and truth. Mandatory attendance is required that you may receive your baptism in truth. It is the precinct of the mind where the essence of peace becomes the promise to those seeking truth.

Peace triumphs in truth but is eroded by uncertainty when fuelled by doubt and fear. Fear is the enemy of peace and is the creation of the lower breed of mind, being the ego mind. You must learn to differentiate the lower mind from the higher mind, so that, you can make the distinct choice of that which will benefit you on your mortal journey. Through the mortal journey spiritual revelation is a natural occurrence, and when one adapts a spiritual focus to their way of life, then one will search for spiritual fruits to enhance his/her evolution. It is the adaptation to spirit that leads to the higher mind where truth finds its crown.

The proverb *"Peace is the master plan, the identity of spirit"*[42], must be pondered upon, so that, recognition may dawn that the author of peace presides within the spirit of each, and thus peace becomes the property of spirit.

The peace posited within your mind and spirit is your prosperity. Vigilance is mandated, so that, it is never inadvertently relinquished or stolen by the turmoil of outer events which evoke emotions resistant to the steady offerings of peace. Peace cannot be acquired through the achievement of outer accomplishments or the gaining of transient goods. Peace is an enduring quality which is owned, and must be

---

[42] To clarify, these are Christ Michael's words through me.

discovered within and channelled to effectively assist you in dealing with, and dissipating potential volatile experiences.

Peace of mind is yours; it dwells within you. You cannot bargain for it or expect that others can offer it to you. Neither can anyone control how you feel. This is solely your responsibility. Choosing a spiritual life, and understanding that in truth your mortal journey is a spiritual one, necessitates the assumption of responsibility for your choices, including choosing the way of peace as a way of living.

Though truth and peace are co-terminus, it is the espousal of faith and experiential faith which will sustain the discipline of a peaceful disposition, peaceful thoughts, actions and response. The power of peace is the anchor of spirit, and even in the most distressful circumstances a spirit that is anchored in peace through the knowing of truth, can display faith in that knowing. This accomplishment clarifies the perspective and perception of the faith holder. Unreserved and unquestionable faith in higher understanding sustains peace, and diminishes the effect that outer circumstances may plague on your emotions.

Peace—Be quiet, is the command given to a spirit that is troubled and demoralised in the absence of peace, through the remittance of faith to fear. The spirit will always recognise its property in peace and wish to reclaim its essence. The wisdom of the spirit knows that peace is its control mechanism for victory over experiences which conspire to facilitate the mastery of the soul.

When you become troubled or anxious and the prize of peace deserts you, sit with yourself, and command that your spirit be quiet and at peace in the presence of and in the name of the infinite spirit of God within. Without vigilance and continuous attendance, the spirit can become lost in the maze created by the emotions of the physical self.

Peace is the legacy I left you, the perennial energy of spirit, the point of rest and stillness that must be mastered that you may evolve into the co-creator that you were destined to be.

WHY?

Why do you need to know the hour of MY coming?
Is it not your decision to make?
MY coming shall centre upon your awakening
For the cornerstone of you abides always in you.
Why do you look for ME in space and count the
numbers of the days until I show MY face?
I AM that formless part of you, your innate self, moved
to life only through your desire to know ME.
Why do you cry in desperation for ME?
I AM the unseen part of you, indwelt,
awaiting your remembrance.
Why do you seek ME on the outer plane?
I AM the heartbeat calling you within
to find your inner fortune.
Why do you petition ME then scold
ME for unanswered prayers?
I AM the unheard voice, which echoes
in your unwillingness to hear.
Why do you cast ME in the den of wrathfulness?
I AM ALL LOVE, which pulsed your very life.
Why do you seek ME then bow to all
the offerings of the world?
I AM the untold "only" truth, the reality of you and all.
Why do you ask of ME for peace?
I AM that peace bequeathed to you by birth
To feel, as your spirit's touch.
Why do you ask of ME to help you change your world?
I AM your deepest vision.
When you can see and be the ME in You
There will in truth, be no world to change.
Why do you ask of ME to rescue you from darkness' hold?
I AM your light, the very light you are.
When you come to know the power of your light
The hold of darkness on your mind shall cease.

Why do you ask of ME to save your soul?
I AM THAT I AM
The soul you seek to save is MINE own.
Yet salvation you will find, the I AM, through.
Why do you seek to analyse ME so?
I AM the Love, the Light, the Truth in you.
Why do you need to know the whys, the whens and wheres?
I AM THE ANSWER TO THEM ALL
THE ONE, THE ALL, THE ONLY
ONE YOU NEED TO KNOW.

When you walk in ME and let ME walk in thee, your moments will illuminate in clarity, with purpose and completeness. The I AM within shall keep you focussed on the Source, and MY plans you shall know with prescience.

THE INSTITUTION OF BALANCE

The soul was a created from a point of stillness, being perfect balance. The spiritual term for that balance is the I AM presence. The centring point is the point of balance. It is the equilibrium point from which the waves radiate. The waves create.

Balance is essential to creation and within creation. I will explain this concept which really should be a practiced and achieved state of being. It is the answer to all your world's problems because your world is not in a state of balance. From a state of unbalanced creation (being that which you create) the results are distorted, unsustainable and lacking in endurance.

Consider a wheel which is perfectly formed, the fulcrum of that wheel perfectly positioned and the tangent of the spokes equally proportioned to create a perfect circle. The centre or point of perfect balance creates a perfect circle, and the wheel can effectively turn with no inner impediments to stem or disrupt its motion. Now think of your world in the form of this wheel. You, the inhabitants are at the centre and are responsible through your thoughts and creations for the spokes which lead to the circle's existence or creation. What was conceived by ME in perfection has been given into your custody. Through your thoughts and actions the spokes of the wheels have become burnished, dented and bent. The wheel itself begins to crack and collapse. The wheel of life has stopped. It can no longer turn. There is no motion, no progress. It stands still in a state of depredation ready to fold in.

I have taught you that Balance creates Balance, but that when you alter your natural state your creations are derived from a state of imbalance. The resulting effects are unbalanced. Do you see, that if your thoughts are the start of creation then balance starts from and through your thought process? When your thoughts are balanced in love and in light, only then can you create in love and light. Balance rests on truth, being love and light. Love and light are the only truth which exists. If you are to function within this paradigm how can your creations be anything but balanced?

As I taught above, balance leads to sustainability and endurance. I would also add that it engenders a state of perfect harmony with all things. Where have you gone wrong? To begin with, you have cast out spirit, either through rejection or forgetfulness, in favour of the ego mind. It is through this mind that you tend to create. What this creates is usually for the benefit of the physical and the individual, not the entire circle which comprises God's creation. As the ego has no reality it cannot bear truth, love or light. Its creations are not birthed from a point of balance.

To clarify, finding your balance in love and in the realm of light reminds you of your inner state, being that of balance. You would have found your centre from which all peace and love emanates, and creation begins. You become in touch with your inner light and naturally your creations are birthed from love. You will know when you feel balanced and are balanced, as this is the time when your creative spark is at its highest and you feel in tune with yourself.

Being balanced in light and love simply means that you will see through the eyes of light and love. It bequeaths a greater vision. If you bring balance into your relationships you will respond always in balance. Balanced response does not mean that you are to accept that which is contrary to the rules or laws of the Divine, meant to bring balance within God's creation. It simply means tolerating the growing pains of others who choose to operate from the point of imbalance to learn their lessons.

You must find balance even with your brothers who have chosen the dark path. You DO NOT support their actions BUT you love them as children of God. Your beloved Master teacher taught that the ultimate test of a God being is to find balance in the light and love towards those who render evil. The souls of MY children are Godly even though their human actions may be cast as evil. Those who choose the dark path operate independent of the Godly aspect of themselves, the soul.

As you live in physical abode you have to harmonise the mental, the physical, the emotional and the spiritual. In other words this is the alignment that must be achieved to find balance in the physical world. However, as your origin is spirit you must find your fulcrum in spirit. Find your point of stillness; connect with your core or Higher self and re familiarise yourself with your natural state and disposition. You will find that this will have a balancing effect on your other bodies.

When you are committed to enlightenment, balance will become your discipline. Let balance be your staple adjective; balanced thoughts, balanced words, balanced actions and balanced creations. Create affirmations from these that they become ingrained as a way of thinking and being.

I AM Christ Michael, your Tutor for today and extending MY Tutelage to you for eternity, if only you will ask and place yourselves under MY Guidance and Mastery. I know what I speak of, for I created you from perfect balance and can bring you back to that point if you allow ME to do so.

Those who seek ME in earnest, you will find ME when you find your balance.

EPIPHANY

The wheels of change churn
And the merciful winds adeptly spiral
in a downward flow
To the rendition of celestial drums
Their catered beats coin grades of energetic plumes
Which meander on the crook of starry arms
To find their home and pour the magic of their potion
Into grounds too far removed from cosmic light
For such the Source of All has ordained
This world to find respite from darkened bliss
That children, origin of first light
Might prize themselves away
From cultures too dispersed
To know the sacred tune within
Their very being
To find their placement
In the height of inner clarity
And hear the purposeful pulse
Of ONE heart
And join with their creative soul
To synthesize that perfect interlude
A welcome programme to initiate
Their baptism into holy terrain
The platform for their journey, eternal
To choose with conscious thought
The higher will
To forge new emblems framed in divine codes
And join the brotherhood of God
That man may find himself in God and God within
And join the cosmic ranks
That earthly roles may find its coordinates
By reference to celestial vibes
And man can breathe into his instrument
Tones and tunes

That they may coalesce in harmony
His inner music to be heard far and wide
That others too may find their inner song
And when his elemental world is put to right
Man will find his kingdom where he's placed
And be the very source he seeks
His God.

WORSHIP—FORWARD THINKING

The concept of worship is affiliated with the religious practice of outwardly honouring God of the religion. This honour is bestowed by those who gather in a specified place of worship, where laud and adoration is attended unto God through the saying or repeating of prayers, singing of hymns, chanting, and the reading of gospels or various other texts.

Worship has become a convention of religion, in that, specified days are allocated when God is to be praised and honoured in a community fashion. Worship has come to signify man's recognition or identification with a God who is Creator of all things, to whom homage must be addressed for gifts rendered of varying nature.

The Father honours HIS children's right to exercise their free will when they choose to approach worship in this egregious manner. HE is moved however by the intent and not necessarily the action. HE recognises that most have been conditioned to see worship through the limited view that religion offers. It has become an imposed practice which many have adopted as a routine in their lives. The form of worship may be distinct amongst religions, but the intent is predominantly the same.

I will provide you with an advanced perspective on worship, so that, communion with God can be fruitful, whilst maintaining the reverent attitude that attends worship. It is by all means worthy for believers to congregate and share in communion with the Divine. Yet, the starting point must always be recognition that as each carries the divine essence of God, God is present within each and in the presence of all when there is such a gathering.

Honour and homage should first and foremost be offered to each other, from the perspective that it is the god within you who honours the god within the other. This births the higher vision that God is almighty within each, and each is sovereign through the existence of God individualised within each member. Praise honour and adoration should be exchanged amongst members of the congregation as an act of recognition of God's presence.

When you come to recognise the god within each then you will appreciate the omnipresence of God and the ONENESS of All. When you worship you will not be worshipping in separation but in ONENESS. You will treat worship as a meaningful communion with the infinite spirit within you, as well as, meaningful interchange with the infinite spirit within others.

When you commune with the infinite spirit within you, you are recognising self and self worth and honouring self as God. This form of worship is motivating and fruitful as it cultivates your thinking which will eventually accept the most incredible thought, that you and God are ONE. Why do you seek to praise and honour God in the first place? What are you appreciative of towards HIM? Are you motivated through love for HIM, a desire to know HIM and be obedient to HIS will; or are your motivations based on the expectations of others, or fear that if you do not attend worship God will be displeased?

True worship is always a result of personal desire to spend time with the god within or to be in the presence of God. Can you accept the possibility that through worship you are seeking to truly know God; to experience what it feels like to be in HIS presence, to be fulfilled in the higher energy and joy HE can bring to your life?

You sing song after song and you become empowered by the energy created through music. Many experience a high, in particular where worship is of a charismatic nature. This high is that which you are seeking to experience, for through it you feel the ecstasy of being in God's presence. It brings radiant joy to your hearts as you feel the higher vibration take control of you, and for many moments everything else is forgotten. Many are brought to tears through the experience and claim to feel closer to God. God is all love and all ecstasy of the purest nature. You therefore long through worship to feel God.

Worship need not be the reserve for Sundays or whatever day of the week your religion imposes. Feeling the presence of God, experiencing the ecstasy of God, and enjoying reverent communion with God should be a daily practice. It should be a willing part of your life; in fact, a priority. Worship should involve the joining of your mind with the mind of God. Daily communion with God shall enable you to develop a personal relationship with HIS presence within you. Worship will then assume a new meaning as HE begins to minister to you in response to your efforts to know HIM and be with HIM.

It is through meditation that you can truly engage in meaningful worship. Let your prayer, love, gratitude and respect be engraved in your heart and this will be your offerings to the Father. Through the meditation process you will be reminded of who you are and guided to fulfil your creative potential in the world to manifest HIS presence. HE is the archetype of what you seek to reflect and you can only truly know HIM through silent communion.

As you come to know the Father within you as yourself, you will live in a constant state of worship. As your consciousness breathes new life of a celestial or cosmic nature your creations in this world will bear the stamp of all Godly attributes. Worship becomes a way of living for you as you honour, revere and love every life force in God's creation as your own.

Your life becomes a living praise through the service you shall render and works you shall do. This type of worship will bring the greatest level of self realisation, and it will create an empowering life built on divine knowledge. You shall live in the presence of the Divine and shall never feel the darkness of separation. You shall be able at will to draw from your infinite resources to create the life worthy of living. You will dwell in the frenzy of joy and see through the eyes of maturity. You will truly love your brothers and sisters as yourself and you will be a God in action. True worship should bring you to this state of being; not the transient state of feeling love, joy and empowerment one day of the week and then collapsing into forgetfulness thereafter.

When you ignore the god within you, you ignore yourself. The Father is not in need of blind adoration. HE knows who HE is. HE wants you to discover who you are, and in that discovery will be a worthy reason to celebrate. It is truly the discovery of God within you that will enable you to see many of your earthy practices and concepts in a different light.

The purpose of worship is to find and know the Cause, and in so doing you will find and know yourself, for it is then that you shall live a worshipful life where all things in God's vast creation will be honoured, praised, revered and adored.

MESSAGE FROM THE PARADISE FATHER (CREATOR OF ALL THAT IS)

Draw from MY breath that you may be propelled into timelessness to experience the ardour of infinite joy. In this you shall find ME, for you shall enter into the nest where I can attend to thee as a Father/Mother would to a child. You shall be weaned and protected[43] and come to a deep awareness of MY love. You will then know MY expectations of thee. You will come to know ME as a loving God who serves HIS children through love, and extends HIS all knowledge to them that they may wish to return to the nesting ground time and time again for nourishment.

I do not require subservience, affected, imposed or unnatural adoration. I do not seek you to love or revere ME out of duty or fear. I desire you to want to know ME, and to experience the fullness of MY love, so that, you can come to know that there is no difference between us. MY actions are exercised through pure love and I wish you to be so motivated. The world does not have to know your love for ME through loud repetitive words, but must bear witness to it through your way of life. The greatest praise and honour you can render to ME is to live a Godly life wherein I AM manifested in all you do.

There are many whose vision is jaundiced and their thinking coloured. They cannot behold reality but simply follow patterns carved out for them. The synthesis of all truth lies in the vestibule conspicuous only through inner sight. Each must choose to see in truth before they find the vestibule.

Solitude is the temperature most fruitful for worship. In your aloneness with me I can reveal myself. You will hear MY thoughts in heightened ways and come to know the ME within you. I will foster you from within and build your inner senses through a network of light, that at

---

43 Weaned and protected from the effects of the outer world.

every point will you be able to receive holy transmission. There will be no need for outer acclamations or praise, for I can and will read that which is in your heart. If you approach ME in reverie I will feel and know the honour and love you project. It is the song in your heart which testifies to your longings that moves ME within to respond, and not necessarily the words from your lips.

I do not require that you worship ME as if I exist beyond you, but do so as if I AM a part of you. Only then will you truly feel MY love and hear MY message to you. The empowerment and comfort you shall experience through this knowing communion will be sustaining.

I know that your current understanding of worship is inherited, and for many it is a practice born out of expectation and duty. Worship placates the soul and allows for recharging in an environment which presumes Godliness. I AM not against community worship, just the manner in which it is executed. I gently encourage, that worship in the setting of a church by whatever name that church is called, is aimed at the sharing of the revelations of the infinite spirit within each, and an honouring of each other as God in manifest. You must come to know and accept that where you are I AM.

MARRIAGE

Marriage is a spiritual institution designed by God for man. It is a creation of "Divine Order", and those who engage in this Holy act must aim to fulfil and outwork the will of God. Always must the parties to this divine union remember the origin and purpose of marriage and seek to dwell in its reflection.

Marriage is the unity of two beings who agree to share the ONENESS of the soul at a human level. It is a higher experience which allows for the exploration of Love's infinite prowess.

At the very fulcrum of marriage is its catalyst, Love. Love marshals the desire for bonding and it is the foundation upon which the union rests. In the stillness and steadfastness of that Love, the pillars of understanding, joy, patience, tolerance, balance, respect, loyalty and honour are upheld. It is only when love is unshaken that the marriage will sustain. Love is unshaken when it is unconditional, and it is this Love that bears the fruits which bestow longevity to the marriage.

In marriage Love is never tested, for true love is beyond challenge, it simply triumphs. True Love rests in its natural unalloyed state, balanced and poised in its own energy, unaffected by the vagaries of human condition. A marriage based on true love derives its strength from the universal placement of God's presence. Blessed are they who see the divine orientation of marriage, for they shall partake of God's vision, and the marriage shall be nourished with the nectar of divine love.

Marriage is love expressing itself through the binding of minds in one accord sharing a common purpose. There is no self in marriage, for marriage manifests ONENESS, and each party must see the whole and strive to maintain the whole. The wise husband and wife will know that the interchange between them must be balanced on the rhythm of giving and re-giving.

There is no property in marriage, it cannot be owned, just shared. It cannot be measured in physical offerings, but only by the wealth of love and frequency of light each party contributes to it.

Marriage offers a sanctum for two souls to grow in an ambiance of one will, being the desires of both, congealed through unity. It is a festival where joy and light-hearted camaraderie are moulded and enhanced through occasional frisson.

Marriage bequeaths the gift of prosperity through the creation of children; it allows for the parties to experience the power and beauty of co-creating with the Divine. As the Father giveth the life of the soul, the parents will give the soul expression through flesh.

The fabric of MY very being is woven into the hearts of men and women, and when two unite in marriage through love they must know that I AM present and I AM exalted.

CHRISTMAS—THE CELESTIAL TRUTH

Christmas is a cultural experience when viewed across the chasm of religious divide. It is no longer confined within the Christian context where it serves as a religious reminder of the birth of the Christ meant to be celebrated.

What could have been a celebration in remembrance, with reverent tones, have become a festival of excess, extravagance and external revelry where even those who have no belief or knowledge of the Christ become embroiled in activities, centred around Christmas which hold no depth of meaning.

The true spirit of Christmas is that of illumination, meaning enlightenment within through the inner celebration of the Christ light, for the Christ is birthed in each soul incarnate. So if this is so, and it is so, then your Christmas should be a celebration of the inner Christ. Christmas or Christ mass is the union or communion with the Christ. Where is the Christ? Did I not come to tell you that the Kingdom of God lies within you? Did I not promise upon my departure that MY FATHER and I would pour the spirit of God onto the flesh of man? Why do you celebrate MY birth as if I reside outside of you? In truth God is everywhere, but for the purposes of your soul's evolution God is within you.

The Christ is within you and any communion or union in celebration of the Christ should take place within. I am not averse to outward recognition or celebration. In fact, the celebration can be used as a welcoming time for each to embrace one another and all, as brothers and sisters within the Kingdom.

You cannot compartmentalise ME to times of the year. I AM whole and I AM within you eternally. I say to you out of love that you should celebrate Christmas every day of your mortal life, for it is within your ability and certainly your divine entitlement to sit with the Christ within, commune in reverence, and in so doing embrace and celebrate the holiness and wholeness of you.

MY very birth was uneventful, not dramatic as it is displayed. I came as man to walk and live as man in humble attire. For those who care, review MY life on your earth, and ponder upon how I lived and worked, as well as, my teachings. This is the Christ within you. Not one who sits as a king upon a throne requiring unending praise. Is not your communion with the inner Christ, praise in itself? There is no real need to celebrate MY birth as much as there is a need to celebrate MY ongoing presence within you. I do not wish you to forever dwell in the stories of old, but to progress through knowing that I have glorified you with MY presence, and I AM glorified when you can recognise this and allow ME to work through you in the interest of your soul's progress.

I want you to think on this. If every day could be a fulfilling day as you allow your communion with the inner Christ to direct your life, will not each day be a celebration of joy and ONENESS? What need will you then have to celebrate an event at one time of the year that holds no significance to the majority?

Dear ones, Christ Michael is not hear to spoil your joy but rather to direct you to the essence of that which will yield perfect joy to you. What you experience during your Christmas celebrations is not joy, but pyrrhic in nature. Most of you cannot even remember the celebrations as you drown yourself in practices which render forgetfulness.

It is time beloveds for man on earth to grow up and seek the truth of that which is real. You can build a life around this truth that will enable you to have a joyful existence.

To start you off on the path of truth I will say to you that what you celebrate is not Christmas. It is a cultural extravaganza drawing from myth, embellished with artistic displays of colour, and indulgences far beyond your needs. It focuses on beauty and bounty unrelated to that which is divine. It is indeed by your reckoning the time when families reunite and the spirit of togetherness prevails. This is the distinct benefit that those who cannot relate to the true meaning draw from the event.

When you prepare to celebrate Christmas, think about what I have said and also think about celebrating the Christ within each other.

I AM THE CHRIST. I WAS KNOWN AS JESUS CHRIST, BUT I AM TRULY FROM THE ORDER OF MICHAEL SONS, FROM THE SUPREME CREATOR OF ALL. I HAVE COME TO REMIND YOU OF TRUTH THAT YOU MAY ACCEPT AND GROW IN TRUTH FROM HERE ONWARDS, AS THE TIME OF GREAT REVELATION SITS UPON YOU. TRUTH IS INDIGINOUS TO YOU. IT IS YOUR NATIVE COSMIC LANGUAGE WHICH YOU HAVE FORGOTTEN. THOSE AEONS AGO MY BIRTH WAS KNOWN BY THE STAR THAT APPEARED IN THE NIGHT SKY. LOOK AT YOUR SKIES AGAIN WHAT DO YOU SEE?

26

Universal Mother-Nebadonia

Let the bud of Love sown in the heart of thy soul
Unfold in gentle sweeps.
Know that in your essence love breathes;
For just as life bestows its breath to sustain life,
Love bestows its breath to sustain Love.
Understand that Love is All and All is Love
And conquer not will it ever be,
For it remains in its timeless form,
Unabridged, undefiled
The constant virtue of every life.
Trust that in its unfolding its joy shall respond,
As every experience will be favoured with its bestowal
In the wake of higher knowing.
Believe that it is your one power
That is incapable of being diminished
And must be allowed its freedom to express its prowess
Always through your making.
Live in its Presence, for it is your very God,
Your very self,
All that you are
And ever will be.

KNOW THYSELF AS GOD

The triumphant glow within the spirit of man is the presence of God. Defeat is never an option, for man is his own victor. It is the sight of man that is short, for he sees his periphery, his surface and not his depth. His inability to claim his godhood comes from not knowing that he is the champion of his own cause. Man's intellect derides him and he cannot conceive his own might. He therefore settles for less than who he is and seldom achieves that which he is truly capable of. He creates a persona which is less than divine that he may search for the Divine. His search is sometime endless, for disbelief parades his very nature, and he denies his ultimate destiny an opportunity to find its goal in his mortal journey.

His inner light is clipped like the wings of a bird, and it is clipped often by choice, yet, sometimes by design. Man has been given the know-how and the teachings, yet, he chooses to be moved by the world surrounding him rather than in the inner world of sprit which is designed to be the guiding force for his worldly endeavours. In the absence of spirit's influence, he fails to find his true self in the miasma that is fraught in his unintelligible world. There is no intelligence in that which is outside of man, yet, man is drawn like a magnet to the outer uncertainties of his existence. He berates the very life within, unconsciously so, when he seeks to deny the existence of God within him.

As the door of creation prepares to breathe itself open once again, mankind is being flooded with divine energies. These energies are breathed in at the soul level, and through the influx, an awakening is being amortized within the hearts and spirits of men and women.

The irreverence which has paled the glow of man for aeons is beginning to subside as many begin to wander in to reclaim what was forgotten. It is likely though that the divine breath will cull the souls not yet ready to partake of their divinity. Truly, separation is called for as the coal is being removed, that the distinctness of the diamonds may show and cast its light through the ailing globe.

These times highlight the need for man to know his perfection, and it is effort and desire that will transport him to that place where perfection lies. The excuses are now redundant. Vision is now called upon that the unearthing and unleashing of divine order within begins its reign. Those awakened to the glory of the inner god must establish themselves in that presence, and bring the light of God alive, in their works on earth. How else can the Kingdom of God be established on your plane? Why do you allow the outer world to conflict you so? Are your needs so great that the god within cannot fulfil? Do you need to hold on vehemently to the trappings which will inevitably bury you in a rut and stifle the divine within you?

You have chosen to take this journey. You know the truth which is buried deep in your unconscious. How can you deny your identity? You are a part of the ONE. In truth there is no distinction because separation is a myth. It is the understanding of the mind that will enable you to grasp this, and comprehend your true nature as God and not man. Who is man, but a creation of himself designed to bring immortality to that which appears mortal. The journey comprises lessons, and lessons well learnt cause the inner presence to grow and glow in awareness.

The lessons are not academic but spiritual, yet, the spirit holds the wisdom which creates the knowing of truth. The presence of God is incarnate within you. It is this presence that calls you and shall willingly guide you home. You need only apply your higher mind and you shall begin to reckon with yourself, and come to know and gradually experience your God potential. It is the knowing that will create the energy fortuitous to your eventual return to your SOURCE.

Disbelief is a sham. It nurtures doubt and on a mindal level separates what is ONE. The Father within each of you is calling you home. Will you not answer the call and free yourself from the bondage of the ego's verbiage which seeks to distance you from your natural heritage?

Know yourself as God and you shall by your own efforts experience the living God within you.

COSMIC GRATITUDE

The glory of the Father resides in each child in-built with the living spirit. That is the spirit of life. To all of you who have agreed to take on mortal countenance to serve the higher will during these auspicious times in your planet's cycle, you are in receipt of great honour.

Your loyalty to a higher cause is noted and streams of applause often flow from the celestial circle of higher authority. You who have chosen to align your consciousness with the Father's, receive more and more packets of light in order to discharge your earthly tasks with greater understanding. Always do we keep your light replenished as you share your divinity with others.

The drums roll in the Angelic Kingdom and love is sent from the spheres of Paradise to embrace your earth for all she has contributed to the rising of humanity. She too has been a faithful servant. The heavens pour into her, gifts of gratitude that she may welcome this energy and prepare herself for greater service.

Many are oblivious to the welcome support we offer freely, and many cannot comprehend God honouring HIS children for their achievements. This is a reality. Just as you speak with HIM, HE speaks with you, and just as you praise and honour HIM, HE praises and honours you. Ponder upon this. A father always encourages his children with talent, offers praise to those who show promise, and those who shine through achievement. Praise and other material gifts may be bestowed as rewards for accomplishment.

The Paradise Father must be viewed similarly. HE too, rewards HIS children when they make balanced choices aligned with HIS will and achieve personal and spiritual progress. HE encourages spiritual development by offering more and more of HIMSELF. HE may not bequeath material effects, but gifts spiritual delights that will enable HIS children focussed on HIM to enjoy greater benefits of HIS presence and wealth. There is no limit to the Father's wealth. HE does not withhold them from you, but offers them freely if you would make HIS will your choice. The offering of spiritual wealth is the expression of HIS gratitude for your determination in choosing to reside in HIS light.

All is fulfilled in the Kingdom of God. There is a flow of natural giving and re-giving, each cycle being expressed in gratitude for the other. Choosing HIS will is the beginning of gratitude, for you express thanks consciously or not when you say, *"Father I desire only to do thy will"*. This is your recognition of the highest will that exits. It is in fact a tribute of thanksgiving. In choosing HIS will, you do not forfeit your free will, but you bring your will in alignment with HIS. This will become a natural choice as you graduate to higher frequency.

This choice of honouring and living the Father's will is the beginning of a kaleidoscope of blessings. Eternal guidance will be offered, but most importantly you can allow yourself the experience of co-creating with the Father. When you are able to flow in HIS energy through the moments of your life, your co creative talents and abilities will surface and you shall begin to indulge in your birthright.

See cosmic gratitude as an extension of the Father's love for you. HE is present and available to all HIS children, but will not impose HIMSELF. HE must be sought and discovered and then chosen. The result of choosing the Father brings certainty, assurance, inalienable peace, righteous joy and gifts of divine gratitude.

When you choose the Father's you will become gatekeepers of spiritual assets, soldiers of the Father in reverent service. This in itself is a reward you have earned, bestowed with divine gratitude.

Fairness prevails in the Kingdom where God exists, and those who find HIS essence within and choose HIS will shall find the Kingdom. When you can experience the Kingdom of God within yourself, you will dwell in the phase of continuous gratitude. What is gratitude, but the harmonious instinct poised and ready for flow within and through the Father's vast creation? It is constantly expressed in myriad ways, yet, can only be experienced by those who are able to receive and accept it through conscious choice of the Father and HIS will.

Some may interpret these words as saying that the Father's gratitude is conditional upon HIS children taking certain steps. Yet, I say that gratitude is an extension of HIS love which is unconditional. Through and by HIS everlasting love you are in receipt of HIS gratitude for your existence, your journey and eventual return to HIM.

Cosmic gratitude is the "Divine presence" reciting codes of love steeped in the mortal hearts of men, that each may find its access and release it to the world. The Father dwells within each child of creation. HE is a constant giver, and HIS love and Mighty presence within each is gratitude in action to HIS little ones who take the long journey of ascent to Paradise.

27

LADY MASTER NADA

I AM THAT I AM
For I AM you and I AM ME
You are you and you are ME
No boundaries can divide
The singleness of ONE
You are an expression of the ONE
The consciousness of the ONE
The unbridled power of the ONE

I AM THAT I AM
The valour of you
The identity of ME
The knowing of you
The loving of ME
I AM THAT I AM

I AM THAT I AM—ITS TRUTH

I AM THAT I AM is the Father's way of saying that which I AM is self and that which I AM is the soul. The "I AM" presence within each who bears the Father fragment[44] represents your God identity.

It is a title that you inherited upon your soul's creation. With every incarnation you are meant to progress in your ability to find the "I AM" within and effort to be that presence. I AM THAT I AM, for you, means that which I am is the soul and that which I am is God. After all were you not created through the light of HIS thinking? HE merely divided HIMSELF in parts that those various parts may experience the realms of time and space away from HIM, but not without HIM. This brief journey of the soul was meant to enrich the Father through its experiences, and enable the soul through its incarnations to reconnect with its Father fragment and make its way back home.

If you were to explain this phrase or title to one who has little spiritual understanding of his origin, you may be accused of indulging in arrogant conjecture to think yourself so worthy or supreme that you dare assume the title preserved only for the most high.

The truth is that these persons live in the downs of ignorance and deprive themselves of the enlightened vision of who they truly are. Subconsciously, they also reject it as they are not yet prepared to rise to the ethos associated and born of that title. The cell memories of their god minds remain dormant as they become subjects of an earthly physical conditioning, in abstinence of spiritual fortitude conferred by that subtle yet empowered presence within.

---

[44] The Father fragment is that which allows man to connect and commune with the Father. It is called the Thought adjuster or Mystery Monitor. All ensouled beings have this fragment.

The "I AM" is real for those who can feel its presence palpably within. The "I AM" is your vibrancy, your passion, your truth. It is who you are. It takes great effort and discipline to access the delights of your powerful soul, that you may be able to propel yourself in the presence of the "I AM". Affirming that you are the "I AM" is one way of conditioning your psyche to accept your true being. The more you warrant that affirmation, the greater the probability that you will behave in a way reflective of that presence.

I wish to make it abundantly clear however that saying it and stating it is insufficient if you do not believe it, for belief is the power which manifests its workings. Yet, saying it, stating and believing it still falls short of its true value and worth, for you will only reap and know its worth when you can discipline yourself through effort to explore its different facets, so that, you may know the "I AM", and begin in earnest to align yourself with its virtues and qualities.

I AM THAT I AM should be a motto, an insignia that man in the new world[45] uses as an affirmation of identity and his spiritual strivings. The Father has bestowed this gift upon you, how will you thank HIM for this? I humbly suggest that you use it with humility yet spiritual pride and consciousness. The Father has said that HE is but you grown in wisdom and presence. Allow this motto to be your vehicle that you may journey, knowing who you are, back to YOU. In so doing you shall find God.

The difficulty in your world is that separation centres all things, for there is a human need for division within the mass consciousness, that man may be ranked hierarchically. The man who stands at the base can seldom feel or experience his sovereignty, because there is always someone above who seeks to discriminate or define who he is. Those

---

[45] We are entering the golden age where through the ascension process the civilization and planet are entering into light. In other words we are gradually evolving from duality to monopolarity.

who find themselves or place themselves in the higher echelons convey a self imposed supremacy defined by man–created laws and expectations. The divide is well and truly conditioned in man's thinking, and in these limiting circumstances man is unable to breach the barriers of human creations so as to discover offerings of higher truth.

The religions of your world have further entrenched man in the false thinking that God is separate from man and must be seen as an entity so far removed, that obeisance and praise must be rendered if man is to ever have hope for salvation. How can man in this cloistered environment think for himself and come to a greater understanding that he and the Father(by whatever name) is ONE? He is merely experiencing life away from home for a short time. It is his experiences that will lead him home to the Source if he is able to find himself in the rubble of his earthly physical existence.

I AM here to tell you that the "I AM" is your salvation, your saviour, your wealth, your guru, your messenger, your counsellor, your constant companion, your creativity, your beauty and essence. Do not reject who you truly are because you disbelieve the eminence of you and your true worth. Allow the motto I AM THAT I AM to define you.

When you use I AM THAT I AM, you must learn to feel its "Divine presence" move within. You must give the "I AM" control over every thought and action. You must be aligned with its virtues and eternal nature. I AM THAT I AM is your cosmic self not your mortal self. The goal is that, as you wear the uniform of humanness you must find the "I AM" and live the "I AM" until your human existence merges with cosmic awareness, so that, your life on earth becomes a life of spirit, and all that is of spirit influences and persuades your actions. Your ascension will be in the measure that you find, know and live the "I AM" presence.

DEVOTION

Devotion is God's eternal love for HIS children. Through the Father's devotion all creation was made manifest. If HE was not devoted to HIS vision HE could not have created its effect.

Devotion can only be achieved if you are willing to extract yourself from the mundane and commit yourself to the reality of who you are. It is uninfluenced by matter. It is borne out of untainted love and bears a magnetic pull to that which you have a passion for.

The subject of your passion will inspire a "feeling", which will be a signal of the measure of your willingness to commit. You cannot be devoted to anything unless that flow of love eternally embraces your passion. There is an expectation of sacrifice attendant on devotion. That is, the need to give up something in order that the subject of your devotion can blossom into the reality it holds for you.

Devotion to God begins with devotion to self, for HE is you and you are HIM. The magic of you is the soul of HIM. When you see yourself as ONE with HIM, love flows inevitably without affectation or confinements of time and space. Devotion comes naturally to those who are moved by deep inner love.

Devotion must be consuming if a "Cause"[46] is to be served. It offers no respite but promises divine rewards. It allows for no distraction, but conquers its own demons which would otherwise cause it to flounder in its bid to serve. Perseverance is an heirloom of devotion and must be treasured, for devotion's posterity depends on it retaining its luminescence. The virtue of patience cannot be unattached from its modem-devotion, for devotion cannot function without the icon of patience activated. Patience wears thin when we allow the mist of doubt

---

[46]   An interest, campaign, movement or crusade.

to congeal. We must ever be alert to the disintegrating factors which veer us away from a chosen "Cause".

The devotee will see that the chosen "Cause" is greater than the effect, and if the "Cause" is served unstintingly the effect will be the result hoped for. Devotion cannot be measured in terms of time for it is attached only to its "Cause" and releases itself from the bondage of linear equations.

When you are truly devoted to the Father[47] you are devoted to all, for all come from HIM and the ONE is not complete without all. When you are devoted to serving HIM you must be devoted to serving all.

Devotion is anchored with onerous responsibility to a "Cause" and requires self preparation. Preparation must originate in the mind which must be strong and closely aligned with the "Presence" within. It is the mind which births the idea and it is the mind which must see the idea through.

The colourful tapestry can only be woven by many hands, derived from efforts abound by all who devotionally serve the chosen "Cause". Only then will the effect become the manifested vision of the "Cause". The "Cause" cannot be superceded by the effect; it can only give birth to it.[48]

Are you prepared to serve your Cause until the vision is manifest?

---

[47]   The Father is also known as the 'Cause' and HIS creation the effect.
[48]   Think of the Father and HIS creation. HE gives birth to HIS Creation and HIS creation becomes one with HIM.

28

MASTER ST GERMAIN

Ferret the folds of fear which fetters the light
And polarizes you from your divine companion.
Bewitch yourself in the knowing of God
That freedom may carve its mark upon your soul.
Renounce the darkened etiquette of fear
Which belabours a mind deserving of celestial manna.
Steer its cultured seeds away from you
That it may find its life on other soil.
Sow instead the seeds of Light which bringeth Love
And know the priceless gift you hold within.
For only then will grandeur bloom at heightened pace
And walk you will the walk of freedom's trail.

FEAR

Fear is not a property of spirit but of the human ego. Fear is damaging to the freedom of the spirit's ability to manifest its power. It is debilitating to the harmonious flow of conscious awareness of man's prized possession, his spirit.

Fear cuts the chord which joins man to God, and creates a purposeful separation which engenders continuous confusion and lack of understanding as to the origin of that fear. Man has for aeons feared God due to spiritual malnutrition. He is not fed with the wisdom of truth and therefore withers in the lack of knowing. What he does not know or recognize is that fear is subversive and a product of his mortal ego, which he unconsciously pays homage to as it directs his feelings that validate his experiences.

This mortal fear generated by the ego cultivates a culture of programming which man responds to automatically. So ingrained is fear within man's subconscious that its response to various circumstances or situations further feeds that wretched emotion, and multiplies the negative effect it has on man's perceptions.

Fear creates havoc in man's mind and clouds his ability to see that the actual situation which confronts him is not in itself fearful, but that it is his perception which casts the situation in fear. Fear is therefore, not extraneous to man but is created by him. It gnaws at his psyche until he believes in it. Were his mind divinely attuned he would know himself as a powerful spiritual being and relinquish fear.

Man fears because he does not know. When man knows he will not fear. Man can only be in the knowing if he knows God. When he knows the God incarnate he will know that he is always in the company of God. This shall confer assurance and security. Fear will not then factor into the equation. The more one remains connected to the Source the less he will be affected by fear. As a sense of ONENESS is experienced you will begin to feel as if you are walking in the footsteps of God, and no mortal emotion counterproductive to your evolution can distress or impede you.

God is the antithesis of Fear, for God is Love and Light and represents the highest frequencies, whilst fear is on the lower vibratory scale. God elevates whilst fear depresses and represses. God knows no limits and creates no boundaries whilst fear imposes limits and boundaries. If fear is the antithesis of God, surely it is the antichrist within man, which brings down the ONE true living God within man. Do you not see that man chooses to be God's enemy when he allows his fear to dominate him? Man cannot house God and "Fear" at the same time. When you entertain fear you reject God. It is only God who can help you conquer your innate fears through the knowing of HIM. HE is the panacea, the elixir that will wipe out that which seeks to debase you and render you slaves to your outer senses.

Fear cripples the joy within you and that joy is the Father's presence. When you are motivated by fear your life loses its edge as you cower behind the fear which provides you with an excuse not to grow.

Fear sours the palette and deprives you from tasting the sweet nectar of life. It is simple; do you wish to choose a life of growth or powerlessness and stagnation? The choice is always yours.

Fear is a dark structure so embedded that it must be weeded out before its thorn and briars create further lesions to contaminate the remnants of your God self and power.

You may say that this is easy for Germain to say, for he sits above and cannot fathom what life is in this 3rd dimension. Well beloveds, as you say, I have been there and done that! I am therefore in a position to show you the way out of the kingdom of fear that reigns heartily within so many, that you may come into the experiencing of the wealth of your heritage.

It is only your knowledge of God, the knowing of HIM from within that will bring you to a point where you will be able to say that, you know HIM as yourself. When you can say and feel this you will be free of fear. This is not achievable overnight and requires a desire on your side to reclaim and live in your sovereignty. When you can find that resolve you shall then proceed to develop a worthwhile relationship with HIM, and through your commitment to stay connected with HIM, HE shall live through you.

Man's fear is birthed from ignorance.[49] The remedy for ignorance is knowledge, and knowledge can only be accessed from within the mind of God which hosts your mind. We have given you the keys time and time again to God's mind. When you can access HIS mind you will find that knowledge, which becomes your power and truth.

Knowledge, Power and Truth which come from God, speaks in light which neither harbours nor emanates fear. Know that when you feel fear, it is your perception born from your outer senses and NOT the word or Truth of God which instils that fear.

You need cast away the unattractive habit of blaming God and giving yourselves an excuse to fear HIM. Learn to see through your inner vision and truth will never be perceived in fear.

Can you expand your mind, so that, you may welcome KNOWLEDGE from God which will give you truth? Often you say, that you cannot find proof for God's word. You therefore deny HIS words and HIM or deny that HE can bring forth such words. My lesson to you is that God's words need no proof. It is not HE who must prove HIMSELF. HE lays the truth on a plate before you and you still deny it. Is it that you fear that HIS truth may destroy beliefs you have held dear for ages? If your fear holds you hostage to denial of truth, do not blame God.

---

[49] The use of the word ignorance is not meant to be derogatory or offensive in nature; it is means unschooled or untaught.

I say categorically and unequivocally that Fear is of Man and not of God, and when you can learn to connect with God and keep HIS company moment by moment, you shall know this wholeheartedly. You come from God and must return to HIM. Many of you seek HIM and HE presents HIMSELF, yet, you reject HIM for fear that HE does not align with your conception.

Relinquish the catastrophic hold which this insidious, infectious fear has on you. Choose HIM WHO gave you life, love, freedom and joy. HE desires that you move forward in growth, and you can only do so without the harness of fear around the neck of your spirit.

Let your fears die within the light of awakened sovereignty. I bequeath to you the violet flame[50] that it may transmute fear's heinous hold, and transform to love, as you move into greater knowing of the ONE.

---

[50] Master St Germain is the Chohan of the 7th Ray which is known for its purifying aspects and transmuting qualities. The Violet Flame is an aspect of the 7th Ray consciousness.

IN VAIN YOU BUILD A CITY WHEN FIRST YOU SHOULD BUILD THE MAN

The repertoire of man's agenda transcends himself, being his spiritual self, as he is influenced by a parochial need to prove himself in this physical world through the acquisition of wealth, status power and fame.

He deigns to be king of his world through the building of empires which glow with egotistical desire to the gratification of his senses while his soul remains in withering absentia.

He channels his energy in constructs of a material nature where his world becomes one which bespeaks to the tune of sensual longings. His worth is measured in quantity not quality. His creations are a product of his senses, not his mind.

There is no spiritual aspiration in the midst of his material, scientific and technological creations. The educational structures currently in place enable man to create without divine purpose. The system is independent of and fails to inculcate the teachings necessary for man to prioritise that which is important for his elevation, or to contextualise the role of the physical experience in man's evolution. Even religious education, is at the most sanguine in its attempt to teach man of God, and at the least fails to complete its purpose.

Man tenders that which is built on foundations of sand with no firm premise. His gift to mankind though superlative, is superficial. Buildings of stones are merely shells without a hint of inspiration, and can be easily disturbed by the winds of change which can imminently sweep them of their "feet".

Man's creations lack gravity. The physical dimension has taken precedence and all that is taught circumscribes man's ability to find his true calling, and thus serve his greater cause which is to find his true worth and sense of God.

Why does man lack in his actions and works the nobility of God character? Man's god is far removed from the light which he truly is. The achievement of man bodes well for instant gratification, but holds no promise for tomorrow. His soul has become cauterised, unable to breathe into man its truth, which will enable man to find and develop his character, based on divine attributes.

Man's nobility is superceded as his perennial aim is to plagiarise the menial practices of others and become pale followers instead of primary leaders.

I desire to teach you that the building must start within each of you. When you become a solid balanced foundation with the knowledge that you bear an unquenchable light which shines immortal values bestowed by that Mighty presence within, you become the bedrock of light in God's Kingdom. You can steadfastly go out into the world to be a seed to help others find and live their immortal supremacy.

It is about understanding that the foundation is what matters. Your civilisation is born and bred by transient elements of avarice, consumerism, lust, self serving agendas and pride. There are hardly any spiritual rays upholding the infrastructures of your world. It is cuddled by the inveterate hold of evil hands which for aeons have conspired to lock man in the prison of his senses, so that he remains dense to his truth.

Your world is devoid of character, innate nobility and divine honour because man lacks the attributes and know-how necessary to build a sustainable civilisation. Any sustainable civilisation must be based on that which endures and only God's laws and processes endure for eternity. The natural laws of universal practice must become the fulcrum of your civilisation.

We have so far identified the symptoms and cause of your civilisation's decline, and must now focus on a remedy that will sustain and create a firm foundation that is unbreakable and immovable. Education is the panacea.

The education I speak of must be addressed to man's mind not his senses or brain. He must be re-programmed to think as a higher universal being, which is what he was born to be. He must be taught that sovereignty is not equated with crowns of material possessions or conferring of status by others. He must see that sovereignty is his birthright and he must be taught how to access his wealth and divine status from within. Man must be taught that life only resides in spirit and that is all that truly lives. Introspective thinking must be taught. Man must learn to place the material/physical dimension within the context of his evolution and be trained to see the real from the unreal.

The laws of God and creation[51] must be re-taught to man, and he must be brought into the understanding that these laws are inviolable if he is to ascend unto higher dimension. He must be taught that these laws are a natural part of his true self which for aeons he has relinquished in preference to man-made laws. He must be asked to take an objective view of his world and to identify the cause of its degeneration, so that, he may for himself come into a deeper comprehension that he contributed to its decline through his participation in those man-made laws which bear no semblance of natural law.

Man must be made to see that he is a fragment of the Divine whose ultimate goal is to become a manifestation of the Divine, and therefore be encouraged to gravitate to all that will create a divine alignment.

Man must be taught that he will not be judged only by courts of law, but ultimately by the Great Spirit within, to which he remains responsible and accountable. To sum it up, man must find God within, comprehend the significance of that presence, liberate his divinity that it can manifest its worth in the material plane of existence, and then accept his divine responsibility to the god within, and to every life force of creation.

---

[51]   The laws of God have been given for balance within the creation. They are akin to the Commandments although more detailed.

Education systems must function to serve the greater cause of man's existence, which is his ascension. Those already educated in this way must serve as living examples to those not fully educated in the ways of the light. Man tends to thrive on associations and what the majority does will set the tone for others.

I invite each of you from this moment to find that portal which offers entry to your soul, so that, you become acquainted with its values and virtues and forge an identity linked to your cosmic origin. It is time for man's soul to become the face of his world. There is no greater honour and beauty than one who wears his soul as his outer cloak that his God light shines in bliss. When you can unlock the jewel of you, you will dwell in your true home and will bring "home", being the light and life of God's domain, into your civilisation. It is only then that cosmic character will be brought into your civilisation and a state of balance reinstated.

Man must be "made" before the civilisation is built, for man is the foundation of civilisation. If man embraces light and life, then the civilisation will prosper.

JEOPARDY

You stand on the brink of a new age, but before this dawns the old matrix must be brought to an end. When chaos rules, this too must eventually come to an end that the genre of peace may take its rightful place, as is ordained by the Creator.

Why have I titled this piece jeopardy? Jeopardy bespeaks of a risk of harm, danger or peril. Its tone connotes a feeling of imminent danger and a warning that there is vigilance. You on earth have lived for aeons in jeopardy of your souls' incarceration at the machinations of dark intent. The light of joy has been jeopardized by the hands of mal intent. You have a game titled jeopardy. What you have not grasped is that jeopardy is a way of life for you. It is your constant reality on earth.

Your perception of what you feel as joy, ecstasy and beauty is experienced in a shell of superficiality. You experience empty joy and beauty derived from the illusion of God's creation, all that is based on matter, and sense oriented. Is this a criticism? No, for you live in a sense objective universe and are entitled to partake of the illusion. The illusion is the pavement upon which you must journey to return to self. It is the facilitator of the greater cause. Yet, many live their lives as the "effect", constantly waiving their divine right to aspire to the "cause". Why? Living as the "effect" offers a choice, and many of you choose mortal contentment, joys of simple or sophisticated lives. You choose to create boundaries which offer mortal security whilst all the time disregarding the higher will for your evolution, thus jeopardizing the health of your immortal soul.

Is any experience wasted? No, but many souls after a mortal incarnation literally hit their "heads" against etheric walls saying "if only I did". You have a long journey and you must make it, or denounce the life, that God intended, to be your immortal soul. Your rejection of the life within the soul will debunk the Father WHO made it possible for you to exist.

EFFORT

Effort is the investment required for the achievement of a goal or materialisation of any project. Effort aligned with positive thinking and the power of visualisation will create. It is the ability to see the end product which will harness and catalyse your inner resource, the application of which endures until a state of completion is achieved.

Effort does not stand on its own; it is not discrete but is propelled by desire. You are beings of action. Wherever there is action effort is required. Where there is inaction no effort is needed. Inaction creates stagnation whilst action births development and enhancement of all things desired.

The result achieved is proportionate to the degree of effort invested. Little effort yields little results whilst great effort brings great results. You are very good at putting effort into your daily chores (jobs) from which you earn your livelihood. You know that if you fail to apply time and ability, you will fail to earn the income necessary for your earthly survival. Your efforts are mostly geared toward the acquirement of personal gain aimed at securing your physical needs. This is by no means a criticism.

The question I have for you however, is, how much effort do you think is required for your spiritual survival? The answer to this depends on where you wish to be in your spiritual consciousness. Do you desire to re-discover your true being, so that, you may effort to live in its reflected perfection? If so, how much work is required before you can drink from the well that hosts your essence?

There are many limitations in your material world conspiring to detract you from achieving optimal spiritual growth. You struggle against non-acceptance from others, disbeliefs and doubts, ego and earthly concerns which impede clarity of vision and purpose.

It takes indefatigable effort to live in accordance with your highest conception of you. Are you prepared to stifle your true self through fear and perceived limitations which plunge you into a state of worldly content, whereby your preference becomes one of fitting in rather than standing out?

It takes great courage and self belief to step out of your humanism and claim your transcendent heritage through the acquirement of cosmic awareness, achieved only through the effort of inner communion with the Source. The choice is yours. Personal ascension to higher levels of consciousness necessitates that you work through devotion, perseverance and discipline. It is a constant journey toward the port of Christ consciousness.

As you ascend to higher spiritual octaves your effort must compliment your moments. It requires moment by moment effort in conscious awareness, to enjoy that peak, to be able to stay there and then graduate beyond.

Effort becomes like strums on the strings of a guitar. Every strum is courted by the vision of a harmonious tune completing an eventual musical rendition, birthed from the inspiration of your creative soul. That song is YOU, your creation. It is one with you. It equals your effort. You become your effort. Effort finds its home in the sphere of abiding love, for any effort glossed by love will yield sustainable results and rewards.

May the violet flame clear the dust which frames your lives, so that, you may clearly see your spiritual desires manifest through the conduit of effort, and reach the fulcrum of your being, the point at which your effort and creations become one.

29

FATHER MELCHIZEDEK, LORD MELCHIZEDEK

"Wisdom is the growth of the seed of God awareness into the blossom of God Knowing and Being."

A MATTER OF INTERPRETATION
OR MISINTERPRETATION?

It is worthy to note the variances between the understanding of concepts and terminologies. Interpretation is mainly subjective as each tends through the influences of his/her conditioning and core values to assign meanings which meet these imperatives.

The mainstream views and projections have largely affected the interpretation and construction of age old terms and concepts. A very large dose of discernment is needed with the additional attempt of man to access his logical mind to exercise reason.

Too often there is the immature tendency to go with the general understanding, viewpoint or collective thought process without independent research or exploration. Man often treats knowledge as an acquisition that must be found in text, books or other external sources. The beginning of knowledge is never himself, but always sourced in something or someone outside him.

The cumulative effect often results in short-sightedness which leads to lack of understanding of the whole. Man's vision goes no further than that which his outer eyes could see and his brain record, analyse and recall. His god mind remains dormant for want of use. Have you ever wondered why, in the days when the Master Teacher[52] walked the earth, that many could not comprehend the teachings in the parables without explanation? Apart from a general un-readiness on their part, it is because they wanted to be told that which was truth rather than think and digest through their god minds, and seek answers from within. There is still in large a culture of "outer reality", meaning seeking outwardly for truth.

---

[52]   The Christ

Man needs to expand the horizon of his thinking, his thought patterns and structures. It is through his desire that he will begin to see concepts in a different light as the God light shines on his understanding, taking him beyond the limits of accepted mortal abilities and showing him the way to a more erudite form of thinking. It is the latter that will lead man to the truth, and it is the truth that will bear him to his freedom that he may live his life in knowing and not in doubt.

Many espouse good intentions but have been sorely misled, and have in seeking to follow the blind, themselves become blind to the truth necessary to direct the course of their journey. Misinformation often flows from misinterpretation.

I wish to give you an example that will illustrate the lesson. A very well used term flouted by new agers in your world is that man must "BE" and in so being resist "Doing". In the state of "Being" man "IS". Does it not have a rather poetic sound? Yet, the meaning attached to the phrase "To BE" or "Just BE" is a rather cynical juxtaposition of man's limited influences, consciousness and knowledge, with copious yet varied interpretations.

Meanings have been prescribed to the phrase which bears little resemblance at all to its profound connotation.

To BE is a state which finds its origin in the God light, the ONE consciousness, of which all are a part.

To BE means, that you must be like God through the reflection of your inner god. Be the God within.

To BE entails being your true self by living your knowing, understanding and truth.

To BE is to allow the spirit within you to champion your thoughts, actions and works.

To BE is to aim for mastery over and of self, so that, you gain ascended status and move into Christ consciousness.

I use the word "aim" as it is impossible for most, to live in consistent alignment with the ONE and in so doing "BE".

Being, requires a great deal of commitment, mental and spiritual effort on your part. Which part of this explanation suggests that to BE requires inaction, inertia or apathy? Can you BE without doing? It may appear so but in fact it is not so. Let us take the example of you in quiet communion with your God self. Through your connectedness you experience divine communion and though it appears that you are just being, you are most times down loading higher rebalancing energies and accessing information from a higher source. When the communion ends you feel rejuvenated, centred and primed. Through that state of communion you were actively being refuelled.

Certainly you must cultivate the ability to be still so that you can forge inner connections, but this stillness must not be confused with "Being". In order that you may BE, you must know how to be still, so that, you may be taught what it means to BE.

When you can be the god within, you will reflect serenity and balance.

God is ever creating from a point of stillness. HE IS, **YET,** HE DOES. So too, must you. You are on an ascending journey, and this requires constant doing on your part, for progress will only be achieved through thoughtful action.

When you have attained certain mastery you will find it easier to be the love essence that God IS. You will understand that love is always in action through doing, be it through a thought, energy projection or positive gesture towards another.

293

To BE is uplifting and venerating and demands being in and of service to others. When you seek to "BE or you are "Being", you will find yourself propelled to take whatever positive action needs to be taken. Action that is not consonant with your desire will take you no further in your "being".

You must BECOME—BE COME like God to Be like HIM or Be ONE WITH HIM. "Become" is loaded with active intent and action. Do not be misguided that it is easy to BE, for you must go through the lessons and training to acquire the tools. You must be able to live in a state of connectedness with your Source and All, to BE.

Do not allow anyone to marginalise or downgrade the importance and necessity of the effort and discipline it requires to BE. Most cannot comprehend its significance.

Be the word of God instead of interpreters of the word. You shall be able to accomplish this when you know God and HIS truth. Even so, being the word means living it and there is no insouciance when one lives the word of God.

All thinking should flow from your god mind, for only then will you be guided how to BE and what to do in furtherance of "being".

The "meaning" must always bear the Truth and the Truth need not be interpreted, just known.

THE VOICE

The voice within often speaks but is seldom heard in the consciousness of its receiver. You have been programmed to hear that which is external through your outer physical ears. The various noises that you are subjected to on your plane of existence contaminate your ability to listen in silence and to silence. That which is on the outside creates confusion and hampers the ability of your spirit to have a voice in your lives. It is this voice in priority to all others that you should be attentive to, for this is the voice which will offer wisdom, truth, discernment, clarity and reason.

This voice is in fact, the voice of the inner god whose utterances are in fact directives which will enable you to secure an understanding, and greater knowledge of your place, purpose and role. It is the hidden wealth you seek during your sojourn on earth. Seldom do you start your exploration within, and there lies your error in judgment. The journey to find yourselves, your motivations, your passion, your purpose, your root, must always as a matter of course commence inwardly. It is the inward journey that provides the petrol which sustains the outward journey. It is the place you go to when you need to refill your engine, so that, you may continue through your life experiences in a knowing way. Many journey outwardly with an empty gas tank. They are not filled from within and therefore seek to sustain themselves by that which is external to them. The external always becomes spent. This engenders discontent which inevitably leads to a hungering for more; the more, being, the material.

There are those who consciously choose not to go inwardly, for they do not believe that anything exists there. Their entire lives gravitate around a limited understanding that conjures mental pictures of greatness, achieved through the out workings of material wealth. This is how they define themselves and present themselves to the world. They form fixed views as to what is required in order to achieve a name for themselves in the world. Frequently they seek to achieve recognition as someone, through the gaining of things, be it money, power or fame.

Yet, their inner coffers are empty, for they refuse to give their inner being (the truth of their identity) a say in their lives. Many decline to answer the call of their inner promptings or merely pay lip service to it. Their lives become either that of a speeding train whose brakes have malfunctioned, or a defective train which makes gradual moves then comes to a standstill for lack of fuel; all because that inner voice is ignored or buried deep below the noise and clutter within the human ego mind. The voice of the ego seeks supremacy and is the voice most listened to and followed. The ego seeks to show off its grandeur through the arrogance of all knowing, and in some cases seeks to assume its rightful place by its measure against the elitist barometer.

Your whole journey on your plane is meant for you to find yourself through inner awareness and discover your most potent sword and shield, being your inner power derived from knowing that God resides within you, and that it is HIS voice and guidance that will assist you in forging a life that is spirit worthy and fulfilling. When you can hear that inner voice, should you decide to follow its directions, you shall find that your path will appear clear. Even though there may be inevitable bumps along the way, the voice within shall always show you how to surmount them, or how to see them for the value they have in teaching you the lessons you need to learn as you journey towards wholeness and mastery.

The voice within always speaks truth and offers balanced perspectives and guidance. It is not there to fuel your ego or to provide unconditional support in your effort to assert your "rightness". It is there to guide and to teach, that through your earthly life you may learn to adopt its voice as your voice, its wisdom and mastery as yours, so that, you can live and be as you were meant to.

If you could spare moments in your days to clear the inner clutter and invite your friend within to speak, you shall hear most clearly and you will begin to know the difference between your inner voice and your outer voice (which is controlled predominantly by ego). You will develop a harmonious relationship with your spirit. You will live your life within the aura of higher understanding and shall constantly effort to extend yourselves to maintain communion with the Source.

To have a voice you must find your voice, that which is real and enduring. It is your inner voice that will transform your outward journey and affect the course of your life on earth.

Be Still!
The voice of greatness speaks
Heard only in religious silence of mind's ear.
Be Still!
The face of greatness shines
Seen only in the light of searching eyes.

SPIRITUAL MILEAGE

The earth is in the throes of her final revolution around your sun as the cycle races to an end.

She is akin to an athlete who agrees to complete many cycles around an extensive perimeter. She keeps going regardless of the heat, the dehydration, the pain, the sweat, the physical weariness and the bombardment of negativity sourced by others along the way.

She is limping, but she is going to make it across that finish line, for she knows that there are many who hold high and great expectations of her. She is not distracted by any surrounding events. She is beginning to accelerate, for she can see the white line, a prism of pure light awaiting her. Even through her aches she can smile, for she knows that she is soon to claim her freedom.

What is the lesson here for you? Do you merely rejoice in her choice and the direction which she has taken, or can you see the run she has had to make to get to this point? She has carried for aeons the weight of mankind upon her back, and has made many cycles with you all. She has been grounded under the burden of too many people, yet, she has never given up on you or sought to relieve herself, of you, deliberately.

She agreed to undertake this task, so that, you too might make the run to find and grow your spirit. Was it worth it? Was her journey in vain? She can account for her mileage; can you account for yours? How far, how long and how much effort have you put into your journey to achieve spiritual mileage? How much mileage in spirit have you covered? This is measurable by the level of attunement you have attained to the spirit of God within you, and the level of mastery you have attained over yourself. I am posing questions to you at this time for all will be required to assess themselves; none shall be excused from this process. The time of balancing is here. Each soul will account for the measure of his/her growth, for it is this that will earn each his/her next assignment.

There can be much joy in the journey, yet, without a goalpost there is little point, as you become lost in your path, devoid of purpose.

Every moment counts in your resolve to persevere to the very end, so that, you can elevate yourself spiritually. Those who are confronting hurdles must strive to overcome, just as your earth has overcome hers. Remember, the greatest development at soul level takes place through the experiencing and managing of obstacles. This is not a time for complacency in the unfolding of your light, but pro-activity. See the obstacles, whether they are created within you or by outer circumstances, as the facilitators of your unfolding. Bless the hurdles on your path, for if transcended they add to your achieved mileage.

Blessed are you children, of the most High. Know however, that you are not merely children. You bear the grandeur of spirit within and must seek to be the grandeur of spirit. How many more cycles must you complete to achieve this? Let the evaluation begin.

I come to give you the push and encouragement you need so that you can reach the finish line at a respectable level of spiritual achievement.

30

THE ARCHANGELS

"Enter into the fold where truth abides and
Godliness condenses into a flow of perfection."
Archangel Zadkiel

ARCHANGEL SACHIEL

"Linger not in the current fields, for we have ploughed for your use new grounds wherein you can sow seeds founded on the fulcrum of love and light that your harvest may yield abundance."

Redefine yourselves and Reach out

Listen with raptured attention. The moments peel away to create new and exciting possibilities. Lean towards us and surrender your hopes and dreams. Allow us to introduce to you the fruit of healthy purpose, that your cravings may be altered to serve virtues of men, in truth and delight.

The offerings are many at this time as man is being reintroduced to the feral nature of spirit. The passion of spirit is asserting itself as many have tasted of its fruit and are indulging in its honest fare. Cradled in the ambience of spirit's consuming energy, you shall plough ahead in certitude to uncover your life's purpose. This doing shall avail you the very object of your livelihood, for you shall soon know that a life without purpose does not exist.

The purpose I speak of is trimmed in a higher frequency and chants of divinity. The purpose is in truth your cosmic duty; duty to God and duty to man combined in the initiative of spirit to foster your inherent talents and skills, to be directed in divergent ways to create harmony in the world. Man must graduate from studentship to mastership. Your world needs more masters to lead the students out of the bondage of infancy into a higher thought system which will elevate the earthly status.

The Angels extend their hands at this moment to all who willingly extend theirs, that they may be lifted from the confusion of their thinking into a world where clarity and truth exists.

The tempers of earthly experiences can cause emotional drudgery, but this need not be as the Angelic realm is at hand to teach you how to escape what you may deem inevitable. We can only offer, never intrude. You must desire change to take positive action. Your visible world cannot alleviate your fears or sustain the comfort you yearn for. The invisible realm can, and will offer the support and energy that will help you to conquer the fear which dwells within and show you the way to true happiness.

We shall teach you that you are in fact never alone, and even though you may not be spiritually ready to embrace your true nature, we the Angels can show you the way to receive the higher guidance you need, to overcome. We work in the sphere of pure light. We come not in our name, but to fulfil the Creator's will for HIS children. We will gently hold your hands and lovingly lead you forward, always with kindness and understanding.

It is not the nature of the Angels to command or to even tell you what you should or should not do. We simply guide in truth and love, and offer higher insights to assist your understanding of events which may beset your journey through life. In so doing, you begin to learn the higher ways and re-accustom yourself to an expansive thinking.

We offer friendship and companionship. When you develop a relationship with us, we are at your side to tend to your cares and needs as best as possible. The more you seek us the more we tender to you. There is a saying in your world that you become like the people you associate with. Accept our hands in friendship. Let us take this journey with you and offer wise counsel and guidance throughout your life, and you may find that in time you will assume the qualities and attributes of the Angels. There will in the maturity of time be sufficient Angels populating your world to create dynamic change.

ARCHANGEL RAZIEL

"Release the rigid ways of thinking that have bolded your lives for aeons. Command that the portals of your mind open to accept and receive new data which will cause an elevation in understanding, and uplift you to experience the cosmic forces of your origin."

Banishment of Mysteries

Mysteries are the curtain behind which the truth resides. Compendious wisdom palpitates in the heart of the holder of mysteries. What is mystery, but the barrier between ignorance and knowledge? The genesis of mysteries finds its origin in the un-evolved aptitude to comprehend the dynamism of creation. Creation originates from the light within the Creator's mind, and all things created manifest energy which has coalesced into matter. Even that, which is absent to the eye, finds its formulae in energy. The answer to mysteries lies in a deeper understanding of energy symbols that run through the circuits of the universal mind.

The term mystery is comparative, in that, what you in 3rd dimension may consider inexplicable may be viewed as mundane by your brethren in higher dimensions of light. It simply becomes a matter of spiritual awareness.

That which you term inexplicable is discoverable through discernment of truth. The pulpit of the higher mind must be sought to attend to the deciphering of unexplained experiences or events. It would be catastrophic if man is to allow mysteries to cloak the very truth which can align him to the cause of freedom. If energies are channelled in a pertinacious way, the curtain of mysteries will fall apart.

Mysteries are the mould which man creates in denial of truth, and are needless voids which must be replaced by understanding and knowledge. I am not indicating here that man deliberately shuns the truth. It is his subconscious that speaks a litany of programmed messages which engages man to see the mist rather than the sturdy tree of truth, behind, what appears to be impermeable. His innocuous vision cannot glean the whys wheres and hows. He therefore assumes the very perplexity of that which he seeks to understand.

The unravelling of mysteries begins with a strident arousal of desire to know truth in a thing, an event or experience. The voice of that which is mysterious to man calls out for resolution, so that, the floodlight of truth may permeate the understanding of man's mind, and pieces of the illusive puzzle found and scripted into reality. When a mystery can be solved the real becomes clear, and that which is engendered is clarity of vision, and reality of that which is natural and original.

I have been known to be the receiver and custodian of divine secrets. Much folklore has been created around my identity. I too, have been charged in mysterious and enigmatic energies as one who is beholden of secrets. WE of the Angelic Kingdom work through revelation of truth and offer such to those who seek. WE are higher dimensional beings of pure light in service to the ultimate Source of All. The truth will always find itself springing from the open well. Truth is an offering available to all. No secrets sojourn in truth. Truth is the illuminating presence of the Divine. How can one believe, that the Divine desires to have the truth of HIS very existence and ways cloistered behind a curtain of mystery?

God holds no secrets from HIS children. HE is all knowledge and perfect wisdom. If only you shall seek HIM you shall find that in truth mysteries are limited conceptual creations of man's perception. What man cannot understand he deems mysterious.

Man has cast the net of his thinking in the shallow waters of his outer senses. How can he therefore, consume of the truth which lies in the deeper waters of the living God Mind resting within his very presence.

There are in truth no mysteries, only a temporary divide. As man grows in spiritual awareness and begins to feel the caress of enlightenment, he will courageously travel into the deeper waters of his soul, and draw visions extraordinaire which will rehabilitate his mind to understand intricacies from higher dimension. He will purpose his life to serve the wisdom of his soul and will never again dwell in the realm of the mysterious.

Man on his transient sojourn on earth plane will come to understand that not all that is inexplicable must be deciphered, but he must choose the mysteries which demand understanding and those which will augment his spiritual progress and prowess.

What of the mystery of a man's soul? Its virtuous voice calls for attention that man may seek to know himself. His soul is the carrier of his divinity. For those who did not understand this I have just clarified a mystery. It holds the seed of man's supremacy. All men have the ability to connect with their immortal soul if they so choose, for the soul is their beginning. It chants wisdom and can direct man to discover his immortality, his purpose and his perfection. Wisdom is the carrier of truth—the very answer to life's untenable mysteries. If wisdom be the prefect of your soul, then surely you must have the answer to all of life's mysteries.

The price of your soul's freedom is the removal of the jacket of mysteries conceived in your thoughts and projected as a belief.

Resolve with me now to banish the riddle of mysteries through the attainment of knowledge. Though you may find the process gradual, once you have found the key, the answers will be unlocked to the freedom of light. The bestowal of light shall illuminate your understanding and bring you into harmony with God's creation.

Knowing vs Sensing

You are the holder of all knowledge. Yet, you often seem to look elsewhere in the hope that you shall be filled. It is true that in your dimension there are many libraries of information, some physical; yet, there is a store house of spiritual knowledge in the realms of spirit which can neither be seen nor accessed in a physical way.

There is a cosmic perspective that is lacking in your physical world amongst the majority. There are disparities in understanding, and also differences in your consideration of the nature of truth.

Man has in many ways carved his truth without reference to his Source. Hence, he continuously seeks on the outside. Should he seek from his Source, then gradually there will be dispensation of truth. Man must come to know that truth is derived from knowing; not from sensing what the five senses tell him is truth.

The five senses are not in harmony with the inner senses which know truth. There is a disparity that must be bridged. You cannot naturally depend on the outer senses to tell you truth, for what you deem as truth is often an interpretation thereof. You do not have all the information from which to form your conclusion.

Knowledge descends from your higher mind, yet, it requires you to ascend within to access it. It requires you to transcend the limits of your physical understanding in your search for higher truth. In fact, the higher truth is who you are. It is what you are. It is not separate from you save in your consciousness. An expanded view is required to gain knowledge. I speak of an inner view that gives you the "inside information". The inside information is that which will direct you to truth.

The beliefs held by many in your world tend to be inherited from others. You are taught certain things and you become programmed to believe those things. It provides the framework for your life and thinking.

It therefore unsettles you when someone comes your way to impart information that runs counter to what you have been programmed to believe. So whom do you believe?

Where do you get the truth from? Do you adhere to your long held patterns of thinking and beliefs or do you seek validation from your Higher self. The fact that the majority may believe in something does not make it truth.

Your journey on the earth plane is to discover the real you, so that, you can begin to harness the light of all knowing and truth which reside at your core, and translate that in a working way to assist you and others on your journey.

It takes a brave person to seek truth, notwithstanding the discomfort that may result from the reactions of others. Truth always bears light. It cradles the highest intent and leads to comfort in knowing that you are your creator and that your destiny is within your creation. You are the driver on your journey.

Knowledge will bring comfort and resoluteness in spirit as you embody the truth, and that cannot be violated. Should you append yourself to the ONE within you from whom you are not separate, knowledge will begin to flow like an endless river without a brook. You will begin to live in the field of inspiration where you are continuously motivated to create. No obstacles can stall you, for you have your bearings, and the coordinates have always been the same. The regency of your inner light is your directive.

When your senses tell you something you assume its directive. So, if the outer activity creates a sensory discomfort, you are directed to think that something is wrong. You allow your senses to rule your interpretation, perception and response. As much as you have been programmed, you can take control of self and re-programme your thinking.

It may be difficult to conceptualise or understand what is being said here if you are seeking to use your brain to interpret it. What you do when you use your brain is that you begin to compare what is told to you with what you think you know, which is really information stored through the observed effects of your senses. You are not integrating the new information, as you have nothing to measure its veracity against. That is because you cannot measure true knowledge. It just is. It cannot be compared to what you have stored in your brain. You can only know the truth of the information given if you receive that validation from your higher mind.

You say that knowledge is power, yet, what type of power are you seeking after? Is it your natural inbred power or is it an assumed power to be earned through the collection of information that will give you a boost in your physical world. All are powerful through the inner circuitry of their god mind. There is no one with superlative power, save you. You cannot be more powerful than your fellow man or vice versa.

You cannot sense knowledge; you can only know it; not through conveyance by others, but through conveyance by the real you—your higher mind. In truth, convictions should be premised in knowledge, and knowledge should be the gateway to a truly meaningful life, where the power of your spirit becomes your anchor, and your physical world assumes a cosmic vibration.

ARCHANGEL URIEL

"You who are called in service hold the vision for tomorrow; you are the architects of the future and the builders of the new earth. See that the foundation of your vision is balanced in the light of cosmic knowing that your creations henceforth shall be purposed for the highest good of All."

Solitude

The nature of solitude is the nature of stillness. The rhythm of silence is that which penetrates the Mind to download vectors of higher knowledge.

The ambivalence of stillness and motion mirrors the causal connection to the effectual creation (Cause and Effect). This simply shows that the effect is created through motion from a point of stillness. If you truly wish to create you must find your solitude, that point of stillness within you, so that, you may through the light of inspiration (gifted through the Mind), express the desire which the light starts to fashion in your envisaged creation. Can you see that it is from solitude that the motion of light is discovered, and you are now able to use this motion as a tool for manifestation?

If you desire to find your power you must find your point of stillness.
If you desire answers to life's questions you must find your point of stillness.
If you desire to create you must find your point of stillness.
If you desire to find God you must find your point of stillness.
If you desire to know God you must find your point of stillness.
If you desire to ascend you must find your point of stillness.

Stillness is the library within the Mind. See "Solitude" as a location within the greater locale of the God Mind. It is that place which you must access and gain entry so that you may be able to educate yourself. This is the meeting place with your cosmic mind. This is where you interact at a subliminal level, where your consciousness expands into a cosmic reality; where learning is ensconced on the cushion of universal spirit.

This is your spawning ground, where you merge and marry with your cosmic identity to give birth to different dimensions to you. See yourself as a multi-tiered being who multiplies after each union with your cosmic counterpart. This is where your servicing takes place, where the moulding starts and where you become complete.

When you hear the call of "Solitude" I implore you to answer, for this is a cosmic call from your Creator friend WHO knows that it is time to merge for your greatest good. As you merge with your cosmic identity your consciousness becomes impregnated, yet, you experience a sense of lightness as you leave the sedentary portals of the flesh to experience the silent manoeuvrings of your soul. You are then home. Home is that place where comfort and nurturing abounds. It is that place where you are never alone, always looked after and guided. Can you see the great security which "Solitude" offers you? This is your point of rejuvenation and respite. Are you now impelled to experience that place of abject bounty, the storehouse of all your treasures?

If you can surrender your conscious mind to the solitude of the God Mind, you shall find that the wisdom of truth shall pirouette its way into your consciousness, and you become one step closer to knowing and experiencing God. Man spends many lifetimes trying to find God. If only he will accept that God is the silent bell within him, he will find his stillness, from which point he can burrow his way through the silence until he clearly hears the chimes of eternity.

A Call for Visionaries

A visionary is someone who has deeper insight that transcends the octave of outer sensory perceptions. Perceptions gained externally cannot be categorised as vision. They are merely a reproduction of what your physical eyes see and record in wave motion in your brain, to be recalled at a later time.

Visionaries are cosmic in making. All ensouled beings have the divine gift of vision, being inner vision. Visionaries are those who have the power and ability to see from within and are ably guided by their inner senses. Those inner senses can only be accessed through a connection with the true you—the soul. The soul is that which contains the inner senses, linked through the seat of the mind. Inner vision is not of the physical and therefore cannot be accessed in the same way as the outer senses can. In fact, your outer senses work involuntarily for you. For example, once your eyes are open you will see, observe and record impressions and images through your physical sight.

Activating your inner vision takes effort and discipline on your part. It requires you to access the "Source" of all knowing within you, and that Source is not physical in nature or what we call matter in motion. It is all that is "STILL".

When man is able to access his inner vision, he will see his true nature and realise that there are no boundaries or limits, and that he is in essence Light. His innate wisdom will be awakened and he will find himself living in a higher dimension within himself, whilst partaking of the world surrounding his physical perceptions to meet his needs, necessary for a physical existence. His inner vision will direct him to the truth of whom he is and who God is. His inner wisdom will magnetically align him with cosmic awareness and truth, so that, he may bring all that he truly is into the physical and transform the physical into all that is spiritual.

A visionary is one who sees through his god vision; he has the sight of God. He sees that which God sees. When he can "SEE", he will "KNOW".

Your world is filled with those who call themselves visionaries, yet, they are merely seers. Your world does not need prophesiers of what tomorrow will bring in the lives of men. Your world needs men and women with God vision who will direct others to uncover their vision, so that, the world can finally see the truth and consciously bring forth the Kingdom of God on earth.

There are so many of you who believe that to "foresee" is vision. It may be a type of vision, but not the calibre needed to change man's thinking and the world.

Visionaries see the needs of the world, as required to raise it to the status of God consciousness. They utilise their inner vision and knowing to assist the world in its journey towards cosmic awareness.

Only God has vision, and when you can find and free your God self, you too will truly see and know.

You all have the competency to uncover your vision through self aloneness and communion with the God incarnate. When you desire to see and to know, and your passion clings to all that is true, you shall see. However, I must warn you that inner vision is nowhere close in resemblance to that which you perceive with your outer physical eyes. Your inner vision is more of a knowing that comes through the all knowing light of God which flashes as inspiration within, and downloads to you that which you seek to know.

You cannot therefore through inner vision record that which you see, for you shall not actually see anything save for light. You shall however come into the knowing. That is why the product of inner vision cannot be reproduced for the purpose of providing others with proof. It can merely be recorded as is given to you. When you come into the knowing, you shall see the Light, and your way or path then becomes clearer. There will be an instinctive knowing of truth that is non-transferable. Man must know truth, for no matter how many times it is given to him, he will not know it unless he receives inner validation for it through his god mind. In other words, he must see it for himself through the knowing.

Inner vision is a resource which cannot be borrowed, bought or leased. You hold the key to inner vision. Your ability to see from within is your treasured asset, for therein lies the light of wisdom which bringeth truth and freedom.

I exhort you to acknowledge that inner sensory perception is equally, if not, more important than outer sensory perception, for it is the former that will provide the directions back to your Source. Accept that you are all capable of being visionaries through the sovereign beings that you are. You must release the culture of wanting others to see for you, or teach you what they know. You must harness your powers to see and know what God sees and knows. When you can experience this you will have started to liberate your true self and emerge into your God power. You will assume a new glow, that of illumination, and others will be drawn to you.

True visionaries walk the humble path, for they see into God's mind and live within HIS Kingdom. They will use the power of their vision to uplift others and guide them home. They will never seek to wear the crown of fame or aggrandizement; neither will they revere themselves or seek to be revered. They will in Godly fashion serve in humility whilst teaching that empowerment is derived from the intangible, invisible receptacle of one's god mind. Visionaries bear an intrinsic power birthed from all knowingness. Only those who can truly see will gain knowledge, and in time experience what it means to be omnipotent.

As you grow in cosmic awareness you will assume the mantle of visionaries. The era that is now dawning must be populated with those who appreciate and recognise the power of inner vision. It will take visionaries to change the face and meaning of your world. Seek ye the vision of God to be thine own, and you shall be shown the way to that portal of greater awareness.

You are all visionaries in the making. Why look for the treasure on the outside when the power you seek lies right within you. Let your inner vision be your guide and empowerment, for it is this vision that underlies your destiny and that of your planet.

The Necessary Pilgrimage

I bring today a new perspective to the concept of Pilgrimage. You see Pilgrimage as a journey to foreign and far places well esteemed for historical holy events. Many travel long distances to places well documented as being the holding places where epic events manifested.

The question is, why does man feel the need to partake in pilgrimages? Reasons may vary from seeking inspiration to discovering one's self, the need to experience "holy" energy, participating in re-enactments or just being present where renowned figures walked, worked or lived. The enjoyment or enrichment which man may receive from such pilgrimages is by no means undervalued. Some pilgrimages may have indelible impact on those who participate. The truth however is, comparatively speaking, physical pilgrimages yield little in respect of mortal transformation. It becomes a story for one to tell later on rather than an experience that has profound and enduring results.

I am here to enlighten you to another view. Your mortal sojourn does indeed have a spiritual bias. It is intended that during your incarnation you will discover your true self, being the God of you, your authentic identity, and cultivate a relationship with the God incarnate. A spiritual evolution will begin which will enable you to be placed on your spiritual path, using the physical body as a vehicle to attain higher consciousness.

The whole purpose of your life on earth is to re-discover your link to God and to seek inner guidance as to how HE fits into your purpose on earth. Many times you have heard that the earth provides a learning ground where you can establish yourself as a God-being and seek and earn God mastery.

You may certainly seek inspiration from past events and even benefit from the recollection or the witnessing, but observation of what has transpired in times past will seldom provide the food for learning, necessary for you to discover your identify and live your purpose. That can only be accomplished through the taking of an "inner pilgrimage". As children of God you bear holy terrain within you. It is this terrain that you must necessarily traverse as you take that pilgrimage from the physical dimension of your being to the spiritual essence—your soul's source.

This inner pilgrimage offers a wealth of opportunities as you journey to re-discover your "Source". You will have to transcend familiar terrain of the physical, and breach barriers to higher understanding before you are able to begin the exploration of the celestial part of you. This is a wondrous pilgrimage to take. It can last as long as you desire it to. As you journey inwards the path can become difficult at times, in that, there may be impediments along the way that will slow your journey or discourage further progress. Yet, it is the most rewarding journey you shall ever take. This travel will cost you nothing, except time, energy, desire and love.

You will become re-acquainted with knowledge well known to spirit, which re-awakens within you as your journey continues. You will meet along the way many who are willing to guide you deeper and deeper into your true consciousness, that you may eventually find your dwelling place in a domain which offers you complete balance, love and light. Never will you be a lonely pilgrim, for when you initiate the inner pilgrimage you enter into a flow of energy that if sustained will eventually fulfil you. You will come to know the great life force you hold within, and this will usher feelings of completeness.

Where does the pilgrimage eventually lead you to? Simply, the Kingdom of God which dwells within each of God's children; a non physical arena where bliss, inner harmony, purity and unclouded love exist; where indescribable peace reigns and where you will glow in the knowledge and comfort of your immortality.

I trust that you are able to understand now how necessary the inner pilgrimage is, for you cannot discover yourself or align with all that is holy unless you find and know "you". You can only accomplish this through the taking of that inner journey, the one true and decisive pilgrimage that each child of God will have to take before he/she reunites with the Source.

ARCHANGEL MICHAEL

"Truth prevails above all things; it questions nothing for it knows itself. It weighs its anchor only in the Divine—its supernatural habitat, and is self sustaining. Seekers of truth must seek the Divine, for herein lies your immortal persona, your liberty, your truth, your life."

You are the ONE and the ONE is you

Behold I am here with you in every way. Know that when you seek to connect with me I am already here. I will be your very breath, the very love and joy you feel at the very moment of unification. I ask that you know me of the ONE mind. Do not look for me in visions or apparitions, for I am pure energy.

We bring you into a new conditioning, a new frame of thinking and spiritual orientation that requires only the knowing and dealing with spirit; that is energy in its purest form.

There is much difficulty associated with the achievement of this thought pattern, as your training has caused you to look for things in matter. Allow your desire for ONENESS to guide you into a higher awareness of what that means, so that, you may begin to see from within, the "Primary Source" as you, and you the "Primary Source". It is energy in its purest that must be known, not perceived, and it is this very energy that you must align with. In the naturalness of its being you will find what you seek, your presence, your truth, your all.

As the pure energy of spirit unfolds within, you begin to transcend the inhabited world, and journey deeper and deeper into the realm of great familiarity. Light bulbs will blink and then begin to shine, as the inner you, true self, God, enters to direct your thinking. It is only through your allowance, your permission, that this magical release takes place.

You will then begin to experience the energetic opening and expansion of thy heart auricle, and the transition from self to ONENESS. The energy within the heart takes on a tubular form, almost hose-like, and it begins its outpouring of scintillating Love; innocent, pure and whole. It then extends in circular fashion to encompass everyone and everything in your periphery of vision. As you enter new segments of inner unfolding and experience, the feeling enhances, and a sensation of peace overtakes and pure understanding dawns.

This awakening will sharpen your focus, and you will begin to relieve yourself of outdated patterns of behaviour and thinking. You shall release all judgement as you come to understand that you are All.

Through your journey in physical projection you will come to an appreciation of the ONE, and in so doing work to achieve mastery over yourself, that you may live in alignment with the ONE. This is not a new message or a new concept, just an expression of what we have brought to you time and time again. Yet, the learning is in the repetition, for many must have multiple experiences before the lessons are learnt. The teaching is always brought in purest love to help you on your journey out of the illusion of the world into the reality of the One, so that, you may come face to face with your power, the very source of infiniteness—YOU.

Love your brothers and sisters, love all life force in your created world, for you are them in another projection and they are you. To project hatred, anger, reviling or condescension towards another is a reflection on you, for your brother is but a mirror of you and you of him. What you do to him, you do to yourself.

Has it become apparent that you hurt yourself when you hurt another? Let love be your fulcrum, your inspiration, your influence and your purpose. Live the love that you are, so that, all barriers of illusion may become extinct.

If you know love and how to love, you will not feel or think hatred. God is PURE LOVE. In the seeking of ONENESS with God and in the knowing of God as yourself, love is the key that will successfully open the portals that gain you entry to the ecstasy that is God. Love must be manifested in your creations and underlie every response. It is the very breath of life. It is the circle that represents the whole. It is your beginning and your end.

You will know when you find yourself in that flow of the ONE. Love will glow from within. Love transforms you into the light that you really are. You will begin to live that which you feel.

Though there appear to be many, your inner thinking and sight will know only ONE, for your perceptions will gradually disappear, and your knowing will replace it. You will see the light of spirit, within all.

Do not be impatient for the unfolding. Know that the frequency of your desire will determine the measure and timing of the experience. Enjoy the expanded feeling of ONENESS as it occurs.

Greater shifts are currently occurring within many during the period of great awakening. In many this awakening will trigger a unified consciousness, and thus will begin another segment of experience towards wholeness.

The move towards ONENESS is the intention which underscores what you term ascension. You must begin to chart the lessons, so that mankind will understand in truth his origin and nature. The Law of ONE can only be taught as the reality of God's Kingdom. Each of his own effort and desire must seek it, for only then will the spirit within man work to release the jewels that will in time enable him to experience and be the ONE.

Hazel Sinanan

The Key is truth, The Burden of the Lie, The Way home

You are the mould, the creative essence, yet, you are the whole. There is no disparity and there never can be. Joy is your illumination, being the very light of your existence. The truth lies only in you for where else can it be? You are birthed out of the realms of time and space through a vision and imagining of self. Your soul is the creation. Your body does not exist; it is the simulated effect of Cause. There is only Cause and you will come to know yourself as this. The lesson requires appreciation, for this perfect truth is the only key to liberation of your thoughts which bind you in the world of matter.

There are many keys in the offering but thus far none has opened the door to the Kingdom. Words without understanding, without knowledge drawn from within, can never influence the dynamic that is truth. It is man's budding ego that inspires interpretation of that which is given, for he cannot believe that truth will be given with such ease. He lives within his own dubious sense and projects this always. When the very truth is laid out before him he seeks to dissect it through comparative research rather than through inner exploration.

He has been told where the repository lies, yet, he deviates from the charted path. Very few have been able to see and know the authentic key. It is this key for which all men seek, albeit many unconsciously. This key will loosen the bindings of matter and free your spirit in totality. That is when you shall have your ascension into life, never again to experience mortal death.

The world erects boundaries, yet, you are without boundary. The simplicity of this realisation will propel you to a state of supreme understanding that you are All. You need not be confined to the physicality of time ad space in the dimensional experience of your world. When you can see this through your higher mind, the tenor of your thinking assumes a new reality which conditions you out of the illusion. Every action will be nurtured by that revelation. You become an aspirant through cherished effort, for your newfound being coalesces in its divinity. For you, the illusory curtain behind which you live will part and the feisty hand of freedom pluck you out of the doldrums of lower vibes. As you achieve this "feat" even in earthly expression, you will work with Light to free the soul fragments yet to uncover their light from the bushel of matter.

When you have uncovered the Truth you will renounce the tale that your growth must take place through repeated cycles on the surface of matter. Thus begins the recall, the reclamation of wholeness.

Let no one deceive you, for you are the sword and the armour. Bring forth through resonance the heart of your being that the world of illusion might melt in the heat of that love. For truly your world does not exist; it is a fragment of unreality. When you can see the world for what it is you will know where your place is, and the purpose of the journey in the first place will become paralysed in the staccato of the all embracing truth that you were always home. It is the mind that holds this truth for the senses are obscured by the boredom of lies and cannot allow for revelation. Ponder upon this. Release your mind from bondage; it has been a hostage of the lie for too long.

I tender to thee at this time in your segment, as confirmation, that the lie must die and only the lie. Sin is not a necessity for learning. It is the lie of sin that keeps man chained in the repetition of incarnations. Sin is valueless, its existence unreal. It is illiterate and must be consumed in the fire of spirit. Anarchy is not man's natural state. It is peace. The world cannot offer you peace, for the world is far removed from the reality of God.

If each can acquire the destiny of his soul even on your plane of temporality, the finiteness of that plane will dissolve, and once again merge into the immortalised realm of timelessness.

You need not gamble with your life by playing with the dice until the numbers fall in your favour. It is not a game of luck and chance. Longevity is your cradle; you do not need to earn it, just claim it. We have given you the tools, being the higher teachings. Your efforts will seal the "deal" as you say. I will simply say that you will awaken from the dream and find yourself back home.

Ponder anew the teachings of old; know that the beginning is always the end and can never surpass or enrich the beginning. The chosen path need not be spent in the delirium of sleep and wakefulness until you enter life through awareness eternal. You need not be born into life ad infinitum to experience life. You are life, never to be any richer than when you departed to seek your fortune before returning to ONENESS, for the ONE is unchangeable.

The enjoyment and diversity you experience in different expressions during the mortal sojourn is a current that sugars the senses and breeds the flamboyant thoughts of enhancement. You cannot be enhanced for you are perfection spiritualised. Perfection cannot be touched as it is its own mastery and holds unbridled incomparable beauty.

You are created in perfection and chose imperfection through perceived separation, yet, never through that perception has there been discontinuity in or of your "life", which forever remains in the womb of its origin. The Light, being the ONE Source, has no capacity for being degraded or diminished; neither can it be renewed or revived, cultured or enlivened. It rests in its own peace; it is its own balance.

The Price of Passivity, The Panacea and The Promise

The price of passivity bemoans the silence of progress. This simply means that there is no movement in terms of action, although thoughts may flow in sequence to produce objectives. There are multiple levels of passivity where the lowest speaks not at all in thought or action, but is voiceless, and rest in the maze of inactivity and complacency.

Passivity lacks the dynamism of thought as the majority are happy to allow others to think for them instead of thinking for themselves. Man does not wish to assume responsibility even for thinking. This is the state of many in the mortal world. The usage of one's time is seldom controlled by self, but by others, and analogous to this is that one's thoughts are seldom influenced by self but by others.

It is true that there is greater awakening dawning now, but there is still inadequate motivation of thought to effect major changes in spiritual morale. The density brewed by the dark forces has impacted on the minds of men, and free thinking has been admonished in the wake of those who seek ultimate control. There are very few gods in your dimension, and this I say in light of man's resistance to stand in the power of the god that he is. Those who hold themselves out as gods do not seek to serve the God of All. Just as temperature can be controlled so too is the thinking of man being controlled by those who manipulate his senses, beliefs and thoughts. Passivity has become a by product of indoctrination.

It is easier to be passive and let someone else do all the work, but that is not how you will earn your way out of physicality. You will have to experience again and again the dimension of physical consciousness to learn to think for yourself and through your "self" before you can graduate. The time for passivity is over. It is declared that man must find his voice through active thinking, and seek to create a future that is based on true values espoused in the harmony of spirit. It is time to rise up, not with arms to fight to the death, but rise up in spirit to fight for life. If man can know himself, he will know the resources he holds within which will allow him to reclaim his sovereign status. Man will then actively use his god mind to think and create his reality instead of being subjected to a reality created by others.

Passivity is not synonymous with peace or being at peace with yourself or others. Passivity is an impediment to growth, for inaction scorns progress. Man wonders why he is stuck; it is because he passively accepts the dictates of others and fails to think for himself. Passivity is the antithesis of creativity, the latter being the god instinct.

If you are ensconced in the comfort of passivity, beware of those who speak laudably and loquaciously, yet, whose actions fail to mirror their words.

Become gods of action through inspired thinking, and rise up in spirit to claim your life back, for truly when you are passive you do not live. You exist in the framework created by others without thought, without a say, as you sashay through your incarnation.

Passivity no longer has a place in a planet ordained to ascend. Take up the baton of spirit and rise to claim the glory of your eminence.

APPENDIX 1

CLEARING MEDITATION

The following is a meditation that you can use to clear old paradigms, beliefs, feelings and programming that you might have developed in this life, brought over from past lives or inherited from your parents or ancestors. They are "God programmes" that are untrue, or limiting beliefs that are impeding you from establishing and enjoying a profound relationship with the Creator, WHOM I will refer to as the "god" within you.

The technique I am about to share with you was created by a wonderfully inspiring lady by the name of Christie Marie Sheldon[53]. She uses this technique in her phenomenally successful Manifesting abundance programme. I have obtained her permission to share this technique with you, which I have specifically customised to deal solely with "God programmes" and limiting beliefs regarding God.

Through this technique you will connect to the Light which is ALL THAT IS, in an expanded state, until your consciousness expands beyond the octave of the human form. It is from this place of all possibilities, that we will clear all twisted and mis-qualified energy patterns or programming that have contained and limited your true self for ages. The more you use these energy clearing statements the more you will release the old blockages.

After connecting to the Light and using the energy clearing statements, you are then going to send out energy asking the Universe to help you manifest what you want e.g. *"What would it take for me to know and feel the Creator's love?"*

---

[53]   See christiesheldon.com

The more expanded you become as you connect to the Light the more you will be able to clear. When the old energetic blockages and beliefs are cleared, you are in fact making room for new energy. This new energy is the truth.

Close your eyes and take a few deep breaths through your nose, and release through your mouth. With every out breath feel every muscle in your body relax. Affirm silently three times in your mind "I am free to be who I am".

- With your eyes closed, roll your eyes upward.
- Project your consciousness/energy way beyond your head as far as you can travel upwards, until you can see, sense or feel the Light which is the energy of the Creator. It is safe and permissible to do this.
- See the Light above your crown, and ask the Light to clear away any energies above your head which prevents the natural flow of the primal life force currents into your body. See the old energies dissolving.
- Now, mentally visualise your crown opening up and the pure Light flowing generously in, opening up all your awareness of who you truly are. Ask the Light to open up all your knowing that you may know divine guidance, wisdom and truth when you receive it.
- Ask the Light to come into your third eye and clear all energies that are blocking you from seeing the truth of who you really are. Ask the Light to open up your inner sight and charge this inner sense with the highest vibration possible, allowing you to have true vision.
- Ask the Light to come into your ears and clear any blockages to you hearing the truth.
- Ask the Light to come into your throat clearing any old energies holding you back from speaking and communicating your truth; and manifesting your spiritual desires.
- Ask the Light to come into your heart clearing old hurts, pain, feelings of betrayal, grudges or self judgment, and to replace

it with unconditional love, kindness, generosity, patience and understanding for yourself and others. Ask the Light to open up the chamber in your heart which holds the three fold flame of power, love and wisdom.

- Ask the Light to come into your solar plexus clearing all old and stagnant energies of unworthiness, inferiority, unimportance, egoism and lack of control. Now ask the Light to open up all the authentic energy, allowing you to embrace your sovereign identity as an empowered being.

- Ask the Light to come into your sacral chakra(two inches below your navel) clearing any old feelings of pain and suffering, victimisation and poverty consciousness, and to open up the energy centre allowing you to feel your authentic self, so that, you can take full responsibility for your life.

- Ask the Light to come into your base chakra clearing any old fears you may have about death, any confusion you feel over your gender identity, or any fear you hold of being your true self. Ask the Light to open up new energies, that you may be rooted in a new reality of yourself as an immortal being taking a journey in a physical body.

- Ask the Light to go into your hips, thighs and legs clearing any old energy keeping you stagnated in old patterns.

- Ask the Light to go into your feet and soles like liquid light, flowing all the way into the center of the Earth where it mixes with the crystalline core of the earth; that blissful place which is warm and full of love.

- Ask the Light to bounce all the way back up your feet, legs, thighs, hips and heart.

- Visualise the Light in your heart like a big ball of energy radiating three hundred and sixty (360) degrees from its centre. You are now connected from above and below right in the center of your heart.

- See this energy in your heart radiate and expand around your whole body about ten to fifteen feet all the way around you. You are this pure consciousness.

- Expand your energy past the place you are in, past your city then past your country.
- Take this energy and expand it past the planet, knowing that you are connected to everybody and everything, and it is safe, right and good for you to be here right now doing this.
- Now, take this energy and keep expanding until you pass the solar system, the galaxy and the universe, and find that you are so expanded that you are ONE with All.
- It is from this point that you are going to start to clear the old energies in the form of beliefs, paradigms, programmes etc on all levels of awareness.
- Anywhere and everywhere you feel stuck in your spiritual life for whatever reason, known or unknown, please delete, un-create and de-story across all time, dimensions, space and reality.
- Anywhere in your physical, mental, emotional and etheric bodies, or your mind, where you are holding or storing in any way, mis perceptions, false perceptions or limiting perceptions about your true identity or true self, delete, un-create and de-story across all time, dimensions, space and reality.

Move on now to incorporate any of the applicable clearing statements on the next few pages.

Delete is to remove or erase the old programme so that it is not part of your awareness anymore. Un-create is to remove from existence in any form, the programme. There is not one iota of energy from the programme that will remain. It will have no identity in your awareness. To de-story is to take the story or lie which creates the blockage in the first place. These words are used sequentially to ensure that the false programme, belief or feeling is once and for all obsolete in your awareness, thus making space for light, truth, love wisdom and creativity.

A—Clearing Statements

It is suggested that for each below, you connect to the Light as described in the preceding page and do the clearing statements first, followed by the energy you wish to project to the Universe; so A followed by A1, B followed by B1 etc.

Everywhere I feel that I do not know the Creator or cannot connect with the Creator, I un-create, delete and de-story across all time, dimensions, space and reality.

Everywhere I feel disconnected from the Creator, I un-create, delete and de-story across all time, dimensions, space and reality.

Everywhere I do not know how to be totally connected to the Creator, I un-create, delete and de-story across all time, dimensions, space and reality.

Everywhere I feel I am not good enough, smart enough, spiritual enough or important enough to connect with the Creator, I un-create, delete and de-story across all time, dimensions, space and reality.

Everywhere I have doubts regarding my ability to connect with the Creator, I un-create, delete and de-story across all time, dimensions, space and reality.

If I have made or was forced to make any contracts in my past life or lives to denounce the Creator's existence and or presence within me, I un-create, delete and de-story across all time, dimensions, space and reality.

Everywhere I have been indoctrinated, influenced or taught by others false information or disinformation about the Creator, known or unknown, intentional or unintentional, I un-create, delete and de-story across all time, dimensions, space and reality.

A 1—Projecting to the Universe the energy of that which you wish to manifest

What would it take for me to know the Creator?

What would it take for me to know the truth regarding the Creator?

What would it take for me to know I am always connected to the Creator?

What would it take for me to know that the Creator is totally connected to me?

What would it take for me to know how to be totally connected to the Creator?

What would it take for me to know how to connect to the Creator?

What would it take for me to know that it is safe and possible to connect with the Creator?

What would it take for me to live my daily life feeling totally connected to the Creator?

What would it take for me to see myself the way the Creator sees me?

What would it take for me to feel that I am important to the Creator?

B—Clearing Statements

Everywhere that I feel or believe that the Creator is outside of me or separate from me, I un-create, delete and de-story across all time, dimensions, space and reality.

B 1—Projecting to the Universe the energy of that which you wish to manifest

What would it take for me to know that the Creator is within me?

What would it take for me to know that I can never be separate from the Creator?

What would it take for the illusion of separation to be removed from my consciousness?

What would it take for me to know that I am ONE with the Creator?

What would it take for me to feel ONE with the Creator?

C—Clearing Statement

Everywhere that I feel I am not an infinite being with God potential I un-create, delete and de-story across all time, dimensions, space and reality.

C 1—Projecting to the Universe the energy of that which you wish to manifest

What would it take for me to know that I am spirit first and foremost?

What would it take for me to know that the Creator is limitless and that I too am limitless?

What would it take for me to know that I am Light just as the Creator is Light?

D—Clearing Statement

Everywhere that I feel that I need to suffer to be close to the Creator, I un-create, delete and de-story across all time, dimensions, space and reality.

Everywhere that I feel that I have to die before I can be with the Creator, I un-create, delete and de-story across all time, dimensions, space and reality.

D 1—Projecting to the Universe the energy of that which you wish to manifest

What would it take for me to know and understand that suffering and death does not truly exist?

What would it take for me to know that the Creator is always with me?

E—Clearing Statements

Everywhere that I feel it is not possible to know the Creator or feel the Creator's presence, I un-create, delete and de-story across all time, dimensions, space and reality.

Everywhere I feel that I can't meditate, don't know how to meditate or it is not safe to meditate, I un-create, delete and de-story across all time, dimensions, space and reality.

Everything that is stopping me from relaxing enough to meditate, including any beliefs, doubts or fears within me or anything outside of myself, I un-create, delete and de-story across all time, dimensions, space and reality.

Every part of me that is afraid to let go and just relax, I un-create, delete and de-story across all time, dimensions, space and reality.

Everywhere I have taken on other people's belief that meditation is difficult, I un-create, delete and de-story across all time, dimensions, space and reality.

Everywhere I feel that it is impossible to connect with the Creator through meditation, I un-create, delete and de-story across all time, dimensions, space and reality.

Everywhere I think the Creator does not have time for me and therefore it is not worth trying to connect with HIM, I un-create, delete and de-story across all time, dimensions, space and reality.

Everywhere I don't want to meditate to connect with the Creator because I am afraid to realize my full God potential, I un-create, delete and de-story across all time, dimensions, space and reality.

E 1—Projecting to the Universe the energy of that which you wish to manifest

What would it take for me to know what meditation is in truth?

What would it take for me to know that I can connect with the Creator through meditation?

What would it take for the Universe to lead me to the most perfect person who can teach me how to go about meditating to connect with the Creator?

What would it take for me to know that it is safe and possible to meditate?

What would it take for me to just let go and relax my mind and body totally?

What would it take for me to hear, see or know clear guidance from the Creator within me?

What vibrational energy can I become to hear, see or know clear guidance from the Creator within me?

What would it take for me to receive inspiration from the Creator within me?

F—Clearing Statement

Everywhere that I am afraid of the Creator, I un-create, delete and de-story across all time, dimensions, space and reality.

F 2—Projecting to the Universe the energy of that which you wish to manifest

What would it feel like to live my life without fear and with total faith in the Creator?

What would it take for me to trust the Creator within me?

What would it take for me to know the Creator and the absolute truth about the Creator?

G—Clearing Statements

Everywhere that I feel the Creator is angry with me and will punish me, I un-create, delete and de-story across all time, dimensions, space and reality.

Everywhere that I feel that the Creator has not forgiven me for past deeds, I un-create, delete and de-story across all time, dimensions, space and reality.

Everywhere I feel that I am not deserving of the Creator's forgiveness, I un-create, delete and de-story across all time, dimensions, space and reality.

G 1—Projecting to the Universe the energy of that which you wish to manifest

What would it take for me to know the Creator as Love only?

What would it take for me to know and understand the Creator's perspective on love?

What would it take for me to know and feel the Creator's love?

What would it take for me to know that the Creator loves me unconditionally?

What would it take for me to know that I am worthy and deserving of the Creator's love?

What would it take for me to feel worthy and deserving of the Creator's love?

H—Clearing Statements

Everywhere that I feel that I have disappointed the Creator or will disappoint the Creator, I un-create, delete and de-story across all time, dimensions, space and reality.

Everywhere that I feel I am not completely accepted by the Creator, I un-create, delete and de-story across all time, dimensions, space and reality.

H 1—Projecting to the Universe the energy of that which you wish to manifest

What would it take for me to know and feel that I am completely accepted by the Creator?

What would it take for me to know that the Creator will never abandon me?

I—Clearing Statements

Everywhere that I am angry with the Creator or blame the Creator for my circumstances, or feel that the Creator has betrayed me, I un-create, delete and de-story across all time, dimensions, space and reality.

I 1—Projecting to the Universe the energy of that which you wish to manifest

What would it take for me to accept total responsibility for what I create in my life?

What would it take for me to know the will of the Creator?

What would it take for me to desire to align my will with the Creator's will?

J—Clearing Statement

Everywhere I feel I cannot know or have the truth about all I desire to know, I un-create, delete and de-story across all time, dimensions, space and reality.

J-1—Projecting to the Universe the energy of that which you wish to manifest

What would it take for me to have the highest truth, being the Creator's truth of everything I desire to know in my life?

What would it take for me to know Creator's truth?

What would it take for me to understand what truth feels like?

What would it take for me to know how to access the Creator's truth about everything I desire to know in my life?

What would it take for me to be discerning of the highest truth?

What would it take for me to know the difference between the ego's voice and Creator's voice?

K—Unconditional Love

What would it take for me to live every moment in the highest vibration of unconditional love?

Everything standing in the way of this, I un-create, delete and de-story across all time, dimensions, space and reality.

Any lower density energies that I have allowed into my bodies, lower than the vibration of unconditional love, I un-create, delete and de-story across all time, dimensions, space and reality.

What vibrational energy can I become to live every moment of this day in the highest vibration of unconditional love?

L—Balance and harmony with self

What would it take for me to live every moment in total balance, harmony and peace with myself and the Creator within me?

Everything standing in the way of this, I un-create, delete and de-story across all time, dimensions, space and reality.

What vibrational energy can I become to live every moment in total balance, harmony and peace with myself and the Creator within me?

M—Balance and Harmony with all

What would it take for me to live every moment in total balance, harmony and peace with every life force in God's creation?

Everything standing in the way of this, I un-create, delete and de-story across all time, dimensions, space and reality.

What vibrational energy can I become to live every moment in total balance, harmony and peace with every life force in God's creation?

N—Higher self

What would it take for me to embody more and more of my Higher self's light and energy into my lower bodies and morphogenetic field?

Everything standing in the way of this, I un-create, delete and de-story across all time, dimensions, space and reality.

What vibrational energy can I become to embody more and more of my Higher self's light and energy into my lower bodies and morphogenetic field?

O—Gratitude

What would it take for me to live every single moment in the vibration of gratitude?

Everything standing in the way of this, I un-create, delete and de-story across all time, dimensions, space and reality.

What vibrational energy can I become to live every moment in gratitude?

It is recommended that you incorporate this technique every day, choosing some or all of the clearing statements depending on your needs; so that you enjoy a more profound clearing. During the process you will be releasing old energies and can experience energy around you or energy moving through you. If you feel any discomfort in your body it is simply a sign of resistance, and you should simply direct the Light to that area and see the resistance either blown up or dissolved. Trust that during this process your Higher self knows what you need. You will receive multiple downloads. You may feel tired, teary, energised, lighter or more positive during and after the process. Everyone's experience will differ. Remember perseverance is the key to success, but it is your desire to know the truth of you and manifest the true you that will guarantee the success of this technique. You must be open to the guidance provided by your Higher self and the Universe in response to the energy you project to manifest.

APPENDIX 2

ARCHANGEL MEDITATION

Sit or lie comfortably for the meditation. Mentally ask Archangel Sandalphon to ground you during this meditation. If you are sitting, visualise roots growing from your feet and connecting to the centre of the Earth. Now, imagine light from the centre of the Earth travelling upwards through the roots, up to your feet, then forming a spherical shape around your entire body. You are cocooned in light.

Breathe deeply and slowly through your nose, allowing the intake of air to expand your lungs. Hold this breath for a count of three and slowly release through your mouth. Repeat this breathing exercise three times. As you breathe in and out, imagine every muscle in your body releasing any tension, through a flow of energy through your fingertips and toes.

As your body becomes more and more relaxed, feel a ball of pure light gently enter your mind; and as the light begins to pervade your mind all thoughts begin to dissolve. Your breathing slows down to a more even breath as your mind becomes more and more still as the light fills it. Enjoy this feeling in the present moment. As the light continues to fill every space in your mind, your mind begins to feel expanded. Your mind continues to expand as the light continues to flow within, and you begin to experience a feeling of lightness.

Your mind has become like a large balloon filled with light. As you continue to breathe slowly, the balloon of light expands and expands and expands until it begins to rise. It is safe for you to take this journey as the balloon is protected by a platinum shield of light. There are two Archangels on either side guiding the balloon to its destination. You are completely safe and protected.

As the balloon continues to rise you can feel it expanding, more and more, and you begin to see colourful lights appear within the balloon. The colours of magenta, purple, violet and mauve all swirl together and fill your balloon of light. You have entered the heavenly spheres; and as the balloon continues to expand you begin to see shapes and forms appear in all different patterns, colours and sizes. This is the language of creation. As your eyes become accustomed to the colours and shapes, you feel a sense of familiarity as if you are coming home. The balloon continues to expand and rise higher and higher and higher, and you begin to experience a new reality. This reality is whatever you perceive it to be at this time. Take the time to observe what you see, sense and feel within.

Now, the balloon pauses and you notice an Archangel appear in the balloon. Take a moment to feel the Archangel's presence and notice what he or she looks like. How does the Archangel appear to you? Breathe, and allow the Archangel's presence to fill the balloon. As this slowly happens begin to feel at ONE with the Archangel. Now mentally send a thought to the Archangel. It could be a greeting followed by a question. Wait until you receive a response. Observe what you feel, sense and hear. Mentally, ask the Archangel for a message just for you. Let the thoughts of the Archangel flow into your mind, which is at this time the expanded balloon. You have now received the Archangel's message. If you want the Archangel to give you a hug, ask for it. With gratitude and love, thank the Archangel. You notice that the Archangel has dissolved into the light within the expanded balloon.

You begin to feel the balloon move again. This time it is descending slowly. You continue to observe whatever appears within this balloon as you travel downwards. As it descends, the balloon slowly contracts. The balloon has now returned to where it originally started, but the light remains within it.

This light is now anchored in your mind. It represents your consciousness which in its true form is the expanded balloon you just experienced.

344

Enjoy for a moment the feeling of this light. Know that this light is always there.

Now, bring your awareness back to your physical body. Begin to feel your body once again. Allow your consciousness to return to your body, knowing that, at any time, you can experience an expanded state of consciousness when you desire. You are now fully back in your body and you realise that everything you seek is within your consciousness, your expanded form, being your mind[54]. Even the Angels and Archangels are there, and you can communicate with them in this way anytime you want.

Make a note of what you observed during your journey and the message given to you by the Archangel.

---

[54]   God is light, the Universal Mind and Mind is Light. This Mind holds all knowledge. Your mind is in truth God's Mind. When you can experience an expanded state of consciousness you can tap into all that God knows. All that you seek and wish to know lies within your 'god mind'.

APPENDIX 3

HYPNOSIS MEDITATION TO RELAX AND CONNECT WITH DIVINE SELF[55]

Lay down comfortably on your back with your arms by your side palms facing downwards. Let your feet rest comfortably apart.

Close your eyes and focus your attention on your breathing. Begin breathing slowly and deeply. I want you to take a deep breath through your nose and visualise that you are breathing in light. Hold that breath and let that light fill your entire body, filling every cell of your body. Now breathe out through your mouth and visualise any toxic energies or tension, anxiety and stress being released through that outer breath. Repeat this three times.

Now, I want you to relax your breathing; breathe in through your nose and out through your mouth; and with each breath that you take feel your body relaxing more and more. And you can silently affirm with every out breath, I am relaxed, I am relaxed, I am relaxed.

And you will notice already how relaxed your whole body has become. Perhaps, you can feel it sinking down deeper into the mattress or couch.

---

[55] This hypnosis meditation contains affirmations. Only those who believe the affirmations at the conscious level, and wish to have them reinforced and recalled subconsciously, should use this meditation. Those who do not understand or believe in the affirmations should not attempt this hypnosis meditation as it is not meant to impose any belief on you against your free will.

Your mind is in complete control of your body, including your muscles; so I want you to focus your attention on your head. There is a wave of energy moving now into your head, causing the muscles on your scalp and around your ears to unwind, and it may even feel like your scalp is sliding down. Now the energy is flowing around your face, and as it moves, all the tiny muscles around your eyes, nose, and mouth let go. Your eyelids have become very heavy. And all the muscles in your jaw have become limp, as your jaw sinks down heavy and tired; and your tongue rests gently on the bottom of your mouth. And you are beginning to drift down deeper and deeper, feeling more and more relaxed with every word I speak.

And this wave of relaxation spreads down into your neck, allowing the neck muscles to become loose and free. Feel any stresses and strains disappear now; and you are feeling more comfortable and relaxed as if you are floating and drifting down, floating and drifting down. This wave of energy continues down into your shoulders now, and as the muscles relax, you can feel your shoulders letting go and sinking down.

Now, the energy is flowing down into your chest and the muscles in your chest becomes loose and relaxed, and you notice your breathing becoming easier and even each time you exhale. This wave of relaxing energy moves to your upper back, gently massaging the muscles and releasing any tension, causing the muscles to relax one after the other.

The energy continues to move all the way down into your arms and your arms grow as heavy as lead. As the energy moves to your fingertips imagine any tension escaping through them, just flowing away as you completely relax. You may even feel a tingling sensation in your fingertips. And you soon become aware of a growing peaceful feeling inside; a feeling of calmness and contentment.

And now the energy flows into your abdominal muscles, waist, and the small of your back. As it does, all the muscles there are bathed in relaxing energy and they unwind like a rubber band, letting go.

This wave of relaxing energy is moving down now, into your thigh muscles causing them to soften and become loose and lazy. Notice all the subtle changes taking place as you continue to relax. The energy flows into every muscle in your legs, your calves and feet, relaxing every cell and fibre. As the wave travels all the way down to your toes you are now completely relaxed from the top of your head to the tips of your toes.

Your entire body is now totally relaxed and feels as limp as a rag doll. You are feeling drowsy, and comfortable, and safe and secure; your entire body is now enveloped in a warm cocoon of energy that protects you. Every cell, every consciousness, every nerve and fibre of your body is totally and completely relaxed. You haven't a care in the world right now—nothing else matters but this wonderful feeling of relaxation.

You are now ready to take a journey to a place where you can just enjoy being the real you; where you can commune with your essence in total comfort. As you lay there enjoying this wonderful feeling of complete relaxation, you become aware of a staircase going upwards; a beautiful winding staircase with thick golden banisters on either side and ten steps carpeted in rich ruby red. These are the steps that will lead you to that place of beauty, and serenity, and solitude, where you will find and commune with your essence.

In a moment I would like you to walk up those steps with me and I will count them off for you one by one, and you will find that the higher you go the more relaxed you become, almost as if you are floating upwards. So when you are ready to walk up the stairs I want you to lightly place your hand on the banister and begin to slowly ascend the stairs as I count them off from One-Ten.

One—deeply relaxed and deeply comfortable, **Two**—not a care in the world, drifting upwards and upwards **Three**—feeling so very light almost as if you do not have a body, **Four**—slowly moving higher like a cloud floating effortlessly, **Five**—feeling peaceful and free, **Six**—getting closer and closer to the real you, **Seven**—feeling a new energy bathe you with a feeling of bliss, **Eight**—feeling safe and secure, **Nine**—enjoying the feeling of floating and drifting, drifting and floating to a higher dimension, **Ten**—so relaxed, so at peace as you enter that higher and healthier level of mind.

In front of you is a veil which opens up as you touch it, allowing you entrance. You take a step behind the veil and there you are faced with the most beautiful and serene garden you have ever seen.

This is your special place where you have come to enjoy your true nature. You notice that the garden is bathed in golden white light which comes from above, and as you walk into the garden you are at once enveloped in a new vibration—a vibration of pure love and total peace. I wonder if you notice how free you feel here, light and totally free. The colourful silken flowers bathe your nostrils with its fragrance sending you into an even deeper state of relaxation. You notice how silent and calm this garden is. You are feeling light in body and mind now. In this moment you are feeling as if you are home.

You see a bench in the distance which you are walking towards. With every footstep you are feeling lighter and lighter as if you are shedding a cloak of old energies for new clothing. And as you reach the bench and sit on it, you notice that it feels like cotton. You feel more comfortable, relaxed and at peace than ever before, and the bench absorbs your weight making you feel weightless. And as you breathe, notice how you become more and more peaceful and quiet like the garden. You feel yourself becoming ONE with the garden, and as this feeling continues you feel beautiful and perfect. You are feeling that this is your true nature.

Gradually you enter into the sanctum of stillness,[56] and as you move deeper and deeper into the silence you are entering into the rhythmic

---

[56] Man's power lies in the stillness of his divine self which centres him. He must connect with his stillness—his divine mind to reap higher knowledge and inspiration. He must forget his lower senses for a while, and sever wholly or partially his consciousness from the seat of sensation, so that, he can tap into the knowingness of his higher mind.

world of imagining, the world of inspiration, the indescribable world of the high heavens; and you are tapping into a whole new awareness. You are merging with the higher mind—your divine self. You may wonder what inspiration you may receive from connecting with your divine self. Spend a few moments communing with your divine self. The inspiring messages are flowing naturally to you.

Now that you have received inspiring messages from your divine self, I want you to silently repeat the following affirmations, so that, every cell in your mind resonates with each affirmation. As you say these affirmations you will come into awareness, a remembrance of the truth of each:

I am ONE with my divine self x3

I am ONE with all things x3

I know all things as ONE x3

I know the light which all things are x3

I know the love nature of my divine self and all things x3

I know my divine self as love x3

I know myself as love x3

I know myself x3

I know I am immortal x3

I AM That I AM x3

You have always known the truth of these affirmations for you are the light of all knowing. That which you desire to know you do know; you have always known. The more you commune with your divine self the more you will accept the truth of these affirmations.

You now know how easy it is to relax and you know what it feels like to be totally relaxed; and every time you do this meditation you will find it easier to be totally relaxed and you will find it enjoyable and easy to connect with your divine self whenever you desire.

In a moment I am going to count up from one to five and at the count of five you will be back to full conscious awareness, fully comfortable and fully refreshed and you will have wonderful feelings flowing through your body—calm and peaceful thoughts flowing through your mind— and these lovely calm and peaceful thoughts and feelings are going to remain and stay with you. You will remember the moments you spent with your divine self and the inspiration you received. You will remember exactly how to re create this experience and you will know that you can have this experience every day.

So—when you're ready

ONE—starting to come back, become aware of your body, your breathing and the room around you.

TWO—moving your legs, start to wiggle your toes and feel a lovely grounding energy travel up your legs.

THREE—moving your arms, starting to stretch, feel the energy moving up your body again.

FOUR—eyes starting to open; and

FIVE—eyes fully open, wide awake, feeling refreshed and recharged and being fully aware of being in the room.